Jet McDonald is a writer, musician and psychiatrist. He is the author of many articles for *Boneshaker Magazine* and has written for the *Idler*. He is a member of the Philosophy Special Interest Group of the Royal College of Psychiatrists.

MIND IS THE RIDE

JET McDONALD

unbound

First published in 2019
This paperback edition first published in 2020

Unbound
6th Floor Mutual House, 70 Conduit Street, London W1S 2GF
www.unbound.com

While every effort has been made to trace the owners of copyright
material reproduced herein, the publisher would like to apologise for any
omissions and will be pleased to incorporate missing acknowledgements
in any further editions.

Material reproduced with permission: 'Suzanne' Words and Music by
Leonard Cohen © 1967. Reproduced by permission of Sony/ATV Songs LLC,
London W1F 9LD. 'Glassmakers' by Attila Jozef translated by Peter Hargitai
© 2005. Reproduced by permission of Peter Hargitai. 'Throwing a
Hummingbird' from *River Dancer* by Ian McDonald © 2016. Reproduced by
permission of Ian McDonald and Hansib Publications.

Text design by PDQ

A CIP record for this book is available from the British Library

ISBN 978-1-78352-939-1 (paperback)
ISBN 978-1-78352-690-1 (hardback)
ISBN 978-1-78352-692-5 (ebook)

Printed and bound in Great Britain by CPI

1 3 5 7 9 8 6 4 2

For Jen and Sol

Contents

CHAPTER 1

The Virtual Triangle

The arrow west read BRISTOL 2 MILES, the arrow east INDIA 4300 MILES. We straddled the bikes, rang our BELLS and slowly, very slowly, pedalled east.

It was time to put on my cycling glasses. I'd ordered them especially off the net, thinking they were what a serious cyclist would need, but hadn't expected super-chunky lumps of plastic that made me look like Elton John in his seventies glam rock phase. I shot Jen my 'Don't say anything about my glasses' look and moved into second gear. Five miles later we stopped for breakfast.

The Bristol and Bath bike path is built on the remains of the Midland Railway, dotted here and there with old platforms. Five miles from the centre of Bristol there is a cafe squeezed into an abandoned ticket room, where dawdling cyclists can get a cup of tea and a chip butty.

Jen having no kick stand leaned her machine against the wall.

I propped mine on its metal legs so that I could fully admire its new paint job and ridiculous freight of luggage. There were two pannier bags on the back, two hanging on the front and one BAR BAG on the HANDLEBARS. Because of all this the WHEELS were obscured, leaving only the central part of the frame in view, a kind of stubby triangle. The spring sunshine projected the shadow of this triangle onto the grass beyond. Commuters cycled past paying no attention.

'Does no one care!' I let my tea cup fall into its saucer and peered at Jen through my rocket-powered glasses. They were light-sensitive and had turned a shade of puce yellow.

'Live and let live,' she said.

I pulled my glasses down my nose so I could look more directly at their seemingly tawdry lives.

After three years of planning, saving, negotiating and ramming stuff into pannier bags it felt as if the excitement was brimming out of my head, and the fact that no one seemed to notice was bizarre, if not a little rude. None of this was lessened by sleep deprivation, which gave the scene an unreal flatness. My attention drifted to the shadow of the bike created by the frame and the early-morning sun. It had a pleasing simplicity. A triangular map. From Bristol to Istanbul to Mumbai and back again.

One of the most famous allegories of ancient philosophy is Plato's Cave. The story goes that a group of prisoners are held in chains at the back of a cave facing the wall. Behind them a series of puppets are danced in front of the flames of a fire, casting shadows on the wall that the prisoners are facing. The prisoners believe these shadows to be the nature of reality. This is analogous to our everyday perceptions, which are not the true nature of things, but merely a function of our sensory organs. Only if a prisoner is dragged to the mouth of the cave would he see the sun, which represents the universal truth, the unchanging ideal that underpins our fleeting perceptions.

A bike shadow is a cyclist's best friend. It's an X-ray of the rider's imagination. Its never-changing geometry follows just behind or ahead, on an icy road, a desert plain, a dual carriageway. And at the peaks of hunger and the depths of exhaustion, it begins to talk with you. It begins to turn you inside out. What is your purpose? What is meaning of the rumbling road? What is the unchanging truth at the centre of the central reservation? Why didn't you remove the WHEELS, PEDALS and HANDLEBARS, put the whole shebang in a suitcase, and take the train?

I called my touring bike Bertle, given that it resembled a beetle and had a dependable 'Bertness', while at the same time retaining a female yoni or *elle* in its saddle-shaped curves (Jen meanwhile called her bike Billy). It was only after the trip that I realised the bike was also called Bertle after Bertrand Russell, a pipe-smoking radical atheist with a profile curiously like that of a beetle. Russell is the author of the handbook *The Problems of Philosophy*. At 165 pages and half the size of a sandwich it can easily be slipped into a pannier bag, and as I dipped into it during those first few days, I began to hear a shadow voice, Russell's voice, like a kind of metaphysical satnav. I imagined him tapping the frame of the bike with his pipe as he navigated a scholarly path through reality.

When we perceive a bike, he explained, we perceive the particular sensory information of a bike – colour, texture, etc. – but what gives the bike its bikeness is a universal understanding of these elements and how they relate to each other. The upshot of this is that while two observers may not agree that my bike has the same particular qualities of colour or texture, both might agree that all those parts together have a quality of bike that is universal. That it is, in other words, a bike.

Iain McGilchrist, psychiatrist, literary don and one-time neuroscientist, is the author of *The Master and His Emissary*, a popular and controversial study of the differing roles of the right and left hemispheres in the brain. In the book he shows a drawing of a bicycle made by a patient with a right-hemisphere deficit, where the WHEELS have been pictured above the larger PEDALS; all the parts of the bike are included but their relationship to each other, in space and proportion, what we might call its bikeness, has been lost. The right hemisphere's tendency towards integration influences our ability to understand metaphor, to bring older meanings together into a new whole, whereas the left inclines towards a representation of things as they are, stripped of context.

A friend who bought a BMX bike but decided that he didn't like the frame took the components off that frame and added them to another. Later that frame broke and he replaced it and kept the original components. But for him the bike still retained the quality of being the original bike he'd had all long. He'd always assumed it was the frame that gave it its identity but here it was several editions later retaining its bikeness.

The bike itself, in the form we know it, has only been around for 150 years. But there is something so right about the way that a bike connects to a human being that there must be a timeless notion of what it means. Bikeness may have less to do with the object itself than with how we connect to it. The first roll down a hill on a bicycle, balance intact, is the joyous swallow dive of youth. Before the bike existed we had no learning-to-ride feet-off-the-ground epiphany, because there was no pedal to push, and yet that moment seems familiar, ageless and universal now because it is a part of being human. Our bodies long ago evolved to ride a bike, it's just the mind had to catch up to invent it.

Two best-selling books about cycling have been *It's Not*

About the Bike, the story of racing cyclist Lance Armstrong (before his fall from grace), and *It's All About the Bike*, the story of Rob Penn, who went around the world searching for the ultimate components with which to build his dream bike. Lance Armstrong's title suggests that the value of cycling is unrelated to the bicycle, rather to the motivations that surround it, while Rob Penn's, tongue in cheek, suggests the opposite. In fact, it's neither 'not about the bike' nor 'all about the bike'. It's all about the apostrophe, the indefinable something that connects the it to the is, that joins the fleeting particular to the immutable universal.

Now a teacher of English might reasonably argue that the apostrophe represents a lapsed 'i', but the eccentric rider through the imagination would argue that the apostrophe is in fact the travelling 'I', the self on a trip between the mutable it and the immutable is, adrift from the workaday typeface on its daily commute from left to right.

The value of philosophy lies in the questions it poses, the process of enquiry rather than any definitive answer that closes the mind to debate. The question in *Mind is the Ride* is what is the apostrophe in 'It's all about the bike'? The joy for me lies in the process of answering this question. That is, the pleasure is in the ride and not the destination, 14,000 kilometres down the road. Jen and I could have easily flown to India. We could have taken the train, the plane and the automobile. But what questions would this have posed other than 'Do we have to pay for the soft drinks?'

I push my rocket-scientist sunglasses back up my nose. A cloud passes and the triangular shadow of my bike disappears. Bertle, my beast of burden for the next year, resolves into all its bungee-strapped glory, with a guitar strapped in a bin bag like a misshapen afterthought.

I watch the commuters pootle along the bike path on their

way to greater and lesser demands. The trees rustle as if they wanted to say something more.

'Come on, rocket boy,' says Jen. 'Let's go to India.'

CHAPTER 2

The Bottom Bracket

The Hard Interchange is the travel interchange at Portsmouth Harbour. It is where the Gosport ferry, Portsmouth train station and the bus and taxi services meet in a kind of Stalinist fortress. It is where Jen and I arrived before we took the ferry over to France. But its name also suggests some kind of transaction, some kind of hard-fought cost, some cosmological pay-off. The Bottom Bracket is the part of a bike that holds the PEDALS in line so a cyclist can drive a CHAIN around a WHEEL and create motion. It is hidden in a shell where all the tubes of a bike frame meet. It too is involved in the hard transactions between passenger and passage, confined in mystery in a sealed cartridge.

The Hard Interchange did not allow cyclists. Though its function ostensibly was to house a cafe and some toilets and a bus information office it looked like a cargo ship that had been top-sliced at the first deck. Someone had decided the domino of PVC bays should echo Portsmouth's naval heritage and the ocean-going liners of yore, but it was a clearly a vessel without a hull, a landlocked cruiser carved into brutalist chunks, a remainder of an eighties functionalist dream. And right on the front, underneath a wide gaze of windows (that in the architect's eye must have been the lookout of a poop deck) there was a sign that read NO CYCLING.

I would remember the Hard Interchange at the salt mines in Romania and the container ship docks in the Middle East. Whatever gives and shoves were going on, whatever deals were being made, a dumb cyclist could only spectate. And yet I still feel quite tender towards the Hard Interchange. There is something about the words that suggests the opposite, that the concrete and non-malleable can exchange with something less tangible; that the physical and imaginative worlds can co-exist despite the brutal handshakes of modern life. And the NO CYCLING sign is just a sign. An indicator of where this process happens. In the mysteries of the Bottom Bracket.

Modern Bottom Brackets cannot be serviced. What mysteries they contain require a heavy shoulder and a chisel. To understand how a new Bottom Bracket works you have to take apart an old one, the relic of a previous generation, and, like an anatomist, make best guesses. The old one is made of a single spindle, a rod of metal that joins the CRANKS, the levers running from the PEDALS to the Bottom Bracket. Two rings lock the spindle into position in the frame, and beneath these lock rings is a metal cone, a lipped saucer which fits into the cup, a circular depression at either end of the spindle. The magic of the Bottom Bracket is in the ball bearings that fit between the cone and the cup. These allow the PEDALS to rotate around the spindle under equal tension and with relatively little friction. These are the hard pips that connect rider to ride.

There are many claims for inventor of the bicycle, but the one to whom the books return is a man with the nippy title of Baron

Karl Freidrich Christian Ludwig Freiheir Drais von Sauerbronn, popularly known as Baron Karl Drais. He was a proto-socialist who by the end of his life would have much preferred plain 'Citizen Drais'.

In 1817 he came up with the idea of a 'running machine', the first self-propelled vehicle with two in-line wheels. It was a device that would allow large numbers of people to propel themselves without the need for expensive horses, coach, groom and feed. The rider sat on a leather saddle on a wooden strut between the wheels, and there was a steerable front wheel and armrest to hold while padding your feet on the ground to propel yourself. What it didn't have were PEDALS, CRANKS (the metal levers attached to the PEDALS) and a Bottom Bracket to join them together. But the fundamentals of a bicycle, two in-line wheels which could be kept upright by moving forward using a steering column, were present. And although practically Drais didn't invent the Bottom Bracket, metaphorically, as we shall see, he did.

In Germany the device was known as a Drasine. It spread to France, where it was known as a *vélocipède* and finally to the UK as the hobby horse or dandy horse. In all these countries riders avoided rutted roads by riding on the pavements and caused enough injuries to pedestrians that they were eventually banned. In Regency England caricaturists savaged them so much that a young 'dandy' on a bike could not escape ridicule and stone-throwing. From the very beginning the cyclist was a fool and a lunatic and a renegade. His heresy was to interfere with the channels of transport, his freedom was a threat to order.

As Jen and I were cycling into Portsmouth a car driver slowed, wound down his window and shouted, 'Get awf in the cycle lane!' A year later coming out of Portsmouth Jen was ranted at for rolling (not riding) her bike across a red traffic light and thence onto the pavement. The woman rang up the police. 'She's got a red top on,' she bellowed to Mr Plod.

But Citizen Drais wasn't only the inventor of the renegade horse. He created the mysterious mixer, the Bottom Bracket, even though, to all practical purposes, he didn't. The palpable absence of CRANK, PEDAL and connector on the hobby horse was sublimated into two of his other inventions, the meat grinder and the typewriter, invented in 1821 and the 1850s respectively. With the eye of the imaginative rider you can see in these two inventions, typewriter and meat masher, the mind–body mash-up of the thinking cyclist. A typewriter is where human thought becomes physical indent on the page, a meat grinder where turning force becomes transformed body. The Bottom Bracket is a composite, the point where the intention of the legs meets the motion of the bike. It represents another kind of hard interchange, the mind–body interface that has entangled Western philosophy.

For much of the past two thousand years Western thinking has been just that. Thinking. The head has ruled the body. This way of reckoning has come down to us from the Greeks, Pythagoras and triangles. Pythagoras made the ancient world go wobbly at the knees with his discovery that the sum of the squares made by the sides of a right-angled triangle, adjoining the right angle, equals the square on the remaining side, the hypotenuse. Which sounds like elementary maths, but in a world where elementary maths had yet to exist was a big deal. I talked about the triangular shadows made by bike frames in the VIRTUAL TRIANGLE, but closer inspection of a bike frame reveals it to be more of a trapezoid made by two conjoined isosceles. And these were the kind of outlaw geometries that couldn't be explained by Pythagoras. Whole schools, academies and cults had been built around the perfect mathematics of Pythagoras, so when his equations didn't fit the wider community of triangles, it was a bit of a let-down. The high priest of the right-angled triangle, it turned out, was a bit of a square.

The ancient Greeks responded by rethinking the way they solved geometrical problems. They reckoned the maths first and then wrestled the practical solution from these 'self-evident truths'. The mind was boss and the body an extension of the outside world, with its unreliable isosceles triangles. This was taken to its logical conclusion by the polymath Descartes in the seventeenth century. 'I think therefore I am,' he said atop the hard pillows of the Enlightenment. He saw not human beings on his daily walks but machines with hats on, typewriters and meat grinders, dumb automatons in service to the mind.

This blunt carving up of human being into two separate halves, mind and body, made reason the kingpin and relegated the emotions, sensations, intuition and imagination (an untrustworthy function of perception) to a lowly second place. Poetry and the imagination were but a feeble illusion.

In those first few days of the trip we had thrift-shop legs, under-the-counter knock-offs. We hadn't done any training and were relying on the journey to give us stamina. Every turn of the pedal was painfully aware, as if our legs were doing their own thing down there in the nether regions of transport. 'Not too far to go,' shouted the hill walkers on Salisbury Plain, waving their stalactite trekking poles. Not too far to where? Four thousand miles to Mumbai? Across the hair-thin divide between Bottom Bracket spindle and pedal crank? The Watford Gap between Descartes's mind and body?

Although Descartes's binary view of existence pleased the more concrete thinkers of the Enlightenment it had an enduring paradox. If the mind and body were so separate how did they interact? Descartes himself recognised this. The mind, he said, could not just be lodged in the body as a 'pilot in a vessel' but had to connect more vitally. Otherwise 'I should perceive this wound [pain] by understanding only, just as a sailor perceives by sight when something is damaged in his vessel.' And how, in the opposite direction, could the mind make the body do its bidding? Make the vessel sail? Through the 'thrusting spirits' of the pineal gland, he announced, the pip-sized organ at the centre of the brain. And with this his philosophy was scattered across the floor like an upturned toolbox.

The removal of an old Bottom Bracket from its shell is like the unearthing of a piece of archaeology. The bearings are inevitably rusted by penetrating moisture and within their cone cage resemble the jewels of an Iron Age ring, plucked from the earth. The tarnished rod, the spindle, is the robot finger, its ridged cup the joint against which the caged ring of bearings is held.

To repair and return a Bottom Bracket it must be steel-brushed, pitted bearings replaced, and everything put back together again. This requires slatherings of red bike grease, which cannot help but look like flesh and blood. Memories come back of anatomy exams, mist lying around the medical school like the ocean around a boat, the smell of formaldehyde, a twinkly-eyed lecturer watching my fingers trace the groove in a bone.

When the Bottom Bracket is lathered with unguent and refitted into the frame, there is a sense that connective tissue has been reunited with its hard centre, the intangible has been relocated to its tangible core, that the interchange has been reset, that the spirit between rider and bike, bike and ride, body and mind, has been repaired. And the journey between here and there, between 'it' and 'is' can begin again.

The mind is not a single brain state or body slice on a neuro imaging scan. It is a moment in flux. The writer and psychiatrist Iain McGilchrist compares the mind and brain in terms of the relationship of a wave to water. The wave exists in the water but is not the water. 'The changing brain states are the mind – once the brain experiences them.'

If the bike is the body then the mind is the ride.

The problem when discussing the mind is that the very act of thinking is involved. And so philosophers and scientists become lost in a vortex of reflexivity where the mind tries to reveal itself only to get wrapped in its own cloak. Our subjective sense of who we are, the mind and self, is a mirage that retreats as we advance towards it. Jen and I had embarked on the ideal of a journey, towards the deserts of the Middle East, towards the Vedic traditions of India, towards the enlightened thinking of a millennial philosophy, only to find it evaporating before us like an elusive spring.

There was no sunset in Portsmouth; the sky was the grey of the concrete car park where we locked our bikes. Below us dinghies were beached in the mud like pockmarks, yet we could taste the thrill in the air, the salt wind of adventure. We hoisted off our pannier bags, barged through heavy fire doors, found our way up to the cafe of the Hard Interchange, ordered cups of tea and stared out across the forecourt of Portsmouth Harbour, pilots of a stranded rudderless building pretending to be a boat.

The cafe of the Hard Interchange was much more appealing than the building that encased it. There was a 1950s Butlin's feel to it, with brass fans on the ceiling and a canteen-style hotplate at one end where you could get your dishes from women with the ample arms of school dinner ladies. The cafe served dishes of homespun comfort to transitory souls – chips and peas, jacket potatoes and stew. And for pudding, the ultimate sop to the homesick heart, custard and jam sponge.

Each pane of glass overlooking the harbour held a different capital letter, laser-printed on an A4 sheet, facing out. Together they read CAFE OPEN, in order that the world beyond might recognise the Hard Interchange had a mushy centre. When we arrived in Portsmouth we took the central table next to the 'O' and gazed out. Spoons dipped into custard and jam and then into our mouths as the masses of travellers gathered and dispersed, into and out of the funnels of transport. We had a long way to go and wanted the comforts of home to outlast the forgetting of travel, the pang of the unknown.

Eventually we rode out from underneath the Hard Interchange, with its NO CYCLING protestations, and into Portsmouth Ferry Terminal. Here, neither pedestrian nor automobile, we found ourselves in the motorcycle queue and, at the beckoning of a man in a high-vis, followed an enormous articulated lorry into the cavernous barrel of a cross-Channel ferry, two small someones into an enormous something. I tried to transfer all my friends' numbers into my new phone from the old one and deleted them by mistake.

Seven hours later we clattered out of the hold with its fug of diesel and onto French concrete, our right of way flipped from left to right. We were tempted to punch the air but instead reached for the cheapest and most joyous part of a bicycle. The BELL.

Ping.

CHAPTER 3

The Bell

The Bell I have in my hand is made of shiny stainless steel, it has TAIWAN stamped on the base and has a crown with a cross embossed on the top. It is the Bell that took me to India. If you unscrew the dome you find a saw-shaped bar attached to a thumb lever. The saw rotates a cog at the centre which in turn rotates a flywheel with washers at the circumference. For each thumb push in one direction you get a free thumb pull as the spring releases and the flywheel spins back. Slow movements on the outside create Catherine wheels on the inside and the crown rejoices. All for £2.99 from the Far East.

The first pinger, in fact the first ding-a-linger, was a cowbell. A mechanical striker on the front wheel of a penny farthing hit a Bell that dangled beneath the HANDLEBARS with each revolution. This was then shrunk into its own independent wheel and fitted onto the HANDLEBARS. By the time of the Lucas

Bell of 1895 you could press a saw-shaped lever on a pivot which rolled against a cog so that both the lid of the Bell and a striking arm were rotated at high speed. The striking arm was pushed aside by a pimple on the base so it sprang back and struck the rotating dome on top. The brand leader was the King of the Road, which had two Bells, one rotating dome on top and another fixed below.

By 1902 Joseph Lucas had moved into car and aeroplane components, and by the 1950s the company were making semiconductors, rectifiers and transistors. By 1996 Lucas Aeronautics had been part-sold to the company which made the tyres for the NASA space shuttle. I like to think that the King of the Road Bell made it into space. That somewhere in the cockpit of the space shuttle there was a double-domed brass apple. And as its crew fled the orbit of the earth, as they stormed free of Newtonian physics, as they embraced the uncertainty of relativity, someone somewhere pressed a little thumb lever and far from Houston a cowbell heralded the infinite everywhere.

Ping.

'Clock' is ultimately derived from the Celtic word *cloche* meaning Bell. Bells were the voice of ancient communities, the chime of peace and war, fair and festival, famine and epidemic, birth and death, the newborn chime of the emerging body politic. But locked into the gears of the astrological clocks of the Middle Ages, subsumed into the anglicised 'clock', they assumed the mundanity of church bell hours and factory gatekeepers. The seasons by which the Greeks and ancient man marked their days were hammered into the brass plate revolutions of the planets and then cleaved into minutes and hours.

Sir Isaac Newton loved clocks. William Blake, poet and visionary of the eighteenth century, hated them, their cold ascetic gears the 'dark satanic mills' of his prophetic verse. For Blake Newtonian physics represented sight without insight. It looked without to the cold tick of the universe but never within to the richness of human imagination.

Ping.

Until medieval times man, and mainly woman, used their bodies like mules. They dug and they lifted and they churned. But muscles develop maximum power when they move quickly with little resistance. Muscles need gears. And medieval man, staring up at the towers of the Enlightenment and a pile of oak beams beside him, rationalised the single-geared capstan into existence so that quick easy movements could be used to move slow heavy loads. Gears upon gears evolved, and the bike Bell, signalling as it did the arrival of the bike, is but a manifestation of that first capstan. Bike Bells are the single-celled cogs of the Industrial Evolution. But, if you take the top off, they are also the fossilised remains of the tyranny of time.

Ping.

When Archimedes was sitting in his bath in the third century BCE not only was he thinking how much water his thighs displaced; he was also thinking gears. Within and without the brain. His mechanical gears were used to create mini planetariums millennia before the medieval capstan and the astronomical clocks of the Renaissance. Now I'm not saying the bike Bell is a planetarium, but with the eye of the imaginative rider you can see its heritage. With the top dome off and the press of a lever, two planetary washers revolve soundlessly around a cogged centre. As such it is a simple answer to the question posed by Plato two centuries before: 'By the assumption of what uniform and ordered motions can the apparent motions of the planets be accounted for?'

Archimedes's solution was a machine in which the sun and moon revolved around a geocentric earth, with the earth as the centre of the universe. This can be seen in the Antikythera mechanism, raised from a shipwreck in 1900 but dating from 150 BCE. It had more than thirty gears and could calculate the positions of all the main planets and calendar events with a turn of a lever. It was the first analogue computer. But the main fragment of it, encased in coral, looks like the single-geared remnants of the inside of my bike Bell. My cow brain.

It is worth reflecting here on the links between Greek science and philosophy. For the ancient polymaths there was no separation. When Aristotle listed the sciences on the back of an envelope, matters concerning the fundamental basis of human existence were dealt with alongside his material on physics, hence metaphysics. Metaphysics, the systematic quest for the nature of the heavens, for the grit of reality, lay not separate from physics but alongside it. But paradoxically it was these first geared models of the universe that pointed to the separation of philosophy and science.

After the break-up of the Roman empire, the highly developed elements of Greek technology were mostly lost to Western scholars and instead went east to Islam and India, where they thrived. It was only in the twelfth and thirteenth centuries that this learning came back to Europe through the Moorish presence in southern Spain. By then mechanical astrolabes and planetariums were being made in earnest but only as carcasses of the philosophical learning and traditions of ancient Greece that were once part of their mystery.

By the Middle Ages these astrological clocks were beholden to a Christian god. They were earthly manifestations of the heavenly machine that the Lord had created. Pendulums automated them so they could act devoid of man, perfect illustrations of God's perfection. They were microcosms of the universe but also precursors of the spring-loaded timepieces that would eventually shuffle the working classes in and out of the factories of the Industrial Revolution and go on to mark Greenwich Mean Time. The revolution of the sun and moon around a central cog was further subdivided into minutes and hours, a multitude of gear ratios away from the movements of the cosmos they were modelled on.

Ping.

The bike Bell, the unholy cowbell, is poetry in free verse, a chime without a clock, a poet calling from the slavishness of the working week, half-dressed in the disguise of puritanical gears, stumbling sideways into the verge of the seasons.

Ping.

Before Plato, before Archimedes, there was Hesiod. In Hesiod's time the seasons of the planet marked the slow beat of existence and his epic *Works and Days* was a seasonal calendar, a poem anti-clock. It used the folklore of seasonal and star change to reap and sow the fields and was sung, like the *Iliad*, to a lyre.

> But when the House-carrier [the snail, in May] climbs up the plants from the earth to escape the Pleiades, then it is no longer the season for digging vineyards, but to whet your sickles...

His shorter list of auspicious days was more silvery, more Bell-like, a ritualistic calendar based around a thirty-day lunar cycle in which different days and associated moon phases meant different rituals, for example 'Bring bride home' or 'Open wine jar.' This reflected a more ancient calendar in which the moon exerted an animate effect on man's behaviour.

Ping.

In the twenty-first century we divide our days into the quartz crystal oscillations of computer time. A quartz clock is devoid of metaphor, containing only ticks and tocks, time increments that service the ghost of a churchly timetable to mortal judgement, and entirely lacking the poetry that marks the richness of human interaction with the natural world.

Ping.

In the land of the cowbell, Hindus and Buddhists have spent millennia maintaining that death is not the end of the line but a gateway to the next cycle of birth and death. Time is cyclical and there are repeating ages. The gods echo a cycle of death and rebirth that itself echoes the turning of the seasons. Greek philosophy once had similar strong ties to both the planetary gods and the homespun business of living. But somewhere along the way Western philosophy lost a sense of purpose, of metaphorical reach or direct influence on our lives. It was hived off into academia for bods with beards. Mechanics ticked into the clock and philosophy into term time.

Ping.

I look at my Bell now with the lid off. I press the lever and the flywheel revolves its washers, its sun and moon; I release the lever and it spins back again. I put the lid back on and this advance and return is made plentiful through sound. It is a childish fantasy that the sun and moon revolve around the earth. But I like this childish time. This plodding, pre-Galileo, pre-Newton time. This time of the cowbell.

Ping.

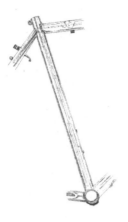

CHAPTER 4

The Seat Tube

On our first day in France we arrived in a campground called Les Forges near Lilleborne. Most sites look like they've been knocked up from a campsite identikit but this one was more roughly hewn. It was overseen by an old lady in a static caravan in the middle, henchwoman to the boss in a nearby cottage, who punched out our receipt on some kind of mechanical typing machine. If tourism represents an attempt to hold back time, to decelerate from the rush of the present into the future, then this place managed it.

We were knackered. We'd cycled twenty kilometres from the coast and it felt like we'd already done the trip. All the expectation, packing and house clearing had knocked us out. We just wanted to sleep. We didn't want to cycle to India.

It was 7 May, the day after the British elections, and the radio announced that the UK had its first hung parliament since the 1970s. Blighty was dangling on the end of a string like a yo-yo, that's lost its 'yo' and we were happy to wait amid the bluebells of Normandy. In the cool of the green forests the bluebells are like a shallow sea. Approach from the road and you feel as if you might go paddling in them. And at a certain angle the colour of the bluebells multiplies, makes such an intense blue-violet it feels like you can see the red in the palette.

The Seat Tube is the large-diameter frame tube between the BOTTOM BRACKET and the SADDLE. The Seat Tube's role in the geometry of the bicycle is in defining the height of the rider above the crank set – those parts of the bike that engage the rider in movement, the PEDAL, CRANKS and CHAIN. The position of the rider along the length of the bike is also partly determined by the angle between the back of the Seat Tube and the horizontal. If this angle is shallow the rider is placed further back along the bike, increasing the load on the back wheel and making it easier for the rider to touch the ground without getting off the seat. This makes for a more relaxed or touring style as opposed to a more aggressive style of riding with the rider placed to the fore leaning over the HANDLEBARS. The average angle of a road-racing bike is seventy-three degrees; ours were considerably less. In that first campsite in France it felt like the angle of the Seat Tubes of our touring bikes was zero. We just couldn't find the momentum to get riding.

One of the delights and challenges of bike touring is that you're in charge. There's no coach waiting at 9 a.m. for you to sling the luggage in the hold. But the price of control is motivation. And how do you motivate yourself out of the bluebells? The chalk roads of Normandy were singing to us, but the bluebell forests had their own siren songs; picnics, croissants sleep, sleep, sleep.

The cafes and *tabacs* have a different message. The posture here is certainly less than seventy-three degrees, elbows over chair backs, but espresso keeps the brain lurching forward. This, I like to think, is how Parisian existentialism was engineered. Sartre realised that someone had to get the groceries and it wasn't going to be Simone de Beauvoir.

Existentialism is built on something called phenomenology. Another big word in a small coffee cup but basically the study of how we perceive the world. Phenomenology asserts that there is no definitive object 'out there' and that we all interpret the world with our own, very personal, perceptive traits. Existentialism claims (unlike Plato and the idealists) that there is no universal and eternal realm, that there never has been an ideal concept of the world and the objects it contains. That there is in fact no preordained essence, in fact no god. We are material objects first. We exist first and then we develop a conscious understanding of the world by our individual perception of it, our essence. Existence precedes essence, like coffee granules precede coffee. The net outcome is that our lives are not preordained. There is no deity making up the rules for us; we map our own paths through life, even if we kid ourselves that we don't and it is fate that is in charge, pulling at our handlebars.

Sartre explained that we are born free, but that this freedom comes with a responsibility, responsibility for our actions. Everything that happens to us and will happen to us is decreed by what we choose to do. Even if we choose to do nothing that is still a decision. 'Not to choose is, in fact, to choose not to choose,' he says. Our lives, our very being is defined not by what opportunity offers or denies us but by what we do, by how we act. 'To be is to do,' he says.

Lying around in a French campsite is a decision. A decision to do nothing. And the argument that I am worn out and not fit for riding would not hold true for Sartre. 'I cannot be crippled without choosing myself as crippled,' he says. This is not an appropriation of disability but rather, 'This means I choose the way in which I constitute my disability.' I could sit around thinking, *Blimey I'm knackered and we've only done a few hundred miles. How are we going to get to Bombay?* Or I can get on my bike and ride. To be is to do.

The existentialist would see the bike journey ahead as something that allows me to function, as something which gives purpose to my life. The actual facts of the road, the potholes it throws up, create the action that defines who we are. 'The resistance of the thing (facticity) sustains the action of man (freedom) as air sustains the flight of the dove.'

Sartre was a fan of the German philosopher Heidegger. Heidegger framed life by the death that awaits it. Every decision in life, he argued, should be made with the finite nature of life in mind. Thus, every decision should be an affirmation of that life, its zing and presentness, whereas a life lived on the basis of avoiding death is a series of tiny deaths in itself.

Although Sartre was around when the ideas of Freud were at their most febrile he was wary of the unconscious. Certainly, he felt that attributing all conscious thought to unconscious process was a cop-out. It was another way of abrogating responsibility so that the middle classes could live a bourgeois life on the assumption that they had no control over it. This passive living of a life, held by the strictures of others and society, blind to the self, Sartre called 'inauthentic'.

We were determined to get off our butts and ride to India. But to do that we were going to have to ride through Germany to Austria and Vienna, the home of Freudian analysis and the heartland of the bourgeois cake shop. We thought it would be easy. But its very easiness later proved to be our undoing (see TYRES).

Back in that campsite there was no brain energy for this. The only thing that could get us off our bums was coffee.

Having been a gentleman tea drinker all my life, coffee came as a shock. Kerpow! You can't help thinking that the reason the existentialists were so into 'to be is to do' is that they were smacking themselves round the head with caffeine every day. The irony of existentialism is that the main protagonists spent all their time sitting round in cafes apparently doing nothing, though for Sartre doing nothing involved churning out philosophical masterworks. A Parisian friend told me that, while he admires the Frenchman's ability to debate over long lunches, he cannot abide their inability to actually get on and do something practical.

The first morning in France I managed to fix the clinking sound that was coming from my right pedal. PEDALS are screwed into the CRANK, the left one clockwise and the right anticlockwise. This is to stop them unscrewing as they are revolved. When I attached my new PEDALS I'd forgotten this. Sitting in the afternoon sunshine at a cafe the solution came to me, and the first *clink* of the trip was quashed.

The second morning in France I had the squits, possibly from sucking the cooker fuel off my fingers the night before. We listened to the election results on a hissing transistor radio. England seemed so far away, hung in the balance of its history, as we started our adventure. And this was the final kick up the arse that got us going again and back on the road.

We were on the B roads, which track across the country like delicate wrinkles, remarking, in a pompous cyclist kind of way, how delightful it was that the shops weren't open on Sundays, how English culture comparatively was so 'twenty-four hours' and the Continent knew how to kick off its shoes and relax, when we found ourselves in a series of villages where nothing was open. Nothing. In rural France Sunday extends into Monday and then Monday extends into Tuesday, and two hungry cyclists with a dirty petrol stove trying to eat the remains of yesterday's

Pot Noodle do not make for a happy couple. 'I don't give a shit,' Jen eloquently put it when I told her that I'd filled the stove up with barbecue fuel and it was no longer working and there was no shop open for fifty miles.

We invented a character called Mr Moped whose job it was to putter across rural France closing all the cafes and *tabacs* and restaurants just as we arrived. He was like those guys on motorcycles in the Tour de France swooping ahead of the peloton for the best camera shot. Except Mr Moped was expressly employed to close all the food establishments just as we rested our fully loaded touring bikes against a wall.

There were, however, some brilliant rides: along a winding chalk path over Normandy farms and through a wild pasture humming with the first hot day of spring, a dusk journey past the battlegrounds of World War I with wooden Christs emerging out of the mist like mystics, an endless downhill through green forests steaming like jungle. And when we did find food. Oh the glory of it. Oh the full flame heartiness of its carbohydrate chains. Most of the time the civilised world sits on its arse and then walks to the pasty shop. But when you are cycling every day a tiny gobbet of food tastes like heaven.

On Tuesday 11 May, outside Gournay-en-Bray, we stopped at what we were told was a restaurant but looked like someone's front room. We expected to walk towards the door and have the shutters quietly closed by Mr Moped but instead we were directed to a few tables in a back room still covered with yesterday's, possibly last week's, crumbs. The old lady who was proprietor, cook and waitress eyed us with suspicion as we tried to explain.

'WE WANT FOOD.' 'JUST GIVE US FOOD, FOR CRYING OUT LOUD.'

She went on to cook us the biggest, fattest omelette that has ever been flipped for two tiny stomachs as her elderly husband watched us from around the door. Ah what delights entered the furnace of our bodies. The crunching of onion like footsteps on frost.

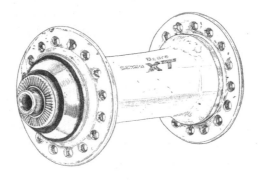

CHAPTER 5

The Front Hub

The hub is that part of the bike wheel that allows it to spin from
the bottom of the bike's forks, which hold it in place. It operates
much like the BOTTOM BRACKET in that there are generally two
surfaces, a cup and a cone, separated by small bearing balls which
allow the surfaces to roll against each other while tolerating
vertical and horizontal loads as the hub is twisted and turned.
These forces become all the more evident when the bike is loaded
with luggage or panniers, which hang on a rack, which on most
bikes is joined to the frame over the WHEELS.

I had front and back pannier racks on Bertle, their weight
bearing down into the front and back wheel hubs. It was from
the Front Hub that I began to hear an annoying *dink* as we were
cavorting down a long downhill section. I thought initially it
was the old *clink* due to the right pedal not being screwed tight
enough into the CRANKS. But no, on further tightening of the
pedal in the correct direction, the *dink* remained.

Our bodies, once filled with calories, found they could perform the tasks we asked of them as we became that bit fitter. Up that hill? That *big* hill? OK. Downhills were the reward for all that climbing but were tainted by the new *dink* that had become a gnarly *donk* in my brain as the bike sped underneath me. Surely the *donk* would become a *clank*, and the machine would fall apart before we reached India.

I tried to ignore it. Lord knows I tried. But when you hear a *dink* every time your wheel goes around, eight hours a day, five days a week, it only serves to remind you that there is a malfunction in the system, that system being the interconnection of bike and man that would take me to India.

Eventually, after flipping the bike upside down and listening to each part in turn as I spun, knocked and wobbled it, I determined that the *dink* was coming from the Front Hub. Now the Front Hub was a mystery. The bike had been bought on the basis that it was worry-free. Each component was top-of-the-range Shimano so presumably top-of-the-range ball bearings.

'Bearings made of strong materials, properly manufactured and finished with high precision, positioned with the proper configuration and kept clean and lubricated, can last for many millions of revolutions,' says David Gordon Wilson, a name you can rely on with three pairs of equally balanced syllables. So why then was my top-of-the-range Shimano XT hub *dink*ing? This was something that I fretted about as if the sound represented all the apparently insurmountable problems that lay between France and India.

In Bresles on 13 May, nearly two weeks after leaving Bristol, a friendly campsite owner and amateur bike mechanic took a peek, shook his head in a serious manner and agreed to transport me and my bike to the out-of-town bike hyperstore. But because it was a national holiday (on a Thursday!) the store's mechanic hadn't come in. Instead my hub was examined by a dude with gelled hair, which reminded me of the gob I imagined slopping round my faulty Front Hub. He tightened up the cone and cup, but still the *dink* remained.

By Saturday 15 May I couldn't bear the sound any more, it pecked at my brain like a little bird. The next hyperstore confirmed it was '*un problem dans le moyeu*,' the Front Hub, but they couldn't fix it. They recommended Jean in the specialist workshop. We cycled to the shop of Jean but Jean didn't work on a Saturday. What did the bike mechanics of France do with their days? Sit in jacuzzis of bike oil drinking cocktails? The third bike mechanic recommended by the second bike shop agreed it was a cock-up '*dans le moyeu*' but that '*Ce n'est pas grave*' – 'Don't worry about it.' But to me that *dink* was a chink in the steely armour of perfection I had assembled for the big adventure.

The fourth bike shop was six miles away from the third. They *Ce n'est pas grave*'ed me so I forced the issue. OK, they said, they would repair it, but only on the Tuesday after the two-day break that all French bike mechanics demand before they have the strength to ride back from their jacuzzi and foie gras. Jen and I agreed to wait till Tuesday in a campsite near Paris and recuperate.

It was then I noticed a spot on my bum. I was tired and worn out and worried that this pimple would turn into some kind of abscess and a volcano of pus would consume me like a sick Jules Verne novel. 'Tired. Burned out,' I wrote in my diary. 'Feel like a kid again.'

After a weekend in the suburban campsite, poised between little islands of dog shit, my spot had gone down enough to cycle, and on Tuesday we pedalled to the bike shop in Senlis.

The surly mechanic looked at me through his eyebrows and then at my heavy touring bike and went, '*Oh la la*.' Which translates loosely as 'Why has God brought me this neurotic

English scum?' However, his colleague, half French, half German, took pity and agreed to do the job. I wondered if I should show him the pimple on my bum but thought better of it.

We left the bikes with them and went into the centre of Senlis. There we met the *patron* of a stationer's shop who waxed lyrical about an exchange visit he'd made as a teenager to Bournemouth in the UK. He was an Anglophile. 'Yes I luuvv England,' he said. 'Elgar and Paul McCartney.' A good sign, I thought. He will transmit beams of positive Macca energy to the French bike mechanics and they will cure the *dink* in my Front Hub.

When we returned the mechanic had completely stripped and re-greased the hub, taken out all the ball bearings and put them back in again. He gave me a wan smile. 'Great,' I said. 'Thanks.' Then we rode back off to the campsite. *Dink. Dink. Dink. Dink.*

Clearly cycling round bike shops in French suburbia was not going to help us get to India. Jen festooned me with kisses and I wrote the following Churchillian entry in my diary: 'We will ride on regardless of the Front Hub and the dink sound. Spread out our maps for the future on the green tarp.' I tried to forget about the *dink*, and with this act of forgetting the spot on my bum disappeared.

We ploughed through the mountain passes of the Alsace region, the Black Mountains of Bavaria, along the Danube and into eastern Germany, but the *dink* continued and I returned to pick at the worry of it. I dreamed of faulty ball bearings revolving in sealed chambers. 'Watch out for the pitted or corroded surfaces,' says Rob Van der Plas in *Bicycle Technology*, 'because soon they will ruin the bearing races and remaining balls.'

Somewhere in the middle of Germany, face plugged into a cake of some kind, I began to fret about the spots on my face. For the past couple of years I'd had a couple of sun spots about the size of the ball in the tip of a Bic biro over my right cheekbone. I hadn't worried about them before. They hadn't increased in size. They hadn't seemed anything to bother about. But then they began to change in the sun; cycling all day had sparked a process of pigmentation, and in the dappled shade of the Danube, bike leaning against a picnic table, I began to worry this was the first sign of a malignant melanoma. By the time I arrived in Straubing in eastern Germany I was a hypochondriac wreck. Whatever you say about the Germans they can sort stuff out. And in Straubing I was recommended both a good bike mechanic and a doctor.

The first bike mechanic in Straubing didn't say, '*Oh la la,*' though this is probably because there is no German equivalent. He put the bike in a stand and put one end of a screwdriver on the hub and the other end to his ear. 'Mmm,' he said, 'this is a problem.'

'Is it a serious problem?'

'No this is not a serious problem,' he said, doing that German thing where they repeat what you've just said in a more muscular manner. 'But I cannot guarantee it will last to India.'

'Is there nothing you can do?' I said pitifully.

'You must go to Mr Braum.'

'Mr Braum?'

'The other bike shop.'

I raced to Mr Braum, who owned a showroom with wheels hanging from the ceiling like unshod hula hoops. Next door he had a garage where he worked on bikes.

He put his screwdriver to my hub and then his ear to the screwdriver.

'Mmm,' he said, 'this is a problem.'

'Yes.' I nodded happily. 'This is a problem.'

'We do not have the parts for this hub. It is a Shimano XT hub. It will take at least two weeks to get another one and we have to rebuild the wheel round the hub. I give you another wheel.'

'No,' I wailed, my wheel had been hand-built in Somerset and had a super-tough tungsten coating. It was a Superman wheel, it was the wheel of superheroes, even if the hub was a bit tremulous.

Mr Braum rubbed at his sideburns and gazed at the hula hoops on the ceiling. 'I will take apart the Shimano XT hub that is already in the XT wheel I have. Take out the cup and bearings and put it in your hub. Then when the new hub arrives I will put the bits of it into my wheel.' A French mechanic would never say anything like this. A French mechanic would go for lunch.

'How long will it take?' I said.

'You must go for lunch,' said Mr Braum. 'It will be ready when you return.'

One schnitzel later I had a perfectly revolving Front Hub in which the bearings moved seamlessly between the runners of cone and cup, enabling friction-free revolution.

It was difficult to believe. I had had the *dink* so long that to not have it seemed a deprivation. If you take the tic out of the neurotic you're just left with neuro, the nerve, a frictionless nervous pathway from brain to foot to wheel. On the other hand, I could at least look forward to exotic nightmares full of bats and serpents rather than small metal balls.

After lunch Jen and I cycled, *dink*less, to the dermatologist, Dr Smirtz.

Dr Smirtz was a well-fed middle-aged man in a white coat. I was glad to see he had a white coat. There's something about the laundry freshness of a doctor's smock that suggests hotel sheets and early-morning starts. We watched in the waiting room while Dr Smirtz greeted his bandaged patients like long-lost pals, acquaintances met over starchy white excisions.

He pressed a looking glass against my cheekbone.

'Good margins,' he said, peering into it. 'Harmless.' Dr Smirtz removed the anxiety from the tic, the *dink* from the friction.

'That's a relicf,' I said to Jen.

Jen launched into a massive tirade. Having put up with me going on about the spot on my bum, the spot on my face and the *dink* in my Front Hub, she was now ready to unleash all her pent-up frustration in a stream of invective.

'There's no need to be hysterical,' I said. This is guaranteed to make your partner hit you over the head with a rolled-up route map of eastern Germany.

It was Charcot, the nineteenth-century Parisian neurologist, who first suggested that not all physical illness had a physical origin, that forms of illness might be 'hysterical'. He demonstrated patients with a paralysis of a limb that couldn't be explained by a lesion of a physical nerve but only by the patient's own interpretation of what such a lesion would cause. He could, under hypnotic suggestion, cause such a paralysis to disappear and then reappear. The patients could not recall or explain what had happened to them. These demonstrations had a profound influence on Freud who recognised, not only that physical problems could have psychological origins, but also that mental processes could be unconscious and still have a dramatic impact on behaviour.

Freud's colleague Josef Breuer experimented with hypnosis on a patient documented in his records as Anna O. Breuer found that if he could get Anna to remember the time at which the hysterical symptom first occurred, and re-experience the emotions associated with it, the hysterical symptom disappeared in an act of catharsis.

The fact that these reminiscences were shameful, painful or alarming led Freud to believe there were mental mechanisms repressing these memories from consciousness. Freud developed his ideas of repression which became the first 'defence' in his theory of the conflicted mind, where neurotic patients wrestled with unconscious experiences of which they were not fully aware.

The psychotherapist Anthony Storr writes: 'The mental state which Freud proposed is analogous to the physical condition of a "blind" boil or abscess which, being unable to find a path to the surface of the body, cannot discharge the toxic matter which it contains. The "surgical" view of neurosis is one that must have appealed to Freud as a medical scientist. It implied that the disowned affect, which was causing the neurotic symptoms, could be excised as if it was a foreign body, an intruder, which was not part of the patient's personality as a whole.'

Freud later went on to posit that these unconscious traumatic experiences were invariably sexual. He even proposed that these traumatic sexual experiences needn't have actually occurred, that they could be unwanted or repressed sexual feelings that arose spontaneously within the individual and which were so shameful they ended up buried in the unconscious, thus provoking neurotic symptoms. Freud, it is fair to say, was preoccupied with sex. And feminists have since argued he used psychoanalysis as a way of specifically defining and confining female sexuality.

Indeed, the word hysteria has always been a code for a certain kind of male fear about female sexual desire. The word itself comes from the Greek for uterus. Plato believed the uterus was an animal that roamed inside women's bodies causing symptoms as it moved. The humoral medicine of the Middle Ages traced hysterical symptoms to the retention of a sexual fluid, common in 'passionate' young women and widows. By the mid-nineteenth century female hysteria was said to be specifically caused by sexual dysfunction and doctors were using sexual massage and vibrators to achieve orgasm and relieve the 'disorder'. (It followed that Edwardian men were more concerned about the rise of cycling amongst young women than about hysteria, believing the friction of the leather SADDLE might lead to masturbation and a frenzy of nymphomania.)

Charcot refused to characterise hysteria as a sexual problem, viewing it instead as an inherited nervous disorder like multiple sclerosis and being present in men and women. Paintings of the time show otherwise, with a crowd of fully clothed men staring at a partially dressed woman in a horizontal and sexually available swoon. Freud said that repressed and traumatic sexual experiences led to the development of hysteria and for some feminists this meant recloaking the inadmissibility of female sexual desire in a different guise.

But regardless of the conflicts at its root there emerged a clear concept of unconscious mental conflict taking physical form, a process later termed 'Conversion disorder'. Now called somatisation, this is the process whereby mental distress is transformed into a physical complaint without clear physical cause. These labels have become increasingly empirical and bureaucratic, the latest being 'Medically Unexplained Symptoms'.

Regardless of what we call it, most of us will, at some point, visit a doctor with a physical problem brought on by underlying mental distress. And this only serves to reiterate the mesh of mind and body. If we cease to imagine a dichotomy between the two there ceases to be a need for a categorical distinction. 'Medically Unexplained Symptoms' merely become the body's manifestation of the mind's distress and no different to a regular pain other than its source.

For people as intimately connected with their mode of transport as Jen and I, cycling more hours during the day than we actually slept at night, the bike becomes an extension of body and thus mind. Bike mechanics should recognise that they are also healers.

Most people with medically unexplained symptoms who see their GP will improve without any specific treatment, particularly when their GP gives an explanation for the symptoms that makes sense, removes any blame from the patient and generates ideas about how to manage their symptoms.

If only French bike mechanics would listen to this helpful advice from the West Midlands Regional Development Centre. Perhaps it's a bit much to expect bike mechanics to have a sense of psychotherapy. A retreat into the mechanics of things is an obvious way of avoiding the more trying mechanics of those that own them. While Charcot understood that physical symptoms can a have mental counterpart it took the Prussian Freud to nurture the mental as a route to holistic contentedness. German bike mechanics get the job done with a kind of concrete empathy, 'yes this is a problem,' they announce seriously. And this is what I wanted. Seriousness. It's not just a spot. It's not just a dink. It's a problem.

(See REAR SPROCKETS for Freud, the unconscious and phalloeroticism.)

CHAPTER 6

The Rear Sprockets

The River Danube navigates western Europe like a snake. Alongside it runs a bike path, smooth, well-tended and almost unbearably flat. I stared up at the cliffs around us and clicked fruitlessly through my twenty-seven expedition gears.

'I feel castrated,' I said to Jen.

But she was already too far away to hear.

Bertle's CHAIN began to slip on the sprockets. In the bike shop in Grein the mechanic scolded it like a dog trainer. 'Bad chain. Gears damage.'

The grit of a British winter had prematurely worn down my once perfect CHAIN and the CHAIN had worn down my expensive sprockets and CHAIN WHEELS. And a CHAIN that no longer meshes with the teeth of its cogs will slowly nibble at them like an introverted cannibal. When you attempt to put on the new CHAIN it no longer matches the old teeth of the cogs and slides off. The only solution is to replace the Rear Sprockets and the CHAIN at the same time. This isn't just a slap round the face. It's a lot of money.

I am a collector of bike mechanics, much like an overenthusiastic boy collects football cards. The one I found in Vienna was a sprucer punkier version of Arnold Schwarzenegger, all symmetry and muscles and teeth, with studs through his ears and lower lip.

'Ya,' he said, 'we can do this but it will be pretty expensive. Do you want SLR or SLX?'

SLR components are good quality but SLX is the best. I knew SLX was the best because SLX is one letter short of SEX. SLX is the most SLXy. SLX is what I wanted. I was riding to India. I was an SLX kind of guy. Jen mentioned our budget, that we still had a long way to ride.

'Ha!' I said. SLX was what I wanted and SLX was what I was getting. I shrugged at Arnold, as if to say, 'These girls they don't get SLX. Not like us guys, with our big eyebrows and tattoos on our biceps.' He smiled and his Austrian cheekbones popped up like waxed fruit.

'I'll be back,' he said.

There is an Austrian symmetry about the Ringstrasse, the ring road built to replace the old walls of Vienna in the nineteenth century. Sigmund Freud, obsessive by nature, would leave his consulting rooms in the heart of the city at 2 p.m. every day and storm around the Ringstrasse before disappearing into the labyrinth of the old town. To understand Freud, and to understand the 'science' of his sexology, you have to understand some of the circles within Vienna itself. Baron Carl von Rokitansky was the head of the Vienna School of Medicine when Freud began his training. Rokitansky did away with the traditional practice of judging a patient's health by the balance of their 'humours', a quasi-magical practice extending back to Hippocrates. Instead he went straight to the formal autopsy of bodies, linking the pathology of the underlying tissues to the clinical symptoms of the patient when they were alive. Freud absorbed this teaching alongside Darwin's emphasis on sexual potency in the survival of a species. He then made sex the perfect leap between mind and body, underlying the thoughts and dreams that his patients experienced and yet physical, with its hormonal drives and anatomical expression. Freud did not invent the unconscious, any more than he invented sexual desire, but he popularised and linked the two in a way that alchemised the Western imagination for ever.

Some regard Freud's work as a well-indexed fiction rather than a science (with testable outcomes and hypotheses). Freud's reluctance to call it anything other than a science left him tainted for many scientists. But to ignore Freud's ideas would be to ignore the contribution he has made to our understanding of sex and sexuality, untethering its impulses from morality and broadening its ambiguity. 'We are all,' Freud said, 'bisexual.'

Jen and I cycled from the bike shop to Freud's old consulting rooms. It was filled with classical statues and archaeological totems. Freud said that the psychoanalyst 'like the archaeologist in his excavations, must uncover layer after layer of the patient's psyche, before coming to the deepest, most valuable treasures'. To Jen and I his archaeological findings looked like shelf upon shelf of antique dildos. How could his patients have thought about anything other than sex?

As the Danube enters Vienna it is partly channelled into the Donaukanal, a canal that thinks it's a river, its mostly turgid waters running with an unseen current. Between the Donaukanal and the Danube, you can find a tacky fairground park, the Prater. Inside the Prater is Vienna's famous Ferris wheel, built from wood and iron in 1897, the same year Freud developed his ideas of 'psychosexual development', the oral, anal and phallic stages of childhood and the genital phase of adulthood. Jen and I climbed into one of the creaking carriages and were swept upwards in an arc above the city. Below us we could see an 'entertainment' carriage where diners in dinner jackets and evening dresses sat for a three-course meal. At each revolution a waiter entered and served the next course. As Jen and I gazed across the park we saw a naked man bent over in gay solicitation behind some bushes. The Ferris wheel creaked upwards, the diners stretched over their napkins, and the man in the bushes was obscured by his flimsy secrecy.

Freud believed that neurotic symptoms were caused by the repression of 'perverse' sexual instincts, which were part of an infant's normal development. It was because of this repression that the sexuality of an adult 'neurotic' was underdeveloped. If the sexual instinct was not repressed but exaggerated it became a 'perversion'. He was at pains to point out that we are all 'perverted' and this was part of the normal range of human expression. Freud was particularly preoccupied with, and, some might say, stuck in, the anal stage. The anal personality was characterised as being obstinate and rigid, fixated on orderliness and cleanliness, reacting against the messiness of toilet training and the inconsistency of worn-out bike parts.

The Rear Sprockets, the metal cogs on the back wheel, are better known as the cassette. They often fit over a spindle in the rear wheel hub called the FREEWHEEL. The FREEWHEEL allows the PEDALS and CHAIN to remain fixed as the WHEEL purrs forward, creating the characteristic ticking sound of a coasting bicycle due to the smaller turning wheels inside it. But because the FREEWHEEL turns so readily when the PEDALS, CHAIN and Rear Sprockets are braced against it, there is a problem with removing the Rear Sprockets. How do you unscrew something built to turn in both directions?

This is where the chain whip comes in, a tool handle with two snakes of chain links grafted on. The CHAIN meshes with the teeth of the Rear Sprockets while a separate wrench fixes onto a locking plate at the centre of the Rear Sprockets. The chain whip is then braced in the opposite direction to the movement of the wrench, as the locking plate becomes undone. This is how the Rear Sprocket is separated from what would otherwise turn beneath it (think of undoing the centre spindle of an otherwise turning record deck). Sometimes a scaffolding pole has to be slotted over the end of the wrench on the locking plate to give it added turning power, exactly the kind of blunt surgery, the kind of fan fiction eroticism, that too often lurks beneath Freud's elegant prose – dismantling delicate things with generic metaphors.

'We do not have SLX,' said the Austrian bike mechanic when we went back to the shop, 'so we fitted SLR.'

'But I wanted SLX.'

'SLR will get you to India.' He wiped the grease from his fingers with a tissue.

I went back to the campsite, took off my cycling shorts and underpants, washed them and hung them up to dry, and then I set off on my newly tuned bicycle into the city, pantless and SLXless.

When you carry enormous amounts of luggage on a bicycle its weight passes for normal. When you stop carrying that luggage the bicycle attains a weightless quality. And here I was in exotic freefall, my hands brushing against the sides of parked cars and tree trunks as I rolled into the main square of the Karlsplatz and straight into a parade of beer-swilling punks waving their fists at the sky. The punks were kicking along the street – I kid you not – a ball of rubbish the size of a lorry, a fly-paper conglomeration of newspaper and flyers and posters. Marching alongside the punks, as if one couldn't exist without the other, there were two columns of suited and booted riot police. *Aha*, I thought, *here is the repressed dreaming of Austria, all those neat wood piles at the side of the roads, finally giving up their sap as a luminous peacock anger.*

Freud proposed that just as man was driven by a life-generating force or Eros (for which Libido was the sexual fuel) he was also driven by its opposite, a Thanatos, or death instinct, a drive to return to the inorganic state of mere matter. The individual directed this instinct towards the self and then out towards the environment, as sadism or aggression. A punk kicking a ball of rubbish is an impulse that veers towards death by kicking it away.

Freud longed to connect the pathological body to the mind but having no science or integrated philosophy to build this bridge he was stuck with a metaphorical tool set. What neuroscience now prides itself on, and what Freud lacked, is material evidence. fMRI scanners knock a window into our skulls and have a peep at what goes where and why. But knowledge of parts is not the same as the knowledge of whole. We can no more say that love is located in the hindbrain than we can say it is located in the physical anatomy of the heart. A purple splodge on an fMRI scanner may be more apparent than a theoretical philosophy but it doesn't make it any more explanatory. The same neuroscientists that sneer at Freud's 'invention' of the unconscious seek to recast this hidden mental realm as a series of parallel processing circuits, sifting through information like choice nuts and bolts on a tray. This ignores the symbolic power of the unconscious, which, whether we like it or not, seethes through our dreams and erupts into the Karlsplatz spitting lager at pantless tourists. We need a scanner to make sense of lesions in the brain but we need a poet to make sense of the paradox of dreaming. Freud was more poet than scientist but would never admit this.

The most valuable part of Freud's work was his process, the journey on which he travelled alongside his patients. It is likely that the generalisations he laboured onto his clients, his interpretations of their dreams, unconscious wishes and sexual instincts, were less important than the hours he spent actively listening to them, accompanying them on a journey from their inner to outer worlds. And for this there is no scanner, no choice words and no compass. It is a partnership through time.

Somewhere in the bucolic Austrian countryside my CHAIN fell off again. I saw Jen ahead, a distant figure looking back. As I propped the bike up on its kick stand, a tractor puttered to a stop. The merry-looking driver waved a crumpled plastic bottle at me. I weighed up the pros and cons of various saliva-borne diseases and then took a long swig. It tasted cidery. When I then kicked the PEDAL down, the CHAIN slipped cleanly into place, and I would not have to adjust it for another three thousand miles.

The border between Slovakia and Hungary meanders from one side of the river to the other. Abandoned Soviet buildings follow one after the other like a discarded concrete chastity belt, and it was here, approaching Bratislava, that we found hundreds of women in bikinis rollerblading along the banks of the Danube. I pushed the thumb lever on my HANDLEBARS, the gears shifted the CHAIN smoothly up the teeth of the Rear

Sprockets, and I slowed down to meet them as Jen rang her BELL furiously.

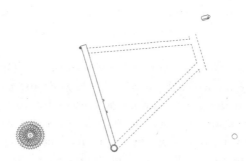

CHAPTER 7

The Tyres

I'd decided that after Vienna the Danube bike path would evaporate and the only way to negotiate the tracks of eastern Europe would be with Tyres of heft and purpose. I'd arranged, therefore, for suitably proportioned 'tank tyres' to be delivered from the UK. We discovered, not unsurprisingly, that after Vienna tarmac roads still existed. And the tank Tyres remained strapped to the back of my bike for the next thousand miles, gazing up at me with a kind of wide-eyed rebuke.

Just as Freud was excavating the subconscious in Vienna a young philosopher called Edmund Husserl was constructing his own philosophical template of human experience. Husserl like Descartes (see BOTTOM BRACKET) began his academic life as a mathematician. And, like Descartes, he subscribed to a world view that emphasised pure thought and reason, the eternal realm of ideas, over the body and its untrustworthy perceptions.

But Husserl became increasingly frustrated with this rational take on reality. To deny our perceptive, sensory, conscious, moment-to-moment experience was to deny the very context in which our reality was constructed, including the science which Descartes's clear reason laid the foundations for. Husserl turned Descartes's famous 'I think therefore I am' on its head and instead proposed 'I am therefore I think.' If Descartes declared that our perceptions weren't to be trusted one iota, then Husserl countered that this iota was all that we have. By emphasising the vividness of these phenomena, his phenomenology, Husserl put individual, physical experience back on the map; the joy ride of being alive. He wasn't seeking to undermine reason, mathematics or science but he was up for having a rumble with 'scientism', the belief that our lives can be determined only by empirical observation, and that our internal world, our private experiences, can only be determined by someone else's spreadsheet.

Any worries I might have had about cycling large distances had long been carried over into the less threatening grid of bike statistics. There are vast car parks of online information that will convince you of the pros and cons of different Tyre sizes, materials and brands. Much of this centres around 'rolling resistance', the displacement of energy due to the crush of a Tyre on the road. After air resistance, this is the most important drag holding a cyclist back on the road.

Rolling resistance is represented by the symbol CR. The calculation of CR is boggling. Tyre diameter, pressure, width, ambient temperature, road surface hardness, the scuffling sideways motion of rubber, the effect of slope, bike speed and wind friction, all have something to add. Even if you just take tyre pressure and bike speed into account you end up with equations like: $CR=0.0051 \{1+(1.09bar/p\}[1 +Fv/3kN) + (1 + Fv/30 kN) (V/39 m/s2]\}$

The Danube bike path had perfectly flat tarmac, and with brand-new, pumped-up-to-within-a-decimal-point-of-their-optimum-pounds-per-square-inch Tyres, it felt like we were riding nowhere, that we were gliding on a monorail, utterly disconnected from the astonishing gorges around us.

Our saviours were the Red Arrows. The Red Arrows were a group of older women on racing bikes, all wearing red cycling tops and Lycra shorts. They had been officially named, by me, after the fighter display team that looped the loop in the skies of my childhood summers. It was humbling to see them disappearing into the distance, only for them to reappear at beer gardens further along the path, where they would be getting sloshed in the sunshine as we rolled past in lacklustre silence.

Without even saying anything, Jen and I pushed into their slipstream. We rode hard and fast, fighting our legs, our bodies, our lungs, our streaming eyes, into the blur of their shorts. And finally. Finally. We began to feel alive.

Martin Heidegger was a German protégé of Husserl and a bit of a Nazi, demonstrating that humane philosophy and humane political conviction don't necessarily go hand in hand. Heidegger said that we aren't just plonked on the planet like golf balls but have a very visceral relationship with the world around us. Central to Heidegger's philosophy is the concept of *Dasein* or 'being there', a subjective, almost indescribable, experience of being alive in the world. His translated writings include stodgy compound words like 'being-in-the-world' or 'ready-to-hand', analogous to the calorific cake combinations so freely available along the Danube bike path (*Kaiserschmarren* or *Haselnuss Bällchen*), labels that give you indigestion even before you swallow them. But all he was really trying to say was 'Wake up and feel the breeze on your face', as death is always on the horizon. Cycling calls attention to the strange freefall of being alive, it wakes us from us our computer screens and cars by relocating us into a whole new merry-go-round of tensions and pressure points, a world apart from our normal experience of movement. Clive Cazeaux, a cyclist and professor of aesthetics, describes cycling as a kind of 'choreographed falling'. And this sense of floating above the road, while also being connected to it, has the power to wake us to the strange physicality of being alive.

'Hey, Heidegger, nice multi tool you're packing there.'

'Yeh. It's a compound bridging experience between the mental and physical realm.'

Heidegger said that tools don't really have meaning of themselves until we put our hands to them. It is we as conscious beings that give tools their purpose. In this way they represent a bridge between our inner mental landscape and the physical world of hard objects. Contemporary philosophers have developed this idea of 'tool-being' into notions of 'extended mind', of a consciousness that spills beyond our skulls. Smartphones contain our photos, addresses, memos and calendars, and represent something of who we are that extends into the environment that surrounds us. We can understand the bicycle as a form of extended mind, a physical tool that can probe and question reality. If we force this idea to its limits, if we pump air into the concept, then we might imagine the Tyres to be extensions of who we are, fingertips reading the road, appreciating the landscape. Cyclists hunched over their HANDLEBARS are also bow-backed question marks. And the question they are asking is, 'What does it mean to be alive in the world?' And the answer that they receive through the Tyres is not a rational description but a ragged jangle of sensation, an experience of presence that Heidegger termed 'being there' and a group of women in matching red Lycra downing steins of shandy might call 'a good ride'.

*

The next day I had the bright idea of going off road, following a path I could see dotted on a tourist map. To begin with it looked like the yellow brick road, scores of butterflies nesting in the sun like stunned ice-cream wafers. But as we went further into the scrub, too far to think about turning back, the road became unnavigable, the mud hardened into runnels and the potholes into stagnant ponds. In the end we had to get off and drag the bikes in and out of the craters like we were leading stubborn donkeys. Then the mosquitoes arrived, and in trying to escape them our arms scraped against the hawthorn bushes either side of the potholes. This was certainly experiential. But did it wake us up with a startling and phenomenological insight? No. It was just fucking awful.

'This time the cake's on you,' said Jen as she swatted her own face with a slap.

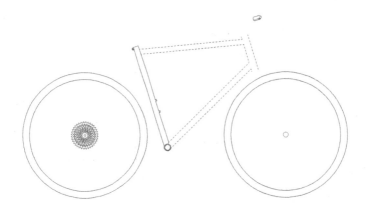

CHAPTER 8

The Seat Post

We heaved our bikes up six flights of stairs to meet Matyas in his Budapest apartment. He pointed at the narrow strip of railing that separated us from the grubby-faced kids in the courtyard six floors down. 'You better lock your bikes,' he said. Romani (Gypsy) families lived in the run-down apartments in the lower part of the building, alongside a drugs and prostitution racket and a police station that didn't care. Leaning against the railings, I had the sensation of falling across the half-demolished apartment blocks, the domed spires and down into the courtyard, a kind of historical vertigo.

Hegel, the big man of nineteenth-century philosophy, believed that human understanding developed historically through a Socratic back and forth, a kind of philosophical ding-dong known as a dialectic. Each era had its own 'idea' which was then thrown out of the ring by the reaction against it, the 'anti-idea' until, finally, a compromise between them was reached. Hegel's big idea was itself wrestled by the weightier misanthrope Karl Marx (larger beard, dirtier fingernails), who argued that ideas were not the drivers of human development but the actual material forces of human existence, the hard push and shove of economics. Historical change happened not because of a dialectic or rallying call in ideas but because of a change in ownership, in material wealth, through the bloodshed of revolution and resurrection. Dialectical materialism, a clumsy left hook of a term, not actually coined by Marx but often attributed to him, was swung hard by Lenin and tyrants like him to justify the Soviet state. If history was a series of revolts and insurrections against capitalism, then the state must wage a continuous battle against it, both within and without, so that all men could become equal and property meaningless.

In one hour a cyclist might make more than five thousand pedal turns and, cycling five days a week over one year, this turns into nine million revolutions. That's a lot of revolution. Even a half-centimetre difference in SADDLE height, determined by the Seat Post's position within the SEAT TUBE, can knock out your knees out like an Ulster snooker cue. I was so neurotic about my knees that I'd marked the point where the Seat Post connected to the SEAT TUBE with a permanent marker. It's not unusual for this point, Seat Post against SEAT TUBE, to become permanently stuck, either mechanically, when an oversized Seat Post is bashed into the SEAT TUBE with a hammer, or chemically, when it is welded into the frame because of rust. To release it you can try putting the Seat Post in a vice and twisting the bike, turn the frame upside down and pour dry ice into it, heat up the outside of the SEAT TUBE with a propane torch, and finally, as a last resort, cut off the end, hacksaw it down the middle and curl it up inside itself like the lid of a sardine tin.

*

Hungarian philosophy has a repetitive bluntness. Marxism, Marxism or Marxism. Like a lump hammer coming down again and again on the subtle complexities of human existence. But this was not always so. After the repressed anti-Soviet revolt of 1956, a more narky anti-authoritarian streak appeared. All states, explained Gyorgy Lukacs, were corrupt, whether they were Soviet, communist, capitalist or otherwise. The common man would always have to deal with not just the hard knocks of capitalism but the despotism of power itself.

Matyas hired out his Trabant to passing tourists looking for a communist fix. The Trabant smells and drives like an old British Mini, the nostalgic whiff of damp carrying through a thin metal frame and every bump striking up from the tarmac, ten inches below your bum. Riding in a car seemed like heresy after so many miles on a bike until I realised, as we were thrown up and down on the road surface, that what I enjoyed so much about the Trabant was that it was so much like a bicycle. After we'd bounced round Budapest in his Trabant, we arrived to find Matyas's wife, Lilla, at the apartment, drenched from a storm. Lilla was employed as a social worker in Budapest, at the interface of the impoverished Romani community and the Hungarian state. She bore circles of worry around her pretty eyes and the black curls of her hair dripped water on the floor. But as soon as we started to talk about cycling she smiled and shook her head from side to side to get rid of the drops. Lilla and Matyas had cycled across Romania on a tandem, up into the Carpathian Mountains, the ancient forests in the far north of the country.

'Bikes,' she said, 'allow the soul to catch up with the kilometres. Planes do not do this.'

We told them that we were bored following the Danube bike path, and Lilla told us we must cycle into Romania and the high ranges of Transylvania, spreading out our tourist map to illustrate.

'You have to seize life,' said Lilla, pulling at the folds like they were the creases in an old dress. 'That is what the Roma do. You cannot follow the same straight road.' (It's worth noting here that the Roma or Romani, popularly but inaccurately known as Gypsy, are different from the Romanians of Romania – see DOG STICK.)

'The Danube isn't straight; it's more of—'

'East.' She jabbed the map. 'Across the Nagy Alfold, straight into Romania.'

Jen suggested that our map might be too small-scale to navigate these bold ideas.

'Matyas will get you helicopter maps.' Matyas nodded placidly. 'After you have ridden through Romania, Bulgaria and Turkey, you will ride through Afghanistan.' We started to protest but Lilla was not the kind of woman who would take no for an answer. After they had gone to bed, Jen and I stumbled across our pannier bags, scattered like a mountain range across our tourist map, and fell into violent dreaming.

Attila Kotanyi was a Hungarian philosopher who searched for a personal response to authoritarian power, finding more of an alliance with the individualism of existentialism than the ham-fisted dialectical materialism of Soviet-era politics. After the failed Hungarian revolution of 1956, he fled to France, where he met Guy Debord, avant-garde Marxist and pioneer of psychogeography, the psychological mapping of physical spaces.

The way to subvert city planning, said Debord, was a purposeful drifting that ignored the state boulevards, the commuter highways and bus routes, and instead created its own revolutionary waymarks through the urban gridlock. This new mapping of old street plans was not a modern trick. William Blake, poet and visionary of the eighteenth century, had long ago jay-walked the tenement streets of London and reimagined them as a new Jerusalem.

The touring cyclist is a border-flouting kerb hopper, dodging down alleyways, scuffling through back roads, rebuilding the world on their own terms and not the diktats of a road atlas. If we are ridiculous enough to imagine a bike as a map, then the tube angles, the geometries, the mitred connections, become an old route plan, refolded and re-welded in a new form.

With Matyas's one-inch-to-three-mile helicopter maps we crept across the flat hot plains of east Hungary, the Nagy Alfold, mile by sweaty mile. It was so flat you could track the sun and its scooped-out path from horizon to horizon. Jen tried to push it down with her finger like a coin into a slot, as I cooked pasta in a ditch. We were forcing ourselves into new places, away from the prescribed monorail of the Danube bike path. There were old men in check shirts riding 1960s bikes, their hoes across the HANDLEBARS, or forty-kilo bags of flour balanced on the mudguards. Even more of these bikes were leaned up against disco bars, full of the same Hungarian men watching the Discovery channel in the humid shadows.

In the middle of nowhere we came across an abandoned railway line marked only by a signal box that had been turned into a clubhouse. Its bullfrog-bellied patrons sat around in their underpants drinking tea. They nonchalantly provided us with our cups as if we were just another set of virtual passengers on the train tracks to nowhere. None of these things were remarkable of themselves, none worthy of indexing in a guidebook, yet they had a glowing quality, visions from the flat plain of the page.

The first maps were really cosmographies, representing the known universe, heaven and earth, in a single depiction. They revealed the ideal realm of the universe, through which the traveller might venture, theologically and philosophically, and not physically.

With the Renaissance a different kind of map came into being. It sought to demarcate an earthly landscape based on hard facts and not the imagination. The poet William Blake had enough skills, as an engraver and illustrator, to be at the forefront of this new period of rational mapmaking. Instead he despised its trigonometry and compass points, its crisp divisions. The visionary and mythological landscape that Blake mapped out, in his poetry and art, owed more to the cosmography of the past than the zest for surveying that was sweeping the royal societies and institutions, whose mapmakers, rather than looking down from heaven, peered out from imperial turrets, from the high points of their own jurisdiction.

With satellite technology and GPS computers it appears we have the ultimate mapping, superseding cave walls, papyrus, vellum, engraving, lithography and colour printing. And yet the information that drives Google maps and GPS mapping is itself loaded with adverts on supermarkets and car parks, the victories of capitalism over Marxism. What purports to a 'real', digital, truth, in millimetre-wide detail, is skewed yet again by the hand that maps it.

When astronauts first gazed down at this planet they marvelled not at the detail but at the spherical integrity. The oneness. Spacemen who had once been airmen, navigating the air with the most detailed military maps that science could buy, came back to earth with a transformed relationship to this newly singular world. Rather than a universal God looking down at the cosmography of the Mappa Mundi, or weather balloons looking down at individual continents, here was man himself looking down at the unity of his own planet. This was the first holistic view of what had necessarily been a part picture, man and woman limited by the horizons that confined them.

And yet to dismiss the 'partial', local, map would be to dismiss the simple sensual pleasure of reading an old map, tracking the line of a road with a fingerprint over the texture of a piece of paper. Just as we are persuaded that every road can be generically mapped for all, the bicycle ride offers a way to reclaim it for us alone, to remap it into our individual character. Like the inverse of a topographical measuring wheel, the bicycle wheel unmeasures the land, it turns it into personal memory and experience.

Near the Romanian border we met Jakov, who asked us to call him Jake. He'd hopped the communist borders after the Second World War and gone to work in a cake shop in Australia. Now retired, he'd come back to see out his last days wallowing in the local spa, one of the tiny oceans of recreation that all Hungarians roll towards in their landlocked country. He lived above a buffet and every day he would get up, read the papers, have his buffet breakfast, bob about in the spa and return to his flat. He clinked his beer bottle against his deckchair as he told us how frustrated he was with Hungary. The country was, he said, living with the legacy of communist culture, a things-were-good-back-then mentality. But soon enough he lapsed into familiar prejudices – 'those Gypsies and the Indians' were stealing Hungarian resources. It didn't matter where Jen and I rode it was always the Gypsies, the stateless Romanies, with no country to call their own, who anchored the prejudice of those around them.

In the vast landlocked heat, beneath the scorching eye of the overhead sun, we rattled down a dirt road looking for Romania. Instead we found a cattle gate and some farm labourers standing around their tractors drinking Tizer from two-litre plastic bottles. I wore a broad-brimmed nylon camping hat and a high-vis jacket, looking very much like a camp cowboy at a long-forgotten rave.

'Is this the way to Romania?' I asked.

The labourers regarded me with the torpid curiosity of workmen sat in a field in the middle of nowhere in the middle of the midday heat. They offered us a bottle of Tizer and told us 'this way' would take us to Romania but that it was an illegal crossing with no passport control. Our helicopter maps had indeed taken us to a version of Romania but not the official one. In the air above us Hungarian choppers could navigate where they pleased. But down here, on the baked earth, it was a different kind of reality.

Five hours later, salt-depleted and sun-blanched, we arrived at a dilapidated building that looked like an abandoned petrol station. This, officially, was Romania, and the first time that we'd had our passports checked since leaving the Hard Interchange (see BOTTOM BRACKET). To have properly travelled it seems you need to be hammered through a space that does not really wish to admit you. The official looked at me dubiously in my cowboy hat and Lycra hot pants.

'Why you want to come to Romania?'

To which I had no answer, other than to hand him my passport.

'Space has always interested me,' said Erno Rubik, architect and Hungarian inventor of the Rubik's Cube, 'with its rich possibilities, space alterations by objects (architecture), objects transformations in space (sculpture design), movement in space and time, their correlation, their repercussions on mankind, the relation between man and space, object and time.' Whereas large architectural structures are made of smaller components permanently fixed, A to B, Rubik had made something where the individual components could turn around each other while the overall shape remained fixed. He attached individual pieces of paper to the smaller cube faces and didn't recognise his object was even a puzzle until he started turning the blocks and found he didn't know how to take it back to its original pattern.

'It was tremendously satisfying to watch this colour parade. Like after a nice walk when you have seen many lovely sights you decide to go home, after a while I decided it was time to go home, let us put the cubes back in order. And it was at that moment that I came face to face with the big challenge: what is the way home?'

An individual Rubik's cube has forty-three quintillion colour combinations. That's a long way home.

Salonta, the first Romanian town we came to, had a Latin feel, almost like a South American staging post. When I close my eyes now I see its reds and oranges, blue shadows underneath the trees of the park square, where the older women wore crimson check shirts and headscarves and the younger women wore Adidas and T-shirts. We ate pizza at a restaurant that also functioned as the dining room for the family who ran the place. The chef leaned over his daughter's maths exercises, whispering advice in her ear as he leaned in to bring the pizza out of the oven. A man who sold radios and televisions let me into his back room so I could use his computer to send some emails. A grocer engaged us in a long conversation about his father, who had gone cycling across Romania. He decided to guard our bikes while we went into the shop next door. When we returned he pointed at a man walking past and dragged at the skin under his eyes. 'Gypsy,' he said. 'Danger.'

Erno Rubik's favourite Hungarian poet is Attila Jozef. Jozef was born 1905 in a Budapest slum, his father a wandering Romanian factory worker, his mother a Hungarian washerwoman. His father soon disappeared and his mother died when he was a toddler. His foster parents called him Peter, saying that Attila was not a good Christian name. Jozef became a lifelong anti-authoritarian, who sought freedom in poetry, a poetry underpinned by both Marxist and Freudian ideas. And yet his writing does not have the breeze block awkwardness of agit-prop Marxism nor the clunkiness of Freudian theory, it is a surreal flowing poetry, guided only by the need to be free; free from ideology, free from power, free from poverty, free from borders, free from the tarmac roads of civilisation.

From 'Glassmakers', 1923:

> ... As the sun sets over the cities and village hovels,
> they spread
> the light. Sometimes we call them
> hired hands, sometimes poets,
> though there is little distinction.
> Slowly they bleed all colour
> and become transparent, brilliant,
> great crystal windows through which
> they can see what is to come.

(translated by Peter Hargitai, 2006)

At the fringes of great cities and countries we come across the most exciting transformations, individuals trying to navigate huge shifts in power and technology. This zeroing in on the detail, from the monumental, from the Marxist, from the Freudian, carries with it an unnerving nausea, a kind of vertigo, that permeates the work of the best visionary writers, as if they are tilting on the ledge of some greater understanding.

'Be the tiny edge on a blade of grass / and you will become greater than the axis of the world,' Jozef says, and only then will you notice the 'rosebushes of your veins' (from *That's Not Me Shouting* 1924 and *Ode* 1933, translated by Klara Papp, 2018).

Colour folds and fades and blooms in Jozef's poems, like the glassblower's glass, like the over-the-shoulder-glance of a passing cyclist. We cycled through Romania, through never-ending villages strung along a single road like a string of amulets. Through settlements of Gypsy Romanies; a woman in a pink chiffon top with a headscarf and medallion earrings, bright red lipstick, gazing at us from the ochre shadows of her doorway, a flash of gold as she smiled.

At dusk we hid behind a hedge, toying with the dry soil in our hands, listening to the clank of cars and the strange tune of another language. And then, hurrying in the darkness, we put up our tent and tunnelled into our sleeping bags. In the distance we could hear the accordion of a Romanian folk tune, closer still, a techno track. The next day we cycled up to the Carpathian Mountains, watery violet in the haze of a departing storm. A stray dog followed us for a few hours up the zigzagging road, and then, defeated, dropped its tail and returned down the road.

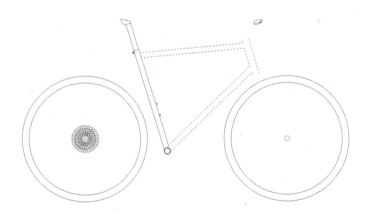

CHAPTER 9

The Dog Stick

In Romania we met the plainly named Alan. Alan was anything but plain. He'd canoed the length of the Danube, bike in the back, and was now cycling across the Carpathian Mountains. The sight of two skinny bike tourists arriving in an empty campsite and scrabbling around for food like badgers on speed clearly pressed his parental button. He whipped out a stick he'd attached to his bike frame and, in a satisfyingly thick French accent, said, 'Thees is the dog stick.'

We marvelled at the long twig.

He swiped it in the air like a musketeer. 'For tha wild dogs.'

Romania has a reputation for wild dogs. And cycling around in shorts you become acutely aware of your ankles, much like a teenager becomes unduly focused on their nose.

'Keep eet under the top tube,' said Alan, 'and where the tweeg branches it goes here, up against the head tube.' He pointed at the front of the bike frame. 'And here at the other end you make a…

uh… notch, so eet press against the seat tube. You put elasteek here –' he wrapped a band around the twig to stop it falling '– and then, when you need it. Voila!' He snatched the Dog Stick from under the TOP TUBE and waved it around his head.

'Ees no good in your bags. When the dog want bite, it bite.'

Jen looked scared. Of course she didn't need to be. I was her man and therefore had a longer TOP TUBE and that meant a longer-than-average twig. Wait till she saw me swinging it above my head.

The Romanian dogs we encountered could be divided into the following four categories:

1. Domestic Leashed
2. Domestic Unleashed
3. Scared Stray
4. Scary Stray

The Domestic Leashed would prick up its ears to your soundless cogs up to a mile away. There then followed a series of yap attacks as each subsequent dog was alerted to your presence, pulling on their leashes like dragging anchors. The Domestic Unleashed was a nuttier proposition: they would either mark their territory at the end of the driveway or, as with farm dogs, your rapidly retreating backside up to three miles down the road. The Scared Stray had suffered enough in this life and, like the most bullied kid at school, would scuttle away with its tail down. Its mirror image was the Scary Stray, the Darth Vader of ankle loppers. With no one to obey, no one to follow bar its own fickle urges, these creatures lived off sweat and bone meat.

We began to encounter these dogs on the outskirts of the larger towns and cities, the legacy of Nicolae Ceaușescu, Romania's cold war despot, who had ordered widespread clearances to make way for Soviet-style urbanisation, guard dogs and sheep dogs alike kicked out from their cages and set free to ape the terrors of their liberator. They needed a very wide berth (including cycling back the way you had come), a light sabre or, failing that, a big stick.

There is a Vlax Romani (Balkan Gypsy) proverb that goes, 'Only in the village with no dogs will walk the man with no stick.' In other words, there are no villages without any dogs, so always carry a stick. Be prepared.

Later, in rural Transylvania, we ran into one of these terrifying mutts. We got off our bikes, stood behind the wheels and pretended to be a double-headed bike monster. The dog was unconvinced, so I swept up my Dog Stick, roared and swung it round and round above my head. This was it, this was *adventure*, fighting wild dogs. A deep-seated masculine drive had finally found expression in a primal act of warrior aggression.

Looking back now, I'm pretty certain the dog was a Scottish terrier. About the size of a handbag.

Some days after we were at a cafe when a Romani woman came up to our table, hand on her heart, the other outstretched and pleading. The Romanian at the adjacent table put down his cigarette and said to us in English, 'Don't give them any money. It's like reinforcing behaviour for animals.' Then he returned to his smoke, as if this was just a reflex pause, and the Romani woman continued on her way from table to table.

Hatred of the Romani people in Romania is centuries old, but years of communist dictatorship dampened it down until, with Ceauşescu gone, it jumped off the leash, snarling. It would be wrong to characterise all Romanians as racists, just as it would be wrong to portray all Romani as saintly. But it was clear to us that the roads here were soaked with anti-Gypsy sentiment.

From the moment they first appeared in eastern Europe, from the twelfth and thirteenth centuries, moving into western Europe and Britain in the fourteenth and fifteenth centuries, the Romani have been variously labelled as Saracens, black magicians, criminal gangs, spies, even creatures from space. Just as western Europe was beginning to characterise itself as enlightened, its view of the Romani people remained resolutely unchanged. Charles Darwin said of the wandering groups that they were not 'culturally advanced', in contrast to those who were 'territorially settled'. In 1960s England it was not uncommon to find signs reading, NO BLACKS, NO DOGS, NO GYPSIES.

Mainstream history overlooks the philosophical and spiritual tradition of the Romani, a tradition otherwise flagged up by writers like Isabel Fonseca or the scholar Ian Hancock. From their work it is clear that the Vlax Romani have a complex relationship with the animals around them, embedded in a tradition of purity. Dogs and cats they consider especially unclean. There is a distinction here between being physically and spiritually dirty. Maintaining spiritual cleanliness is important for an overall sense of balance in the life of the individual and the community. And there is a division between the inside of a home, which is kept meticulously clean, and the outside, which is sometimes less so. In a similar way, the inside of the body is considered clean, while the outside, and especially that part below the waist, is impure. A bar of soap used to clean the body is considered dirty and is not used anywhere near the same sink as that for food preparation. Dogs and cats which eat unprepared flesh and lick themselves all over are considered unclean, unlike horses. Romanies would never consider having dogs as pets in their home, unlike the non-Romani, the *Gadze*.

The beliefs of the Romanies, *Romanipen*, is a community lore. They abide by rituals of purity and decontamination to provide balance – Kuntari – within their own lives, that of the community and the wider universe. This sense of balance has its roots in the ideas of dharma and karma, the central tenets of Hindu philosophy and identity (see HEADSET).

Westerners often see the Gypsy as harking back to a rural idyll, an unfettered freedom from job and state and commitment. And the Romani, wary of the persecuting non-Romani, have done little to alter this ideal and their artificial separation from those around them, which is as much a difference in philosophy as a physical boundary. In this way the Gypsy people have become a blank cinema screen onto which the technicolour dreams of the *Gadze* are projected, a fantasy of unfettered freedom which contains within it the fear of what that freedom could lead to, the impulses of the thief, the criminal, the harlot, the womaniser, the murderer, the unregulated energies we ourselves cannot admit to.

Among the hills and valleys, the delights and defeats of travelling within Romania, it took a robbery by a Romani family to challenge our idea of the thieving Gypsy.

Jen needed a pee halfway up a rural road and disappeared into the bushes. Fast behind a Romani horse and cart approached. (when I say cart – it was more of a pallet on truck axles, with a polythene tarp as a roof). Before I knew what was happening two girls had jumped off the back, popped open Jen's BAR BAG and snatched out a plastic sack with her passport and credit cards. Jen jumped out of the bushes and ran after them as they hauled themselves back onto the cart. And I, having been frozen to the spot, rode after them waving my stick. The girls, following an urgent consultation with the moustachioed man driving the cart, dropped the plastic bag off the back of the cart and onto the road. Jen peeked inside. Her passport and credit cards were all there but not her head torch. So I cycled ahead of the cart, the horse trotting at a nonchalant pace, and screamed at the driver. He looked at me placidly and, after a mild remonstration with the two girls, handed over the torch. He then asked for a cigarette. I said I didn't smoke. The girls, skinny, hair tangled, on the back of the wagon, looked down at their swaying feet as the cart moved away.

Later in Romania I would start reading *Bury Me Standing* by Isabel Fonseca, probably the most well known account of Romani life. It describes Fonseca's stay with an Albanian Romani family and her take on the history and culture of the people. The book has its critics and its own preconceptions, but it personalised the Romani for Jen and me, gave them an identity beyond the 'pack of thieves and liars' we'd heard so much about.

In a poor Romanian village, where everyone travelled by donkey and cart, a brand-new people carrier pulled up alongside us. The window slid soundlessly open, releasing a waft of air con, and the driver began the following conversation in fluent English.

'Where are you from?'

'England.'

'Have you flown from England with your bikes?'

'No, we have cycled here from France, Germany –' we rehearsed the list of countries for him as the driver hit his head with the heel of a hand '– to Austria, to Hungary, to...' The driver repeatedly hit his brow. Our trip wasn't just a revelation to him, it demanded self-punishment.

'You are crazy,' he decided.

'Yes,' we agreed, 'we are crazy.'

Then he noticed the tent on the back of my bike.

'You are camping...?'

'Yes.'

'It is dangerous?'

'No. People are kind.'

'People are kind?'

'People are kind.'

He shook his head as if this was the craziest thing he had ever heard, and then reached into his car, located an ice-cold can of Fanta and passed it through the door.

The lesson of bike touring, with very few exceptions, is that people *are* kind. But people too often want to hear the inverse; not only is hatred better gossip, but it also reinforces long-held assumptions about who we are, in opposition to others, and provides a convenient get-out from experimenting with the possibilities of intimacy. But, despite the kindness of strangers, which would increase exponentially the further east we travelled, we began to yearn for the kindness of home, the acknowledgement that we weren't just two people passing on bikes, we were somebody's son, somebody's daughter, somebody's brother and somebody's sister, somebody's friend and somebody's neighbour.

If too much time is spent with the *Gadze*, who do not respect Romani rituals or beliefs in cleanliness, there is a draining of spiritual energy – *dji* (probably related to the Sanskrit *jiva* (see HEAD TUBE) and Hindi *ji*, meaning life, soul, spirit, mind). To recharge this *dji* a Romani must spend more time with their community to encourage *baxt*, a mixture of spiritual and physical wellbeing. This helps me to understand the crowds of extended Romani family, who appeared at the wards and accident departments I worked in as a junior doctor. A Romani patient must wrangle with the uncleanliness of the *Gadze*, despite their sterile wards, and by doing so risk a state of pollution or *marime*. The presence of the extended family can help restore *dji* and spiritual balance. All of these ways of thinking suggest a different definition of identity, in which the individual self is more intrinsically connected to everything around it (see Atman and Brahman in HEADSET). The Romani do not see the non-Romani as untouchable, only different. A friend of mine who went cycling in the Ukraine surrendered himself, like many bike tourists do, to wild camping, washing in rivers, taking his food where he could find it, shaking off civilisation like an itchy shirt and getting properly 'dirty'. One night he ate some wild mushrooms, fell into a toxic coma and awoke to find himself in a Romani camp being nursed back to life with a thin gruel. Another friend was kicked out of a squat for drug use and ended up on the streets. He was saved from homelessness by a group of Romanies who, for a short period, gave him shelter.

On the way to Sibiu in Transylvania a Romani boy, aged about ten or eleven, rode alongside us, frantically pedalling to keep up, one hand on his HANDLEBARS, the other alternating between his heart and us. 'Money. Please. Give me.'

Not having the normal option of just cycling away, I said, half playfully, 'No, you give me some money.'

This tiny purgatory continued out of the village and along the road, the same back and forth again and again – 'Please. Money. Give me.' 'No, you give me money' – until we reached a hill, and the boy dropped away behind us, feet on the ground, staring after us, expressionless, as we rode on.

The exact origins of the Romani can't be known. But their language overwhelmingly suggests they migrated out of India. Some say they came from northern India, after resisting Muslim invaders in the eleventh century. They left the Indian region as either prisoners of war or victors, into what is now Pakistan, before travelling through Iran and Turkey. By the thirteenth century they had arrived in Byzantium, the Christian empire extending from Europe into Turkey. It was during this period, in the high plains of central Turkey, that the Romani language was forged; a mix of Hindi, Greek dialects, Persian and Turkish. When the Islamic Ottoman Empire eventually conquered Byzantium in the fifteenth century, they brought these tribes with them as they advanced through the isthmus of Istanbul, into Europe, and right up to the gates of Vienna. The Romani had long ago ceased to understand themselves as coming from Indian castes, as their cultural and philosophical identity, aggregated from all the lands they had travelled through, was now their own. Over the next five hundred years they were subject to slavery, torture and genocide. And it was amidst these constant external pressures that Romani culture and philosophy, *Romanipen*, turned inward. A hundred years after they arrived in Romania, in the sixteenth century, the Romani people were taken as slaves by feudal Romanian overlords. ('Romanian' is from the Latin Roma meaning Rome. 'Romani' is from the Roma language Rom meaning man or husband.) These Romani slaves included 'scopiti', men who had been castrated so as not to present a threat to Romanian noblewomen. Slaves were bought and sold in batches in the Romanian principalities of Transylvania and Moldavia. In the sixteenth century, you could buy a Romani child for 32p whilst in the nineteenth century they were being sold by weight. You could buy one and a half slaves, a woman and her children, and exchange a slave for a pig. They were forbidden to marry without their owner's consent, speak Romani, practise their customs or play musical instruments. Those that escaped into the Carpathian Mountains were described by a nineteenth-century observer as 'half wild, half-naked, eating dog meat by the absence of anything else'. The Romani sense of identity and cultural cohesion, itself based around a spiritual cleanliness and balance, entirely at odds with 'unclean' animals, was debased by slavery into a caricature, in which they became those dogs. Not only was the Romani identity stolen (and this is the real essence of the 'thieving gypsy') it was savagely redrawn in the minds of those who enslaved them. By the Middle Ages this slavery had been carried into Spain, Portugal and Britain, and from there, around the world. You could find Romani slaves in Scottish coal mines, Virginia colonies and the Caribbean (where the women were traded as prostitutes). Commonwealth slavery of the Romani ended with the Abolition Act 1833 but it continued in Romania late into the nineteenth century. Vlad Dracula (a template for Count Dracula) was the fifteenth-century Romanian who delighted in torturing his Romani slaves. And in Romani myth, the Vampire, who is a *mullo*, one of the living dead, takes the virginity of a young woman and kills her mother, father, husband and son, so that by the time the story is done the floor is 'swimming two hands-breadth deep in blood'. It is not hard to read the devastation of a people into this.

> I like the constant change from extreme comfort to extreme discomfort, that is an essential part of living a good healthy life, and I like the feeling of uncertainty of never knowing quite what's round the corner though I might know the area well. I like the feeling that, come what may, I will be able to win through in all circumstances, as long as I rely on myself and remain a Romany...

> (Manfri Fred Wood, Welsh Romani in the early 1900s)

The loss of identity that accompanies us, far away from home comforts, is in contrast to the presumed strength of a Romani community that travels and lives together. Romani travelling identity, idealised or otherwise, is one of movement *and* rootedness, dispersed and grounded, common to all nomads, but more jarringly obvious in Europe where these beliefs have otherwise been lost.

The journeys that Romani have taken around the world and the story of their exodus from India to western Europe, puts paid to the idea that the road to India has a clear beginning and end. In our local play area in Bristol you might find a Vlax Romani 'Roma' family playing alongside second-generation families from India and Pakistan and Poland and Lithuania. The Romani remind us that India is already in Europe, practically and philosophically, part of a journey that has been going on for almost a thousand years. The white, non-Romani, British, will have traces of Romani blood in their ancestry whether they like it or not, with Romanichal (English Romani), Kale (Welsh Romani) and Nachins (Scottish Romani), travelling and settling in the UK for the past five hundred years.

Outside the Tesco of my local Bristol high street you can find, most days, a Vlax Romani man, with black moustache and crumpled grey suit, playing the violin. You don't need to listen carefully to that violin to know the sound of an aching melancholy, not just a romanticised notion of 'Gypsy' life, but a living evocation of a people. There on the wet British paving, amidst the plastic bags and the theme pubs and the cash machines.

One Vlax Romani story tells how a woman sacrifices her whole family for the Devil's violin; the body of this violin is her father, its strings her brothers, her mother the bow. The sound of that violin is the sound of an identity being stretched, not across any one individual but generations linked over hundreds of years and thousands of miles to a self that was forever being torn apart and left behind. In the malls of the UK, in the tourist squares of Bavaria, in the *piatas* of Romania, you can hear this yearning threaded with the Byzantine and Ottoman melodies of the Middle East, an oriental chromatic scale and, ultimately, the Indian bhairava, and the Ragas of the Indian subcontinent, with their chanted stories of Hinduism, of the gods Shiva and Kali, meditative ciphers for unity from division.

The violin busker's cardboard sign in Bristol is, using the English Romani language, a *'kosh that pookers the drom'*; a 'kosh' (signpost), that 'pookers' (tells), the 'drom' (road); a milestone that leads backwards through time and continents to a philosophical wrangle with the very nature of self, to the Hindu Atman, the individual soul, and Brahman, the complicit universe (see HEADSET). The shoppers, huddled into their raincoats and their smartphones cannot know this, yet how can it not seep into them, through their skins, their pale eardrums, and into the lopsided lope of their bike ride home? And in the sounds of the Romani musicians along the road, in the drone whistles of the Balkan men we rode past on street corners, in the Dastgahs and melodic structures of Persian music, how could we not hear those same echoes, clip clopping towards us from the East?

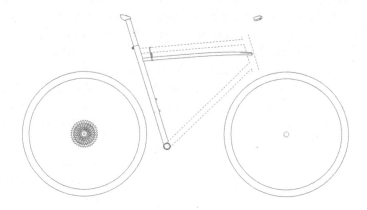

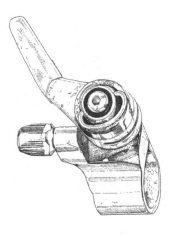

CHAPTER 10

The Gears

Matyas and Lilla, our friends from Budapest, had long ago persuaded us to cycle to Stana de Vale, a hilltop village and winter ski resort in the Carpathian Mountains, but the sweep of Lilla's biro on a tourist map turned out to be a sheer zigzagging road. I recorded the incline as a 1:2 in my diary, a 50 per cent gradient, but this is impossible. Perhaps this was just how it seemed. So we did what any man and woman with cake-shop legs would do. We stopped.

I awoke the following day to the sound of bleating. I poked my head out of the tent to discover two shepherds with crooks. *This is it! Ancient. Biblical. The real deal.* Then one of the herders pulled out his smartphone and started texting as he waved his crook at his animals with the other hand. Didn't he understand *my* needs? Our journey here had been so gradual there had been no culture shock. And yet I had wanted this. Some jolt or swipe around the face. Something to match the incredulous gradient we were climbing.

*

Gears allow a cyclist to maintain their pedalling force, regardless of speed, by changing the diameter of the CHAIN WHEELS at the front to the diameter of the REAR SPROCKETS at the back. You can generally judge how far into the wormhole of cycling a rider has descended by their approach to Gears.

Most people know a bike has Gears. Though often not. Then there are those who know the difference between derailleur Gears (where the gearing is on the outside of the WHEEL axle) and hub Gears (safely enclosed). Then we come to the mechanically minded, those who know exactly how many cogs their Gears have, the teethed rings of metal fore and aft, and how many teeth each of those rings has. But total Gear freaks will be able to tell you the ratio of the teeth on the CHAIN WHEELS at the front to the ratio of teeth on the REAR SPROCKETS at the back. And it is this ratio that determines the ability of a bike to tackle both those ridiculous hills and the flat plains beyond. A higher ratio means the bike can better tackle large hills while reducing torsional forces through the knees. But the price of this wider cog ratio, with its lower knee-racking forces, is a higher pedalling speed, hence the whirring legs of a cyclist on a hill, spinning their smallest 'granny' wheel at the front. Jen and I had granny wheels. And grandpa legs. And it occurred to me, as I spun endlessly up these hairpin bends, that we were cycling in the opposite direction to India, the reason for taking this trip in the first place. The net result of this was the following conversation, punctuated only by the creaking sound of a CHAIN stretching against spinning cogs.

'We could have followed the Danube all the way through Hungary, you know.'

'*We* agreed it would make the journey more *interesting*.'

'Have you got any bananas left?'

'You ate the last one.'

'How are we going to get up this mountain without any bananas.'

'Eat the biscuits.'

'But I don't want the biscuits.'

'Then put a sock in it.'

'But I don't have any clean socks.'

Creak. Whirr. Creak. Whirr. Creak.

In the myth of Sisyphus, he pushes a boulder up a mountain, only for it to roll down again just as he reaches the top. This is Sisyphus's punishment for outwitting death: to repeat himself for all eternity – push the boulder to the top of the hill, see it roll it down and push it back up again.

The French existentialist Camus wrote a long and famously gloomy essay about this, insisting that Sisyphus echoed the predicament of modern man and woman. If there was no longer any god, religion or explanatory force for human existence, then what was the point in being alive? Man must repeat the same daily tasks without any higher calling, and with no eternity to salvage his death. But despite this (and the essay being a long meditation on suicide), Camus believed that Sisyphus returned to his task with *joy*. Sisyphus was the ultimate hero of absurdism. He had dissed the gods, put two fingers up to death and now he was putting his shoulder to the meaninglessness of life without any hope that someone would relieve his burden. His hopelessness gave him a paradoxical kind of freedom. Freedom from the disappointment that hope can contain, freedom from the weight of disappointment. Sisyphus's rock was heavy, but it was *his* rock, and no one could take it away from him.

There was an absurdity about the whole proposition of cycling to India. The actual process of spinning our legs round was endlessly repetitive. You wake up, you cycle for eight hours and then you go to bed and wake up and repeat, heading towards a destination that seems impossible to imagine. And yet there was a choice in this 'stupidness' (as my Trinidadian grandmother would have called it). It was *our* ridiculous choice. It didn't belong to the workplace, the government, the state or God. It was *ours*.

'All Sisyphus's silent joy is contained therein,' says Camus. 'His fate belongs to him. His rock is his thing...'

And, I thought, as I pedalled up an interminable mountainside in Romania with no proper food, this fucking heavy lump of steel is *mine*.

The top of Stana de Vale revealed a bossy woman in a caravan who was keen to introduce us to every single biscuit in her 'shop'. We also found a concrete Soviet-era hotel that served meaty soups beneath an enormous flatscreen television showing global sports events. And from there we acquired a stomach bug that led to a knock-kneed power walk to the campsite lavvies, where, after depositing my bum skew-whiff on the lid, I found myself staring down at the decapitated body of a dead pigeon.

Emil Cioran was the son of an Orthodox Christian priest from one of the prettiest mountain villages in Romania. And yet Cioran quickly denounced Christianity and came to scorn the peasantry of his ancestry. Cioran's philosophy was one of apocalyptic nihilism, and his parting gift to Romania, before he left for the existentialism of Paris, was the jauntily titled *On the Heights of Despair*. Sat in the darkness atop a drop toilet, atop Stana de Vale, looking down at the body of a decapitated bird, I found some solidarity with Cioran. These are his words aged twenty-two: 'The deepest and most organic death is death in solitude, when even light becomes a principle of death. In such moments you will be severed from life, from love, from smiles, friends and even from death. And you will ask yourself if there is anything besides the nothingness of the world and your own nothingness.'

And yet, like Camus, there is a blithe joy in his despair. If all there is to life is a long drop into a smelly pit of decay then this immediately opens up the possibilities of what to do in the interim. For Cioran, like Heidegger (see TYRES), the zest of life lies in a lyrical state close to, or considering, death, where utter despair is the 'negative equivalent to ecstasy'. Cioran was a philosopher in love with the lyricism of 'great and dangerous contradictions'. You don't go to him for a gentle pat on the back but for a shove out the door. And so the swing gates of the toilet cubicle flapped behind me like inverted wings.

Climbing through the hills of Transylvania, weak from our stomach bug, yet still we climbed. Eventually we came to a plateau with steep sides, and alongside us other hills like islands in an archipelago. On the hill next to us was a lone shepherd with his flock. Everything was frozen and silent.

We rolled down a rocky path and skidded to the feet of an old Transylvanian woman in a traditional black lace dress. At her side were young twin girls with cropped hair and a silver earring in each ear. The girls and the woman said nothing, and then all three, the twins with emerald-blue eyes and the woman with pupils lost in the creases of her face, looked directly at us, with our plastic pannier bags and sweaty synthetic clothing. I went for my camera and Jen pressed her hand against my arm to stop me.

Bike Gears are basically pulleys, circular levers. A lesser force is needed to move a fixed weight if it is applied over a longer distance. The pulleys of a bike WHEEL apply force over the longer distance of a bike CHAIN, around the pivots of the cogs, so the body can be carried more efficiently over the surface of the road.

All of this is so that we can use our muscles most efficiently. If the force required exceeds the fuel cell capacity of our muscles, for example if the hill is too steep or the gear too high, then we have to rely on anaerobic exercise. And this is far less efficient, leading to a build-up of lactic acid. The secret then is to fine-tune the demands of our muscles to the amount of oxygen available. And this fine tuning is the selection of Gears.

On a normal hill, with carefully used Gears, a cyclist will always be faster than a walker because of the extra efficiency that those Gears allow. But when the gradient exceeds 1:5 cycling becomes less productive than walking. So why then do people still cycle in places where they should get off and walk? Because every uphill gives a lottery win of a downhill, and the descent always gives more oomph to the cyclist than the pedestrian.

There is another way to read Sisyphus. His story has persisted over thousands of years not because it replicates the *lack* of meaning in our lives but because it helps us understand who we are, because it *gives* us meaning. In the longer version of Sisyphus's adventure, before he begins his endless trek up and down the mountain, he cheats death, not once but twice.

The same story, of hoodwinking mortality, is told in different forms across the world, with the doctor taking a lead role. In an Icelandic myth a doctor asks Death to wait until he has finished his prayer. Death agrees but then has to wait for a hundred years until the doctor tires of living, and comes to the end of his prayer. In the Grimms' tale 'Godfather Death' Death explains that the position a doctor takes at an invalid's bed determines the duration of the sickness and whether the patient recovers or dies. *Aha*, thinks the doctor, turning the bed of the patient around. But because of this the doctor himself must die.

Age thirty-nine, cycling from the UK to India, I was wresting, or so I believed, a hunk of life from its chronic final stages. But I soon discovered that cycling across continents demanded another kind of chronic wear; pedalling five days a week, for every week, for every month. In escaping a repetition of vocation, I had taken on another; an endless re-treading of a hill. It is the waking up to this repetition that characterises the mid-life transition, that the potential for the new, that marks the beginning of life, leads inevitably to the rehearsal of the old, and the inferred finality of our single span. And yet there is also something about a long cycling trip that extracts the riches from this predicament. Life may repeat but that does not mean that every repetition is the same. In each new kilometre we gain a subtly changed perspective on the road behind. In this way we rescue an ounce of the new from the old. And within those seemingly endless minutes, hours, days, of legs spinning round and round and round, there is the passage of other people's lives and the flowing variability of the landscape around us. It is not that we remake the world anew on a bike but that we repeat it more clearly. And if mind and body are just different aspects of the same thing (see BOTTOM BRACKET) then this very physical activity also represents a mental exercise; we are working out what repetition means by repeating it, hill after hill after hill. Perhaps in this way we can let go of the intoxicating potential of new beginnings, and get on with the simple process of being alive, mile after mile after mile, those apparently banal moments, exotic with slivers of newness.

Some have suggested that Sisyphus goes further than its Greek etymology, that the susurration of the sound Sis-sy-phus is an echo of our breathing, of something more ancient than even classical myth. And that by penetrating into the world around us, it echoes the swing of the sun from east to west, the endless tides of the sea, even the advance and collapse of civilisations, the inevitable cycles of time.

*

South of Cluj Napoca we joined the steep-sided gorges of the E81 highway, barrelling downhill over river basins on a stilted road. The rumbling trucks were like hammer drills pounding through the mountains, and it felt like we were part of those same hammering vibrations, excavating the tunnels. I acquired a thigh-wide graze when I smashed into a crash barrier and Jen nearly catapulted over the top of me. But that evening we followed a quiet path down to the riverbank away from the main road. Here we found a jetty where we sat and said nothing as the water moved silently underneath and around us. It was a moment that seemed all the more still for the change that surrounded it: the slow-flowing river, the evening mist curling above the water, the silhouettes of distant mountains and, on the other bank, a farmer pitching hay into his barn with a slow hypnotic rhythm: fork, pitch and return, fork, pitch and return, fork, pitch and return...

Lucian Blaga was a pre-war Romanian poet-philosopher who believed that Romanians were born from the Mioritic Space, an imaginary well that shaped Romanian identity, growing not just from their shared culture but from the outlines of the mountains themselves. He took the name from the folk ballad 'Miorita': 'Where the mountains mate / there is Eden's Gate / They're approaching lo! / And downhill they go / three fair flocks of sheep / which their shepherds keep / one Moldavian / one Transylvanian / one a Vrancean man.'

His contention was that such folk ballads were created on the *plai*, the meadows on the slopes of a hill, while the culture of the Romanians' Saxon counterparts was forged on the flat plains lower down. Blaga went as far as to say that the variation of accented and unaccented syllables throughout the poetry of Romanian ballads represented the ups and downs of the land itself.

Constantin Noica, a contemporary of Blaga, spent much of his life on a mountain top in Transylvania. He understood living as a process, not a birth into a definitive object or identity. He did not divide reality into the particularity of things or the universality of ideas but tried to condense all of these perspectives into the form of a wave. He was influenced by advances in physics, believing that matter could be understood both as particle and wave. He paralleled this by saying that the best a poet could do was ride the wave through the metaphor of poetry, following its rhythmic cadences, ebbing and flowing to the end of the poem, bringing us from birth to death, from light to shadow, from hill to valley and back again.

With a vast sweep you might attempt to connect the myth of Sisyphus, the rising and falling of the sun, the susurration of the tides, the wave theories of Noica and Blaga, the quantum chemical reactions that allow our muscles to go up and down hills in the first place, as pure *movement*, a relentless advance and return.

Somewhere between Sibiu and the E81 highway the index shifter for my Gears broke. This is the mechanism that clicks the Gear cable into predetermined spots so the CHAIN is pulled onto the correct set of cogs. Without indexing, without its *click*, there is the possibility of the CHAIN landing neither on nor off the sprocket teeth, but somewhere in between. This mattered very little until we came to the bottom of the highway, and the next hill. My solution was not to fix the indexing but to 'read' the positions of the gear lever beneath my thumb on the HANDLEBARS, an endlessly nuanced series of pauses. OK, so this wasn't Jedi levels of intuition, but it did feel like the start of a man making allowances for the rough edges of adventure, the raggedness of being alive.

As we waited for the ferry to take us across the Danube border, sulphurous clouds blew across the banks from a nearby industrial complex, while young Romanians took dips in the river. Eventually the ferry arrived to take us, the only passengers, to Bulgaria. We were greeted by a breezy Romanian man coming back in the other direction.

'*La revedere*,' he said. 'See you soon.'

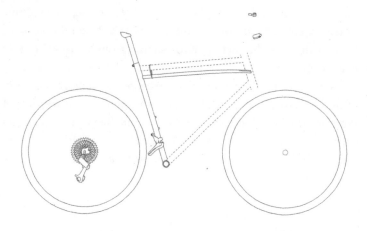

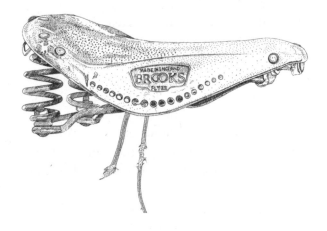

CHAPTER 11

The Saddle

After the food poisoning on top of Stana de Vale we tried to keep rolling but couldn't keep our breakfast down and stopped every ten minutes to rush into the bushes. We had no water, Jen had only swallowed half a biscuit, and I was beginning to wonder if we would make it to the next village. So when I heard a distant puttering sound on the deserted road, I imagined it would be an old Lada, a friendly farmer come to nurture us back to health with sweet broths and sleep. Instead, over the brow of the mountain pass there came a middle-aged man in a baseball cap on a petrol-driven skateboard. He acknowledged my frantic waving, thinking I was only wishing him well, before he whizzed on past. The demands of crapping in the woods and staring up at the stars as pine needles scraped at our bums had left us without clean underwear, and so we rode pantless and shortless beneath our trousers, the springs in our leather Saddles creaking as our listless bodies swung from side to side.

A piece of leather, taut and riveted, supports the sitting bones of the rider and *not* the fleshy buttocks, otherwise known as the backside. Saddles made of plastic gels or padded foam may appear more comfortable but soon smear the backside, the skin, the fat, into a flaccid balloon. Leather crafts itself to the deeper sitting bones of the human pelvis, a ring of bones that suspends the weight of the human torso. A broken-in Saddle carries the rider through the deeper frame of their bones, almost as if that skeleton, and the bike frame itself, have a seamless line. 'The bicycle like the human body is built around a frame. Bones make up the body's frame, metal tubes make up the bicycle's. Damage the frame – or the body of a bike – and everything can crash to the ground' (*Boys Life Magazine* – 1986).

The tubes that comprise a bicycle frame are made by heating a steel rod up to over 1000°C. It is then pierced and drawn over a cylindrical core called a mandrel. The resulting tube is thicker at the ends and narrower in the middle. Bike frames are now double, triple and quadruple butted, each increment adding to the strength and width of the cylindrical butts at the ends of the cylinders, while the numbering and suffixes of the different brands – Reynolds 531, Columbus SL, Ishiwata 022 – explain the alloy of the steel used. When I was approaching adolescence, with my own accelerating long bones, those names and numbers were an incantation. It felt that by just rehearsing them out loud you were spelling magic in the air.

The story of René Descartes's skeleton after his death is an extraordinary tale of theft and deception that weaves through the philosophical dilemmas that Descartes himself raised, notably his division of mind from body. Descartes spent many hours dissecting the calves and oxen that had been slaughtered near his house, and analysing their organs and bones. It was only a short step to plunge the blade into their brains. It is one of history's supreme ironies that, after Descartes's death, his head was stolen and the rest of his remains buried elsewhere, the skull and the torso never properly reunited.

Having creaked across that mountain pass, with its startling view of the Carpathian forests, I let go of the BRAKE lever and bounced down the road on my pelvic bones, looking for shelter. The first *pensione* we came to took one look at us, pale and grubby and destitute, and waved us on. In the next village we met Matei, a Bucharest city worker who had returned to his childhood home. His family were proud of him, and he was proud of the leap he'd made from this Transylvanian valley into the world of global commerce, addressing us in fluent English and by implication including us in his participation in the modern world.

'We will make you a banquet,' Matei said by way of welcome.

Jen and I still had stomach cramps and stared at the plates of food we were offered that evening with bewilderment. 'More *polenka*!' shouted Matei. As far as I could tell, *polenka*, a potent liquor and cure-all, exerted its magic more through inebriation rather than any pharmaceutical action. As the *polenka* flowed, Matei translated his uncle's oratory from the head of the table. 'The weather is changing. Before we have no mosquitoes in the mountains. Now...' He slapped his arm to make the point. 'When my daughter was born in the spring we use the traditional clothing and the wood fire. Now, her birthday, we never use the wood fire.'

Matei told us he had watched Al Gore's film *The Inconvenient Truth* about global warming but was unconvinced by its arguments. He believed the rising temperature was caused by 'flames in the sun, solar flares. Scientists want to give us another story to make the oil expensive.'

It was a star-picked evening as we crossed the valley back to the *cabine* where we were staying. Matei's softly spoken cousin knew all the statistics as he pointed up at the solar system: how far it was to the planets, how this distance could be divided into human steps, and how long these steps would take.

'Do you believe in aliens?' he asked us through Matei.

Jen and I looked up at the stars, the hundreds of thousands of stars, and we all laughed.

We cycled along the coast of Bulgaria and the crocodile's tail of concrete beach resorts. The coastal road has no hard shoulder. The region is also host to a particularly infuriating version of the summer fly. They follow you about in a black cloud, like the cartoon version of a bad mood, feeding off the sweat created by cycling in high humidity. It was either death by truck, torpor by package holiday, or torture by flies. We eventually toppled off the coastal road and onto Irakli beach, one of the few parts of the Bulgarian coast yet to be claimed by developers. There was wild camping in the woods and naturism on the beaches. But Jen and I, in a fit of conservatism and sick of pitching in roadside puddles, opted for the official campsite – a fenced compound with a toilet block and showers. We found a bit of shade under a few trees next to a swampy river, watched cows slop in and out, and then meandered onto the public beach, populated by big-bellied Bulgarian men and their much slimmer girlfriends. *What are all these men eating?* I wondered. *Their girlfriends' puddings?* Next to the toilet block was a canteen-type building that appeared to have been set up to feed all the backpackers living in the woods further down the beach. 'Come to the woods,' their cut-off jeans seemed to whisper as they queued on the other side of the fence. 'It's groovy, man.' The campsite was just a foot in the door for the developers, and we, by implication, were part of that exploitation. But something kept us there, a need for shade, a semblance of civilisation, perhaps sheer bloody-mindedness. By the second day we couldn't stand it any more and cycled up the nearest hill to the village of Emona.

Jen and I peered at the crowds milling around in what should have been a village backwater. And it was then that Rosa toppled into our life. Rosa looked like Kate Moss in shades, and her mouth moved at a monumental pace powered by Bulgarian-inflected English. She explained we had arrived on the first day of the Emona Festival of Arts 'by everyone and for everyone'. The gathering crowd were the bohemians of Sofia, and now, thanks to Rosa, we were part of the mix. She handed us some white wine, a blank white canvas and some paints and instructed us to paint the apple tree in the courtyard of her friend's house. I made a picture of an apple and stuck kidney beans in the corners with a cross on them, using the sap oozing out of the tree. Paskal, Rosa's boyfriend, who was collecting the sap in a spoon, waved a beer at me and said he was 'superglue man'. Rosa introduced us to a group of uber-hip musicians from Sofia. Somehow, we had gone from being flunkies of capitalism to Sofia scenesters.

Rosa was prone to exuberant generalisations, so that even criticisms of her fellow Bulgarians had a generosity about them. 'All Bulgarian men over forty are drunkards,' she said, waving her glass of wine around the table like a toast. She made it quite clear to us we would not be cycling back down the hill to the 'compound'. 'Tonight,' she said, 'you dance with us.'

We were bundled into the back of a jeep and sent off to the very top of the village, where we found a crumbling monastery and Vasco, the 'Eric Clapton of Bulgaria', who was doing a secret show there, playing rock tunes on guitar and harmonica.

I got talking to a German artist called Arnt, who told me about the unusual wildlife you could find hereabouts, snakes with venom so poisonous you only had an hour to source the antivenom, 'two hours if you don't move', and a roach-like scorpion. He said this corner of the coast was about to change and that all the backpackers camping on Irakli beach 'needed somewhere to shit'. Some days, he said, you could smell it wafting in from the beach.

I wandered with a beer to the small monastery on the hill, which had been lit up with spotlights so you could see its timbers and strips of lath and plaster. Its walls were scooped into pleasing domes and arches, daubed here and there with names and dates in Cyrillic. Rosa said they were the names of conscripts from the nearby radar station who had marked their end of service with graffiti. And then we were whisked off to the White Rabbit pub, where the other Sofia musicians were jamming and riffing and everyone was plastered on fig brandy. When we eventually stumbled back the down the hill, to the main part of the village, we came across one of the rare roaches that Arnt had mentioned, crossing the road. We gathered round as a jeep full of musicians rolled up beside us, and the driver, misinterpreting our shouting and waving, swung the jeep around the corner and over the scorpion. We returned to have a look at it, squashed but still wriggling, its juices leaking out from its exoskeleton and across the chalk road.

That night we slept in the garden shed of one of the artists, twisting and turning on the travel towels we'd made into makeshift blankets, the bones of our bodies hard on the wooden floor, dreaming fig brandy dreams of crunched scorpions and the broken lath and plaster of a graffitied monastery.

Separated from their skull, the bones of Descartes's torso were buried with Roman Catholic ceremony in Paris. A hundred and fifty years later they were saved from the chaotic looting of the French Revolution to become a trophy for the new secular state. It was only twenty years after this, in 1819, when Descartes's coffin was opened in the presence of members of the French Academy of Sciences, including the Swedish chemist Berzelius (responsible for the notations and shorthand of the modern periodic table) that it was finally discovered that Descartes's skull had gone AWOL. Berzelius returned to Sweden (the place of Descartes's death), where he happened to see a classified ad in a paper advertising the 'skull of the famous Cartesius'. He bought it from the casino owner who had secured it at an auction and arranged for the skull to be transported back to Paris to be reunited with the body.

When the skull was taken out of the box it was found to be covered in graffiti, the signatures of its previous owners. Among those signatures was Olof Celsius, whose nephew had created the temperature scale of the same name. Then there was Johan Fischerstrom, whose lover Hedvig Nordenflycht was Sweden's 'first feminist' and a poet of 'nature and loss'. The skull had spent many of its lost years in Sweden in a series of cabinets of curiosities. These glass-fronted dressers, a phenomenon of the Enlightenment, were places where the reasoned mind turned its focus on everything that had previously been the domain of a Christian god. And so the skull of Descartes was kept alongside the trophies of pygmy head-hunters, the fossilised remains of flying monsters, phallic totems, dried flowers and pinned butterflies, suggesting that the entirety of the natural world might be contained and ordered in separate boxes. In fact, these tiny museums were more studies in random association, places where Descartes's skull could exist next to the bony shell of a scorpion's exoskeleton.

Aged nineteen and freshly arrived at Birmingham Medical School, I haggled a skull off a third-year student. Like many others I wasn't able to afford a whole skeleton and had to make do with the head, which I kept in a box underneath the drop-leaf desk in my digs. The floor spaces of those terraced houses were a thriving labyrinth of rodents, which I could hear scurrying beneath my feet from one underheated rental to the next. I remember waking one night to feel my pyjamas brushing against my nose, until eventually, half asleep, I grasped at whatever was there, opened my eyes and saw that I was holding one of the furry animals in my hands. I jumped out of bed, screamed and threw it against the wall. Then I took the sawed-off vault of my skull, still unboxed on the drop-leaf table where I had been studying, trapped the mouse inside, replaced the skull cap and then released the animal in the garden. I spent many winter nights hunched and shivering over that skull, listening to the mice scratch beneath the floorboards, my young hands tracing the sutures, the sawtooth joins between the plates of bone. Never once did I wonder where that skull had actually come from. To whose skeleton had it been attached? To what human being had it belonged?

In nineteenth-century Britain, the appetite for skeletons was such that it led to battles in graveyards between grieving relatives and medical students. The Anatomy Act of 1832 gave medical schools the rights to some unclaimed bodies and stopped the thefts, but even then demand could not match supply, so bones were exported from India to Britain. In 1984 India was still exporting 60,000 a year, most of them stolen, until their export was stopped the following year. However, the trade then continued illegally, and in all likelihood the skull I owned, bartered between medical students, had once belonged to an Indian man or woman, perhaps dragged from a funeral pyre as soon as the relatives had left.

In Hinduism it is believed the body becomes impure immediately after death, and its burning is thus a ritual cleansing, allowing the spirit to leave and find reincarnation. The ashes are returned to the River Ganges by the relatives, returning the container of the spirit to the physical world.

Seen in this context, any skeleton 'belonging' to a medical student may once have represented a Hindu soul trapped in its worldly domain. Is this the price of reason? The dissecting scalpel of Cartesian doubt, the stripping caustic soda of rationalism, right down to the bone? There can be no doubt that the advances of medicine in the last 500 years have allowed us to live longer and sometimes happier lives but it has not always allowed human beings to be other than the bodies that contain them.

Until the nineteenth century the medical profession in the West based most of its treatment on the four 'humours' of Hippocrates and Galen, the pillars of ancient Greek medicine. The humoral theory of illness stated that we are made of four substances, blood, black bile, yellow bile and phlegm, related to the four seasons and the four earthly elements, air, earth, fire and water. Every individual had their own humoral balance based on the proportion of their humours, which emphasised the integration of mental and physical characteristics. Illness was caused by an imbalance of the humours, and it was the physician's role to diagnose this and restore equilibrium using techniques like bloodletting, emetics and laxatives. From the Enlightenment perspective the humoral approach was quackery, an antiquated distraction from the pathophysiological study of disease, the dissected corpses, the microscopic slides, the centrifuged blood samples, and later the X-ray pictures and the fMRI scans. How ridiculous might we now think it to offer the cancer victim a leech? How punitive to give the psychotically depressed old man a purgative? But humoral medicine does at least recognise the mind, body and environment in confluence, their interaction in element and season in a way that the insularity of hospital medicine ignores. This may not extend our lives but, when interpreted in other ways, could deepen their meaning and value.

When not studying bones, first- and second-year medical students could often be found in the 'Path' Museum of the main building. It was here that diseased organs were kept, boxed and alcohol-preserved, named after the Enlightenment scientists that had discovered them; Crohn's, Behcet's, Cushing's... And amongst the shelves of boxed organs we would sit and study at long tables, minds on overtime, bodies restless in their seats. What I can remember from those years is not the cellular structures or even the broad outline of those boxed organs, but how, at three in the morning, when the security guard at the main reception was asleep, we would stack the end of one long study table on top of another and use it like a playground slide. Or, better still, clear the tables away from the centre of the hall and then, taking a running jump onto our white lab coats, go sliding the 400 yards of the polished wooden hall, flying and tumbling and falling on our sit bones.

We couldn't sleep in our make-do bed in Emona and instead cycled down the hill to our tent in the municipal camping compound and the fierce sun. Our plan had been to sleep off our hangover and get back on the road the next day, but we hadn't reckoned on the heat and another bout of food poisoning. Our toilet block was fiercely guarded by a stooped caretaker who intermittently tried to prevent the young backpackers from using the facilities, a hopeless task doomed to failure, but the caretaker regarded us as two of his own, and the hippies on the other side of the fence as the enemy. The following day, while Jen was inside the tent, vomiting into a plastic bag, I was approached by a couple of the wild campers who'd sneaked past the caretaker and into the compound.

'Why don't you camp in the woods?' said one.

'There's lots of shade, free space and community,' said the other. And then they sneaked back to the wild side.

'Jen?'

'Uh?'

'I have to go and see what it's like on other side.'

'Bluuh.'

'It might be good for us.'

'Bluuh.'

After a long hot trek I came to the point where the sand met the coastal forest. Various groups had set up base in the cool shade of the trees with hammocks and makeshift tarps, but you could not escape the smell of human shit. It hung in the air with a sickening sweetness, and everywhere you could see wet wipes, curled and folded and discarded. It was far better that the backpackers were here occupying the beach forest rather than the bulldozers and the concrete foundations of yet another casino, and yet and yet and yet...

I reported back to Jen that there 'wasn't enough space on the planet'. As if we both didn't know that already; brave intercontinental adventurers that we were, shuffling from one small square of shade to the next, vomiting into plastic bags, running to the toilets to add our contribution to an already overpopulated ceramic basin. But, and almost despite my scepticism, the migrating starlings chirped in the trees, and the cows staggered down from their pasture to drink lazily in the swampy lagoon.

In 1910 the Seine broke its banks and so much water flooded Paris that a million people were made homeless, the clocks stopped working, the lamps fused and the trams came to a standstill. The polluted waters found their way into the galleries of the Museum of Natural History, where Descartes's skull was now being stored. Descartes said that his philosophy of rational doubt would make people 'lords and masters of nature' and his rational 'method' would unlock the world with a single mathematical flourish, but when the curators of the museum tried to the locate his skull, they had to admit it had been carried away by the flood waters. A Cartesian method in science, morality and culture is a quest for certainty. The Hindu practice of throwing pulverised ashes into the Ganges is a cipher for a wider distribution of death back into the uncertain energies that nourish life. Where the pulsing streams of life in living bones begin and the replenishing minerals of the flood waters end is less clear. The boundaries between who we are and what there is are a lot more fluid than Cartesian science allows. Our journey towards India was an adventure towards another way of looking at the world, but it was also a journey *away* from a particular kind of Western cynicism, a headbound intellectualism. Cycling long distances is a surrender to the joys of ambiguity, always moving, always going, always living in the unknown. And, intermittently, vomiting into plastic bags.

If Descartes's philosophy of doubt has cut away some of our ties with the natural world, continental philosophies like phenomenology (see TYRES) try to rebuild that connection, understanding that the tools we use to shape the natural environment can also be the tools that help us reconnect with it, from the interior of our mental landscape to the physical contours that surround us, and it might be that cycling is one of those renewals. It would be wrong to characterise reason as the sole force in the alienation of the natural world; religion – and Christian belief in particular, with its characterisation of man being made in God's image, with an implicit mastery of the Garden of Eden – has a lot to answer for. But to reiterate that science and technology and reason harbour the only answer to environmental catastrophe is to ignore the disconnect, the 'othering', that is implicit in rational doubt.

We have a pervasive need to make a connection that supersedes our individual identity, that reaches beyond the first-person monologue of Descartes's 'I think therefore I am' and often beyond the religions of a monotheistic god. Cycling is not the Universal Convention of Human Rights, nor the Ten Commandments, nor the Five Pillars of Islam. It's a ridiculously humble little tool by which ordinary people get to meet ordinary people living their ordinary lives over extraordinary distances. Can any other tourism, can any other travel, bring us those same conversations? Not so intimately and not under our own steam, bringing the land and its people together into a very physical experience of unity. And if that sounds too mystical, then I suggest you suspend your doubt, hang it like a sun hat on the back of a Saddle and keep on riding (see TOP TUBE).

Eventually, in that hot, squat, ugly, ring-fenced compound on Irakli beach, Jen stopped vomiting and we got back onto our bikes. We had to get to Istanbul to apply for our Iranian visas and then navigate the almost unimaginable distances across Turkey. So we veered inland, away from the turgid coast, through an endless series of industrial estates with windowless abandoned factories and the echo of dogs, through unnamed shanty towns until, finally, we found ourselves across the border and in Turkey. Was it us or was everything much friendlier on the other side? The first town, Kirklareli, a whirl of taxis, painted carts, fruit stalls and families getting ready to break the Ramadan fast. There was a heightened energy, and everyone appeared to move around each other in a new way, as if the space itself had been folded differently. And everywhere there was the sound, the sight, the taste of Islam: the call to prayer, the spires of the mosques, the frenzy of Ramadan, the plates of hot rice and flatbread. We were on the road to the Middle East, our Saddles finally worn to the shape of our skinny bones, and we were famished.

CHAPTER 12

The Top Tube

We cycled along the Bosporus and met Shukran, a twenty-year-old student, outside a McDonald's in Istanbul. Not the most glamorous meeting of West and East but it was a start. We heaved our bikes up five flights of stairs to his flat. It was Ramadan and Shukran was spending all the non-fasting hours of darkness drinking coffee, smoking and listening to Johnny Cash. I gave up trying to get any sleep and opened a map under the streetlight bleeding into our room. It quickly became clear that Turkey was *massive*, nearly as wide as Europe. Everything about it would follow the same template: the breadth of the roads, the rope coil of the moustaches, the acreage of the circular *pide* bread, the magnanimous hospitality. How were a boy and girl from Dorset and Wiltshire to get across it, to span its vast distances? To answer this the reader must join us on a longer journey, to a more distant horizon.

*

The Top Tube is the upper part of the bike frame and connects the SEAT TUBE to the HEAD TUBE. It's the part you carry over your shoulder or swing your leg across when you're ready to ride. The height of the tube above the ground is important for sizing a bike, and if there's a couple of inches between it and your groin, then the cloth is cut to the suit. But the length of the Top Tube is equally important, even responsible, for the reach of the rider over the HANDLEBARS. Traditionally bikes were built only with the height of the Top Tube being taken into account. Which meant that tall cyclists might have enough leg room to reach the PEDALS but their upper body was crammed, like a lobster in a pot, over the HANDLEBARS. Modern frames are built with more proportion than this, so the longer cyclist can now stretch their whole body into the ride. No matter how far it is.

We used our time in Istanbul to visit Hagia Sophia, a Christian basilica built in CE 537 at the beginning of the Byzantine empire, and then converted into a mosque in 1453 after the Ottoman victory, before finally becoming a secular museum in 1935. It is a testament to the grandeur of the building that you forget about the thousands of tourists and look up, through a thousand years of Christianity, five hundred years of Islam and fifty years of museum entrance fees, standing at the gateway to Asia. If West meets East anywhere this is probably where you'd stick your flagpole (though there remains a reasonable argument for the McDonald's car park). It has a huge central dome onto which four minarets were later bolted. Christian mosaics co-exist with gold Arabic script. What I remember most is not the enormity of its gilded domes but the young woman outside, dressed in a hijab, with her arms, legs and most of her face veiled in black, sporting a battery-operated, luminous bubble gun, delivering glowing spheres of washing-up liquid into the dusk. Up. Up. Up.

In the third century CE the Egyptian philosopher Plotinus developed the notions of Plato (see VIRTUAL TRIANGLE) into the hybrid philosophy which we now call Neoplatonism. Plotinus travelled east from Egypt into Persia, where he absorbed Zoroastrianism (see WHEELS) and Indian beliefs (see HEADSET), which he incorporated with the ancient Greek philosophies of Aristotle, the Stoics (see INNER TUBES) and Pythagoras (see BOTTOM BRACKET). For a time Neoplatonism was the go-to philosophy of the West, but in CE 529 the Byzantine emperor Justinian ordered the Athens school of Neoplatonism to close because of its 'pagan' sympathies with ancient Greek learning and cosmology. The Neoplatonists had little choice but to take their learning with them to Alexandria in Egypt, into Syria and across Persia. It's hard to overemphasise the loss this was to Western thinking. Much of ancient Greek philosophy disappeared during the Dark Ages of the West, while in the Middle East these concepts, if not allowed to thrive, were at least tolerated. Some of the surviving Neoplatonists subsequently moved from Alexandria to Constantinople (the Byzantine name for Istanbul), where Neoplatonism continued until the fifteenth century, influencing Islamic philosophy and theology.

Adapting Plato, the Neoplatonists suggested the universe was based on a single fundamental principle, which Plotinus himself described as the One. The One represented the universe, of which we are all part but do not have direct knowledge. Plotinus described moments of ecstasy in which he stood outside his own body and recognised the One, using techniques of passivity and contemplation comparable with practices in Hinduism (see HEADSET) and Buddhism (see FREEWHEEL), in which meditative or physical techniques are used to further a philosophical understanding based not on reason (see BOTTOM BRACKET) but on an intuitive process. Plotinus suggested the interrelation of mind, body and universe could only be appreciated in moments of irrational wonder. He did not construct the One as a theological god, nor did he suggest that there was an afterlife. Instead he made the radical suggestion that happiness could be achieved in this life through philosophical contemplation. Some Islamic scholars used Neoplatonism to underpin Islamic theology, but without the heretical proposal of salvation in the here and now.

Islam developed in Saudi Arabia in the sixth century when Muhammad received the word of God as transcribed in the Koran. It spread through the Arab states, across the Middle East and Persia, and later into North Africa, eventually making inroads into southern Spain. Islamic intellectuals were fascinated by the Neoplatonic idea of a transcendent unity, who for them could only be Allah, the God of Islam. There then followed centuries of rancour about the role, or not, of philosophy in Islam, and of Neoplatonism in particular. There continued to be a tension between the literal word of the Koran and the open-ended questioning of philosophy; a questioning that was interpreted by some as a godless heresy and by others as a way to improve Islamic law. The Islamic philosopher al-Kindi said that the truth should be sought from 'whatever source it emanated' while the sacrilegious Al-Ma'rri believed there could only be 'reason and no religion, or religion and no reason', a view closer to the rationalism of the European Enlightenment. Against this stood the fury of the Islamic literalists, who believed in an unarguable doctrine, which they enforced by sword and blood.

But where Neoplatonism really struck home was in the sect of Islam known as Sufism, embracing neither the pure reason of rationalism nor the strict scripture of the Koran, instead seeking a mystical, personal inward path to the One, a unity understood as Allah within Islam. Like the Neoplatonists, Sufi mystics believed that the relationship to this unity, the transcendent God, could only be approached by a suspension of reason, and that some kind of physical rather than intellectual process had to intervene.

Some Sufis took the ascetic route much like the Christian monks of western Europe, rejecting worldly pleasures and attracting the name *sufi* – wool – from their coarse woollen shirts. In the thirteenth century Sufism developed into collectives or fraternities, gathered round a single spiritual leader. Their rituals took the form of prayer, meditation, repetition of the divine name, and later music and dancing, in search of trance-like experiences and an intuition of the One. Its fulfilment could involve a loss of self and discovery of a kind of selflessness known as *fana*, equivalent to the state of *samadhi* in Hinduism (see HEADSET).

Long-distance bike riding demands, if not exactly asceticism, then certainly a kind of self-sufficiency. You leave behind the comforts and familiarity of home for a harder sense of the road. You deliberately throw yourself into the hills of discomfort and push yourself to the limits of endurance and the dizzy reaches of hunger because the efficiency of a bicycle's mechanics allows you to reach these extremes (see GEARS). The word 'ascetic' comes from the Greek *askesis* meaning exercise or hard work. Are bike tourists reaching for inner enlightenment by rejecting worldly comfort? Probably not, they're more likely to be reaching for a credit card as they hobble into a cake shop. But those who ride long distances are signing up for more than a credit agreement, they are entering into a contract with a certain form of hardship, one that defines the mushier contours of who we are and may even begin to change our self-identity, who we imagine ourselves to be. The skinny hairy wretches who return from these rides do not appear unlike the ascetics of medieval faiths. So what then are these latter-day seekers seeking? A good story? A mile count? Selfies?

Like most consulates the waiting room of the Iranian visa office in Istanbul had the air of an unfriendly bureaucracy, all plastic chairs and tapping feet. Except scattered among the tired Turkish,

Kurdish and Armenian faces were a few button-bright travellers enjoying the thrill of the visa lottery. Having slid our forms and passports through a gap in the glass-fronted counter we were told by the bureaucrat, with the whiff of fast on his breath, to sit. A TV on the wall showed Iranian state news with disconcerting English subtitles: 'Minister says foreign blockade will not affect us' and 'Minister says Iran is best example of an independent state'. I nervously twisted the corner of Jen's headscarf until an official beckoned us through a side door and behind the counter. After a strange few minutes in which we had to provide our fingerprints and I dabbed mine in the wrong boxes, he returned our paperwork complete with our visas, passports and a beatific smile. This was to be our experience in Iran, a troubling, and troubled, bureaucracy that hid a boundless hospitality (see WHEELS).

Istanbul's Grand Bazaar is now more of a shopping mall, but tucked away in its innards we came across a young man sitting behind a laptop with no apparent wish to sell us anything. We got him to put aside his laptop and sell us the fake wedding ring that would get Jen and I through the Middle East without too much attention. He told us we needed to eat more meat and protein and also, oddly, that nuts were a good aphrodisiac. We weren't sure what had prompted this, perhaps it was the 'wedding' ring. Or perhaps it was the webpage on his laptop, reflecting its molten glow against his face, in the shadows of the Grand Bazaar.

The joins of a bike frame, the SEAT TUBE to the Top Tube and the Top Tube to the HEAD TUBE, are held together by the chemical bonds of welding or the alternative process of brazing. In welding, a rod of the same material as the frame (in our case steel) is introduced into the mitred gap between the two tubes, sealing them together at temperatures of 2000°C. In brazing, a rod of a different metal is introduced into the heated gap between the two, which is drawn into the space by surface tension and capillary action. This creates a ring of metal that is stronger than the tubes it joins. I once built a frame using brazing under supervision. The trainer issued terse commands like 'More rod, faster, slower, backwards, forwards, shallow' as I stared with intense focus at a space that didn't seem to exist, pouring flaming heat and puddling metal into creases of reality so finely aligned as to be indiscernible. Afterwards, as the frame cooled and hissed in the rain, the world itself seemed different, as if for a period I had slipped into an alternative universe, focusing on a single point that dissolved into nothing, before returning to a newly aligned material existence. Later I finished the joints with a coarse 'bastard' file and then a more delicate nail file and then an instrument so smooth I could hardly feel its grain as the brass braze became one seamless transition with the tubes it joined together.

From Istanbul we cycled through rural Anatolia during the Bayram festival, the end of Ramadan in Turkey, when families get together to share breakfast, wear their best clothes, visit their neighbours, honour their relatives and load up long-distance cyclists with fruit. A ridiculously steep downhill stretch released us into a valley abundant with apples, blackberries, rosehips and grapes, all loaded onto us by farmers along the road. There were so many people wanting to wave us down and drink *cai* – Turkish tea – that we just had to wave back and roll on. When we asked a man at the side of the road for water he took us to his house, where we met his mother, father, daughter and shy wife, who gave us watermelon, grapes, baklava, walnut bread and, eventually, fresh water from their spring. We camped as the sun set near a mountain pass. I watched the slopes of the crag opposite recede from pinkness into black like the gum of a shark's tooth. The sky turned violet and the peaks flattened into a shadow puppets' stage set, with the white ring of a waning moon above. At dawn the call to prayer began, reverberating through the canyons, each voice replying to the one before until, oddly, there were two loud *beeps* as if a mechanical answering machine was on the cusp of launching into its spool.

Islam has always been structured on hospitality. Traditional Arab Muslim greetings include 'My home is your home' and 'Peace be upon you'. As Islam conquered the regions of the wider Middle East, they took on these traditions, honouring the Hadith, the habits or actions of the prophet Muhammad. 'When a person is invited to a feast and he does not accept (or reply), he disobeys Allah' (Hadith 26.5) and 'Gather together at your meals and you will be blessed therein' (Hadith 26.14). The sharing of food binds Muslims together and attains particular importance during Ramadan, at the breaking of the fast each day, and joyously at the end of the Ramadan calendar itself. This is emphasised in Anatolia, where to be a guest is to be privileged with the best that a host can offer in copious cycles of tea.

At first glance it might appear that kindness in Turkey, indeed kindness throughout the Middle East, is just pious duty rather than true selflessness. But it is difficult to define where etiquette ends and a more informal kindness begins. There is something about the offering of gifts that dissolves formality into appreciation, that opens us up to the interior world of others, an elusive oneness stitched through the teachings of Islam and Sufism.

It's likely that those we met on this extraordinary ride were reaching out in the context of their faith, but it had a wider and exultant effect on all of us, loosening a putty in the frames of mutual suspicion. The original meaning of 'kindness' is kinship or sameness. The experience of cycling long distances through Turkey was peculiarly intimate, as if through receiving these gifts we were revealing something of ourselves. As Adam Phillips and Barbara Taylor note in their book *On Kindness*, the act of kindness changes both parties in an almost molecular way. It 'mingles the needs and desires of us with the needs and desires of others' and is 'more promiscuous than sexuality by involving us with strangers'.

Kith (as in 'kith and kin') is a less-used word that once went hand in hand with kindness. As the writer Jay Griffiths describes, kith enlarges our sense of kin into the landscape of our childhoods. Kith grows within us from the streams and fields and parks where we grow up. To take the fruit straight from the branches of the land is also to risk the intimacy of nature, to fling open the conservatory doors to our own childhoods.

Our shock at the kindness of Anatolia begs a second, more pressing, question. Why the shock? Why should we consider those of other lands, and the land itself, to be so unkind? Our shock at the kindness of strangers is related to a forgetting of what kindness actually is, which, at its most severe, is an amnesia for what it means to be human.

The ancient Greek Stoics thought of self-sufficiency as being generated not through personal reliance but a shared sense of community. The Stoics espoused *oikeiosis* – an attachment of self to other that spread like ripples in a pond, from the individual to close family and then wider society. Christ's 'Love thy neighbour as thyself' was a plea for kindness or caritas that was originally universal in its outlook – to pagan, slave, woman and child. Subsequent holy wars and Church corruption undermined the Christian ideal of kindness and permitted Enlightenment thinkers from the seventeenth and eighteenth century to shove it to one side. People like Thomas Hobbes, who suggested that kindness was a sham, the disguise of an inherently selfish animal.

In the opposite corner we have the Swiss-born Jean-Jacques Rousseau, who suggested that we are born with an innate kindness, a generosity only society can corrupt. Rousseau's ideas unleashed a revolutionary socialism across Europe that ended with the French Revolution, a movement that undermined its own moral authority through the terrors of the guillotine. This left the door wide open for the brutishness of capitalism, which claimed 'enlightened self-preservation' as the natural mode (see BAR BAG). To exploit others, the rational economists of the West explained, was the natural order of things. Kindness, if it existed at all, could stick its drippy nose in the handkerchief of charity. And so the idea has wilted into the twenty-first century as weakness, a failing, an illusion. What we used to perceive as the will to good is just selfishness in another guise, sentimental self-gratification.

The ebbing of religion in the West, and the self-reliant capitalism that has replaced it, has allowed a simpler, more binary version of kindness to develop, of supportive family on the one hand and hateful foreigners on the other. To imagine that strangers in the Middle East are generous is to allow a tonal shade into our emotional landscape, which demands a redrawing of these barriers, not dictated by the lines on a map but by the smudged ambivalence of our own backyard.

There is no screen on a bicycle, no glass divide to separate us, we are thrown into the vividly populated world whether we like it or not, at a pace that will carry us far from those we know and close to those we don't. The further Jen and I rode the more we became aware of this journey into kindness. The real myth in long-distance cycling (as in many kinds of adventure) is of self-reliance when in fact the cyclist is inextricably connected with those they meet along the way. With a hypermetabolic need for clean water and food, we are involved, whether we like it or not, with others. But this is also the journey's blessing. Cycling propels us from the self-denial of unkindness towards the ordinary kindness of being fully alive.

In Anatolia we met Javier, a quiet Christian in his mid-twenties, walking in trainers and baseball cap from Switzerland to Jerusalem. He had a small rucksack, a staff he had fashioned from a branch, a wind and click camera and a Walkman tape player. He had no tent and went from village to village hoping for shelter. He did not evangelise and seemed as genuinely awed and surprised by the kindness he had received as we were. We took a picture of him, grinning, with our digital camera, and he took a snap of us with his old Kodak. And then we went our separate ways.

It was only with the Islamic invasion of southern Spain in the thirteenth century that translations of Islamic philosophers, and the Greek learning they had harvested, filtered back into Europe. Greek advances in science and medicine, cultivated in Islam and the East, re-emerged in the West (see BELL). The inductive methods of the thirteenth-century British philosopher Roger Bacon, which led to the empirical testing of the natural world, and which we now call evidence-based science, were directly informed by Arab Muslim philosophy. The idea that Islam and the Middle East generated a formulaic religion that Western science and reason has now supplanted is not correct. The seeds of Western reason were sown by Islam.

On Sunday 12 September, four months after the start of our trip, we awoke from our wild camp on a mountain pass somewhere near the town of Tarakli, ferociously grumpy. The stove wasn't working and there was no coffee. And so we climbed the next forty kilometres in the midday heat, getting into an argument and sharing the bottom of a bag of fruit and nuts in the shade of a bus shelter. We asked a tractor driver in the next village where the nearest restaurant might be. 'Nallihan,' he said. Fifty kilometres down the road. We stopped at a petrol station, which had a single cheese sandwich on offer, lying limp and forlorn in a chill cabinet that someone clearly hadn't been able to chill. The owner and his little girl looked at us curiously over the metal counter, as if even they couldn't quite believe we were going to eat it. As we forlornly tore the sandwich in half, the tractor driver we'd met before strode in like a gunslinger, all dust and moustache and bravado. And *demanded* that we put the sandwich down and go to his house for food. We pedalled after him, up the main road, off a track and into the hills, chasing his tractor as best we could, as he waved and cajoled us on.

Hasan lived in a house on stilts, built on an incline next to a path. He introduced us to his whole family, his two daughters Ayra, aged twenty, and Mysha, sixteen, and his wife and mother. Hasan had a habit of tutting a lot, for example when we suggested that we should lock our bikes under the house, but underneath his bristly exterior he was very much a softie. We ate on the floor around a very low circular table that you could spin, with a cloth that emerged from underneath the table and over our knees as a napkin. We ate with our right hands from lots of small dishes, all washed down with cups of *cai*. Ayra and Mysha served us, new dishes emerging before we had finished the plates already in front of us: red aromatic cold rosehip soup, stuffed vine leaves, mushroom with eggs and a paprika sauce garnish, freshly baked bread and on and on, like a fairy tale. Jen and I managed to transmit our thanks with sign language. After dinner we settled around the television with the family. A neighbour popped in with a new headscarf for Jen and then the daughters left us to light a wood fire for our shower. Jen was provided with traditional Turkish baggy slacks for her pyjamas and we went to bed on a mattress on the floor, with a heavy, comforting quilt. We slept deeply till the call to prayer at 5.30.

Breakfast began with the whole family back around the circular table eating Bayram flatbread, fresh honey in broken honeycomb, potatoes and fresh goat's yoghurt. All of this prepared and delivered by Ayra and Mysha as Hasan looked on proudly. The night before we had asked them if they were at college, and they said no, as their father, 'beba', wanted them to stay at home, look after the house, wear the scarf and fulfil the domestic obligations of Islam.

We left with cheek kisses for Jen and a formal but somehow intimate knock of the head for me. Finally they handed us a bag of their tomatoes and some Bayram bread, still warm, which we tucked into our pannier racks and returned to the main road. Regardless of Islamic duty, regardless of the traditions of Bayram, regardless of our own shyness, there was an ordinary kindness at work here. We had felt a change in each other, a nervous intimacy that carried with it a pride: us, for being their honoured guests; they, for the food that they had shared, an abundance we'd never expected from this harsh land.

Back on the main road we found Javier once more, plodding along with his blisters and his staff; he too had stayed with a family and woken before dawn. We shared our stories about the kindness of strangers, finding our own tiny community, and, after saying farewell once more, let go of the BRAKES and began an everlasting downhill on a perfectly macadamed road, with the hills and mountains resolutely still and unchanging, as if neither us, nor the bikes, nor the land were changing, all of the world rolling in the same pitch, captured in an ever-present moment.

Rumi, or Jalāl al-Dīn Muhammad Rūmī, is one of Persia's most famous poets but he was principally an Islamic Sufi and preacher who settled in central Anatolia in the thirteenth century. Known as Mevlana from the Arabic word for master, Rumi established the Mevlevi order of Sufis, known in the West as whirling dervishes, spinning devotees of Islam who reached for intuitions of the divine through music and dance. Rumi captured the imagination of Western tourists who, awakening from the rigid classifications of the Enlightenment, once more sought an instinctive unitary connection. However, the Western reading of Rumi is clearly a romanticised one, representing what some

Arabic intellectuals describe as Orientalism, the projection of Western needs onto a complex Eastern culture that it has been unwilling to properly engage with. Rumi's mystical poetry and teaching is part of a centuries-long tradition in Sufism that has a number of practical purposes in Islam. Championed by ordinary people, it aspires to convey the central truths of the Islamic faith and establish an experience of oneness with Allah without the need for formal religion or the set texts of the Koran. Rumi reaffirmed the physical means by which this understanding might occur, recognising that poetry and metaphor were intertwined with music and dance. Much as poetry sought to bypass the rigid knots of intellectual reasoning, so too could a repetitive physical action conjure an ecstatic experience of closeness to the 'One', a unifying experience of God. However, much of Islam, particularly Wahhabism, has disowned Sufism for its emphasis on the personal aspects of worship and its allegorical stories of sainthood. Many young Muslims believe Sufism to be a turning away from the outward realities of their faith, and many Middle East intellectuals are more likely to ally themselves with Marxism (see SEAT POST) or socialism. But for hundreds of thousands of working people in North Africa, the Middle East, South East Asia and Slavic and Russian states such as Chechnya it remains a living belief system and a physical philosophy, couched within the religion of Islam.

Tradition dictates that Rumi was walking past a goldsmith and started to dance in a whirling movement to the sound of the goldsmith's hammers, and it was from this that the dervish ritual began. But it was only on Rumi's death that dancing, music and chanting were formalised into the rituals that we know today. The spin of the dervish is inseparable from the music it is performed to, and both are known by the same word, *sema* – 'listening'. In other words, active listening is more important than the music itself. Rumi highlighted the way in which the reed flute of the musician and the reed pen of the poet are similarly parts of the same flowing engagement: the poet is pen becoming poem, the musician is flute becoming music, the dancer is body becoming movement. And had Rumi been alive a millennium later, he might have versified the cyclist as bike becoming ride, an indivisible choreography in movement.

The Sufi dervishes of Istanbul still wear tall conical hats, originating from central Asia, and black coats cast off to show the white garments beneath. As the dervish turns, at first slowly and then with increasing momentum but never with loss of control, in time to the music, the right hand is held up to heaven and the left down to earth. For Rumi there would have been no formality or ritual or performance. The dance was merely an expression of the interconnection of creativity with physical movement.

Mustafa Kemal Ataturk, the army officer who established Turkey as a modern secular state in 1922 (and whose image is replicated across the country in *cai* shops and restaurants and public places) outlawed dervishes. Their only public performances were to be for tourists. Rumi's mosque in Konya, like the Hagia Sophia in Istanbul, was subsequently converted into a secular museum. Sufism has continued to suffer persecution in Turkey while still surviving as a living mystical tradition whose practices are not window dressing but the very path to understanding reality. As we cycled away from Hasan and his family, on that endless downhill through Anatolia, there was a change in the way that I engaged with the landscape, a change that was experienced more than reasoned. The Sufi understanding of turning movement as an intuitive method for experiencing the interrelationship of all things has an overlap with this other way of interpreting cycling. Beyond the fairly obvious comparison that its movement is a revolution of sorts, that the arc of the leg around the CHAIN WHEELS echoes the dervish's spin, there is an underlying blurring of meaning – that what you do, that what you make of yourself, becomes one with who you are. As the later Sufi poet Shabistari explained in his long poem *The Secret Rose Garden*, 'travelling, travel and traveller have become one'. This movement is not a pedometer-measured kind of distance, it is a metaphorical leap into the shadows, where what we experience as matter (bicycle, desert, landscape) and mind (thought, ideas, beliefs) become inseparable. The awareness of a boundless or infinite nature to existence is at once the god of Sufism, what the modern Arab poet Adonis describes as 'another country, but it exists about us and in us'. If we understand cycling as a creative process in which the individual creates the moment of his own movement, then the cyclist, the bike and the ride integrally affirm the condition of oneness at the centre of the Sufi Mevlevi experience. It is within this ecstatic realm that reason loses its kingpin place, and in a multiplicity of physical experiences we become lost in the process of movement.

The dervish uses the regular chanting of prayer to induce a trance-like state, whereas in an endless downhill the FREEWHEEL, the workings of the rear wheel hub, tick their repeated charm. As with the *sema* of Sufism it is not the character or meaning of the sound, it is the listening that matters, the flickering of the freewheel, the *whish* of the wind, the *burr* of the tyre on the road. Within *sema* the Sufi may experience *fana*, in which individual identity dissolves. *Fana* means annihilation. 'Die before you die,' explains the Islamic Hadith. When I see those bucket lists, those reminders of the top ten things to do before you die, I wonder if this should be the number one point, and thus render the tick boxes underneath if not redundant then at least unboxed, so they contain no space at all.

You could argue I am just another cultural voyeur of the East here, a scrap-metal merchant searching components of all-encompassing faiths to screw into my virtual frame. I would hope, instead, that I am weighing the resonances or overlaps between these philosophies, faiths and cycling, so that we can understand each from a different perspective, to investigate what makes riding a bike such a transformative experience for so many people. It is not a religion, but neither is it a sport. It generates a living culture around it and for some can be as revolutionary as faith itself. How and why it does this is as hard to define as the space into which cycling is always rolling.

A recurrent analogy that occurs again and again in Sufism is the journey of a single raindrop, to merge with the ocean, so that the circle of evaporation and condensation can begin again:

...You will be freed from the spell of self.
Then will your being, as a drop,
Fall into the ocean of the eternal.

(from *Wine, Torch, and Beauty*, Mahmūd ibn 'Abd al-Karīm Shabistarī, CE 1320)

A few days after our ecstatic downhill in Anatolia we were riding from the town of Beypazari, across slow hills and descents, beneath the sun, sun, sun. At dusk a gathering thunderstorm turned into clouds of black pillowcases and forked lightning. There seemed to be nothing between the storm and our steel bikes out there in the pancake plains. We found ourselves cycling just behind the lip of the storm front, as it moved in exactly the direction we wanted to go. It was less storm-chasing more storm-lagging, the forked lightning flashing on the road ahead of us.

In the next town of Haymana we treated ourselves to a hammam. I was an object of some fascination with my cyclist's 'farmer's' tan, Jen even more so in the women's section, where her skinny cycling body was observed with much glee. After using the sauna, bathing pool and ladling cold water over my head, I sat on a bench beside a window that took up the whole of one side of the changing rooms. There was no need for towels, the heat of the setting sun pouring through the glass evaporated the water from my skin as the man next to me chanted a prayer.

Two days later we took shelter in the shade of a caravanserai, the remains of an ancient Silk Road staging post. Some stonemasons who were renovating the building invited us back to their canvas shelter for *cai*. As their boss passed round the cups he said, as if by way of introduction, 'We are Batman.'

Jen and I tried not to appear nonplussed as they looked over their drinks expectantly.

'We are Batman,' the boss repeated. He opened my road map and his fingers travelled east to an area we would come to know as Kurdistan, and there was the town of Batman. And Batman, as they reiterated between cups of *cai* and plates of raisins, still on the vine, was *'çok güzel'* – very beautiful. If anyone embodied kith it was these quietly kind, fiercely proud Kurdish stonemasons, who had, through the power of international English, become both their place of birth and the comic-book hero of my childhood.

The enormous miles and hills of the landscape dragged at our legs. On 1 October, after yet another mountain pass, we pulled our bikes out of the grain store where they had lodged, and began a ride through the arid canyons and roadworks of eastern Turkey until, among the sandstorms of jackhammers, we arrived at a river in full flow, brimming from the storm of the night before. Here we found dappled shade and green green grass but most of all there was the sudden shock of the river in full spate. Feeling bone-tired, ill from the latest bout of flu, and not having seen any greenery or running water for such a long time, I burst into tears. 'When you see something you least expect but perhaps most want, it stands out and grips you all the more – like a river, like the kindness of others,' I wrote in my journal.

If there was ever a golden age of Sufism it may have been in the twelfth and thirteenth centuries. The natural world runs through these Sufi poems, as an expression of divine unity, as a bird in flight, as a raindrop, as river and ocean. There was an emphasis on travel and pilgrimage, as an allegory for a spiritual or imaginative journey. Often both were combined, with creatures migrating towards wisdom.

The Persian Sufi, Fariduddin Attar, produced his allegorical work *The Conference of Birds*, using five thousand poetic couplets. It tells the story of the hoopoe bird, elected by the bird kingdom, to guide them over eight mountains to their king, the *Simurgh*. Only thirty birds find their way to the Simurgh and the words 'Si – murgh' mean 'thirty – birds' in Persian. In other words, the destination is the birds themselves, they are the Simurgh, and the Simurgh is them.

Pilgrimage towards self-discovery is not, of course, exclusive to Sufism or the East. It is found in the Chaucer's *Parliament of Fowls* and *Canterbury Tales*, in Dante's *Divine Comedy* and Joseph Conrad's *Heart of Darkness* (later remade as the film *Apocalypse Now*). In all of these cases, there is a search for meaning abroad, with an eventual recognition that what we consider to be foreign, in both the landscape and its people, is merely an unravelled aspect of ourselves (see also HEADSET).

The more we rode into the barren, wide-open spaces of Turkey, into the unceasing clarity of their clear blue skies, the more I began to write songs in my head. Were these echoes of songs I already knew, or were they imaginative reflections of the country I was travelling through, an allegorical journey through a landscape I was becoming part of? I'm not claiming these songs as visionary masterworks but I find it hard to see their themes now as anything other than metaphysical. 'I am the bird above / I am the snake below / I am the ocean river melting snow / I am the soil in your hand / black upon the spade / I am the rose light wandering / from the morning shade / I am all things to everyone / cold and bright beneath the sun.'

In Attar's *The Conference of Birds* we meet the Heron, a melancholy bird, always at the water's edge, appreciating the ripples but afraid to join the wider ocean. I was raised by my mother for the first two years of my life with a lot of input from my grandmother and grandfather. My grandparents nursed me through the intemperate summers and snow winters of the Dorset countryside, when their natural home was the West Indies, where generations of their family had lived before. My grandfather, John Archie McDonald, was an expert in agriculture and managed several plantations in Trinidad. But his father, and his father before him, were doctors. My great-grandfather was a much-loved GP on the Caribbean island of Antigua, and it was also here that he built a small coastal home to make best use of the cooling offshore winds. Throughout my childhood I would visit this island and coastal house, and the shores around it became part of who I was. When my grandmother offered to take me swimming in the Caribbean, I said, 'But Granny, it's so big.' My grandfather transmitted his awe of medicine to me, and this played a large part in my choice of career. It was my grandfather who sent me money to buy my first stethoscope, and it was in the middle of a forty-eight-hour shift in Shrewsbury General Hospital, a few months into my first job as a junior doctor, that I found out he'd died. When I next went to Antigua I sat outside my grandparents' house, listening to the waves crush and collapse, and return to the reef, and it felt as if I understood then, if only for a moment, that the land and the sea and my grandfather were all part of the same turning cycle of loss and renewal, and that I, sitting there with my skinny backside on the rock, was part of it all too.

My grandmother died a short while after, and my aunt said that the single white heron that accompanied her funeral cortège was my grandfather, who had come to see his wife's final journey. My aunt, born into Catholicism and raised among the carnival spirits, would always weave stories of the saints into visions of the Caribbean. That my grandfather was the heron would have been as natural to her, and now to me, as the transmigrations of poetry.

My great-grandmother, Hilda McDonald, wrote collections of lyrics based on nature and the Caribbean. 'The clamouring Silence spoke insistently, / It cried aloud to me / That heaven itself might be / A moment – prisoned in Eternity' (from 'A Moment', c.1956). And my grandfather, despite his longstanding appreciation of medicine, astronomy and the science of agriculture (becoming a lecturer in physics and meteorology at the University of the West Indies) inherited his mother's interest in mysticism. In the early 1960s, in a short book called *The Promise of the Stars*, a title taken from one of his mother's poems, he elaborated on these themes. 'The Seers, mystics and prophets of past civilisations, by withdrawing from the world and living a life of contemplation, seem to have been able to achieve a trance-like state, akin to sleep, in which their active minds were subdued and quietened ... Perhaps in their visions and prophesies these old-time philosophers attained a power of the mind that has been temporarily lost by modern man, obsessed by the physical and mechanistic interpretation of the world around him.' Of his mother's poetry he said, 'the simple belief that God shows his presence in all the beauties of nature can challenge the inspiration of the scientist or the devotion of the religious mystic'.

My uncle, Ian McDonald, the next generation of poets after my great-grandmother, is still writing in his eighties.

*

these lines make no particular point
just if any reader sees them
they might suggest that everything
is miracle and mystery all one's life
my study window overlooks the garden
a branch of bougainvillea trails upwards
within my reach this last month
this morning a hummingbird tangled in it
fluttered and fell onto the desk
stunned and still I seized it quick
I swear I felt its beating heart
saw closer than I ever will
the soft green feathers at its breast
threw that green-gold shred of light
soaring flashing heavenwards again
this happened once in eighty years

('Throwing a Hummingbird' from *River Dancer*, 2016)

In Anatolia, with the harsh light flashing off my spokes as I hunched and heaved over the HANDLEBARS and then rolled down, endlessly downhill, I wondered if I was reacquainting myself with what I already knew, a childhood education I didn't even know I had had, obscured by shelves of science books and skulls kept in shoe boxes. Riding a bike across continents is not the clearest route to mystical enlightenment. It is mostly chafed bums, acres of boredom, hunger, exasperation and unedifying sweat patches. But at times it can approach the sublime, like a bird swooping down through a valley, to the river, to the sea, like a boy still waiting at the edge of a shore.

We camped at truck stops where the waiters seemed to be running off brittle caffeine highs. On the road to Diyarbakir we took *cai* with the village elder, a dapper man in a checked headdress with a spruce sergeant-major moustache. Word got around that there were tourists on bikes, and a gaggle of pasty-hatted villagers wanted to make it very clear that this was Kurdistan, not Turkmenistan. Three mobile phones appeared. 'This English phone,' the elder said, dropping a scuffed old handset; 'This Turkish phone,' dropping an even older Nokia; and 'This Kurdish phone,' pushing the latest slimline smartphone into view.

In Diyarbakir, the major city in Kurdistan, we went on a wild goose chase looking for some spare INNER TUBES, being led around by a character called Azad, sharp-suited with chunky gold rings. Azad spent most of the time ringing young women and asking us to speak to them on his mobile, while treating us to an ongoing monologue: 'I like it when people live their lives... Hippy is happy... I want to buy a German car... You can teach English here at the kindergarten; I will get you a job, you will get a good salary.' What we didn't find in Diyarbakir were INNER TUBES. Instead Azad recounted to Jen a love poem he'd written as a romantic goodbye and I spent the night patching a many-punctured INNER TUBE to make a new spare, eyelids half closed with weariness.

We were harried out of Diyarbakir by homeless street kids, no older than nine or ten, begging and hustling. I embarrassed myself by pulling out the DOG STICK and waving it around my head as they yanked at the bags on the rear pannier rack. We later found a roadside repair shack that sold INNER TUBES and I threw my patched one to Jen, who threw it to the mechanic, who threw back fresh ones to her, who threw them back across the waiting traffic to me.

The plains of Kurdistan burned into black as the farmers cleared the land. Later, as dusk fell, with the fields still burning, we pedalled into Batman, the hometown of the stonemasons we had met a couple of weeks before. And as if on cue, as the light faded, the bats appeared, criss-crossing a dishwater sky, as kids chased us shouting, 'Money money money.' The next day we turned a corner in Batman to find a troop of young men with scarves across their faces running from police in full riot gear. We dodged into the only place open, a cake shop, which made us cheese on toast. The waiter said that the exiled leader of the PKK, the Kurdistan Workers' Party, had come to speak in a nearby mosque. The PKK was agitating for Kurdish nationhood, and had its own armed faction.

There was a long downhill from Batman towards a green plain, spread out like the Nile's fertile fields. At the last hairpin a pack of stray dogs jumped out at our wheels. I pulled out my DOG STICK and turned to face them. As I did some Turkish sentries ran out from one of the concrete barracks that lined the road and booted them back into the oncoming traffic. That evening we slept on the roof of a *cai* stop, halfway up one of the mountain passes. The customers were keen to reassure us we were in good hands, and a villager went to the extent of ringing his English-speaking brother in Istanbul. Sleeping on the flat roof beneath the stars we felt truly adventurous. Until the heavens opened and pissed on us.

Further up the mountain road a squeak developed in my CHAIN, even though I had oiled and maintained it to within an inch of its engineering. The green ravine beside us had been turned into a smouldering landfill site and a sign in English said EU FUNDED LANDFILL RENEWAL PROJECT. Yellow smoke drifted across the road like mustard gas as I ducked between the trucks to retrieve the glove that had fallen from my pocket, smudged like road kill.

Mystical experiences such as those found in Sufism are described in Christian, Judaic, Native American, Amerindian, Buddhist, Hindu, Aboriginal and Celtic pagan rituals. But they also occur in our everyday lives without any ceremony. Scientifically they are described as aberrations of the occipital lobes, the right hippocampus or the left amygdala, induced by magnetic fields or psychedelic drugs, while sociologically they are constructed as the explanation of a particular belief system; the power of the holy spirit in Christianity, the life force in shamanism, the nearness of Allah in Sufi ritual. All of this analysis, scientific or sociological, tries to objectify the mystical experience, as if it is something that can be separated from subjectivity, imposing the headlight of reason on an unknown that can only ever be particular to each individual.

But this shifting perspective is not a human condition. We prefer the oppositional, mind or body, science or solipsism, and all we allow ourselves is a fleeting travel across the border of reason and mysticism. It is unlikely the matter-ists and the visionaries will ever meet peaceably in a modern American or European conception of self; all we can do is reach across those boundaries and enjoy the fierce paradoxes in extending ourselves so far.

Peering over the edge of the ravine of the 'EU Funded Landfill Renewal Project', it felt that even this might be a bit of a jump. Operating alongside any mystical elation, in our felt relationship to the natural world, there also has to be a more complex response, that acknowledges its material loss. Just as we might admit an ordinary kindness that acknowledges the potency of love but also the pain of its loss, then we must also admit the possibility of a mystical grief, that the oneness of any union must also embrace the possibility of its separation; that the 'EU Funded Landfill Renewal Project' must now co-exist with the green mountain valley. Cycling is one way to navigate this painful landscape, winding between an ecstatic alignment with the natural landscape and our complicit role in its loss; any transcendent aspect to cycling will always be connected to the nuts and bolts of a frame that is endlessly rattling apart.

Before Jen and I embarked on our long bike trip, before we (re)discovered cycling, we went to see a lecture by the futurist James Lovelock, now in his nineties. It was he who came up with the

Gaia theory of the world's interdependency across natural systems, including weather fronts, ocean flows, species diversity, and how man was altering this interdependent equilibrium irrevocably. He told the audience that the 'Four Horsemen of the Apocalypse' were galloping over the horizon, and that the migrations and wars and starvation that climate change would wreak would spell the end of civilisation. His answer? Build more nuclear power stations. I still don't know if I understand his argument, but what James Lovelock unleashed, in me at least, was a terrible fury. I queued at the signing for his new book, *The Revenge of Gaia*, and, like an indignant schoolboy, ranted at him. How did he know that nuclear power stations were the only answer? How could he say that we were all doomed? How could our relationship with each other also be our downfall? Jen ushered me away from the table. This was not the way to treat a distinguished intellectual in a Bristol art gallery. Outside the environmentalists and activists huddled into their Afghan coats against the cold.

Later that spring Jen and I bought touring bikes and we cycled from Bristol to Pilton Farm for a work weekend in a community garden that would, that summer, be at the centre of the Glastonbury Festival, the largest outdoor music and arts event in the world. At that time it was just empty fields embedded with hidden litter. I thought I could see the ghosts of old revellers walking past in ecstatic travel. We were at the beginning, I see now, of a far longer journey, towards and away from my anger and confusion, banging my fist against the table of a book signing, making impotent ripples in the wine glasses.

It was mid-October in Kurdistan, and we were at the higher altitudes of the frontier with Iran. This gave Lake Van, near the town of Van, an icy purity. We shivered on its shores as I cleaned and reoiled my bike CHAIN to get rid of the squeak in its links. Jen's picture of the lake shows it glass flat with a coronet of mountains, the ellipse of a single bird hovering in the cloudless sky above. What the picture doesn't show, just below the frame, is a municipal tanker disgorging sewage into the water.

We decided not to take the lakeside road and instead headed off into the surrounding mountains, where the path wove between the peaks rather than over them. This, I decided, was how a pastoral utopia *should* be: teenage shepherds tending their flocks and whistling from distant farmsteads, a dusting of snow on the ragged ridges, the leaves on the lower slopes an autumn tamarind, a child holding out a small red fruit for us as he chewed on another, his cheeks a ruddy shock of colour, women in hand-knitted tops rubbing their shoulders and pointing up at the mountains to tell us to keep warm, the familiar see-sawing rise and fall of the bicycle along the road.

The city of Van was a legendary staging post on the overland 'hippy trail' that led from Europe to India during the 1960s and seventies, a countercultural echo of the trade routes that had passed through here for centuries and a reflection of the adventures of the Romantic poets of the eighteenth and nineteenth centuries, their rejection of rationalism and pursuit of a different kind of enlightenment through sensory derangement and dislocation in travel. The archetypal Romantic poet Arthur Rimbaud specifically advanced a project of sensory derangement and 'tramping' in his broken boots all over Europe, and is even said by some Arab poets, like Adonis, Alī Aḥmad Saḥīd 'Isba, to have been working in a similar way to the Sufi tradition, with his wilful derangement of the senses in search of a more coherent whole. Rimbaud was a hero of the beat poets of 1950s America, whose early adoption of LSD created a ripple of experimentation in literary circles and then a wave of psychedelic drug use across America and Europe. A generation of 1960s Americans and Europeans were taking these trips at a time of disillusion, both with religion, and with the nationalist politics that had replaced it, a recognition that there was a deeper layer of meaning to reality but no tradition or allegory to translate it. Hence the long exodus to the East, towards the 'other' of a different philosophy and religion, in search of new meanings, a journey that inevitably led back to the self they had left behind and, for some, the anchoring materialism of 1980s capitalism.

The bicycle tourist travels a different route to India today, literally and metaphorically. The evergreen possibilities of the sixties have long been replaced by a more knowing cynicism, in which the once-sought-for utopia of the East has hardened into the fundamentalist jihadi or the sexually exploitative guru, while the physical route has been obstructed by spreading wars in Afghanistan, Pakistan, Iraq, Syria and the fluctuating embargoes of Iran. Our perception of travel has turned in on itself and then out again once more. We no longer travel to see the world; we travel to know our place in it.

There was a whiff of lawlessness about the region upstream of Lake Van. The PKK survived by taxing drug and people smuggling over the porous border with Iran. A kilo of heroin fetched $5000 and each smuggled migrant $250.

We followed a slow mountain pass up to 3000 metres and then a narrow, twisting valley, as if we were on the highest level of an arcade game. When we stopped in a lay-by, four men peered down at us from a ridge, leaning on sticks that could have been rifles. Then there were the army checkpoints every fifty kilometres or so and the rumble of armoured personnel carriers. In the town of Baskale we found a dormitory with a corner room that had metal drums of hot water you could ladle over yourself. The windows opened onto a ravine, beyond which we could see the frontier peaks, cuticle pink. The next day we were halted at a Turkish checkpoint by shouting soldiers. The trees beside the road flared orange, burning to autumn like a match struck along a box.

At the border with Iran we had to wait while our bags were unpacked and checked. I had a hundred euros in my socks 'just in case'. We carried on over a barren undulating plateau, our legs turned to mush from the repeated mountain passes. We went over the brow of a hill to discover the infinite plain of Iran stretching far below us. Was it a trick of perspective or was there a sheer drop into Iran, as if we were landing from a long flight rather than cycling? We set off on the downhill, with no pedalling, just coasting, as the smooth looped hand of Farsi signs went whirling past. There were no shouting kids, no gaggles of earnest young men, just the half-curled waves of astonished pedestrians. We rolled past, too fast to stop, too fast to see their faces, our heads raised to the wind, 'rising to the world of bliss, / With necks exalted as racers' (Mahmoud Shabestari, fourteenth-century Sufi).

Later, in our hotel room, we would watch the wedding ring I had bought for Jen fall from its bathroom shelf and roll towards the shower, a silver circle going round and round and round, gathering momentum towards the plughole, until it was gone (see WHEELS).

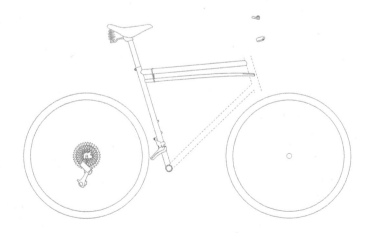

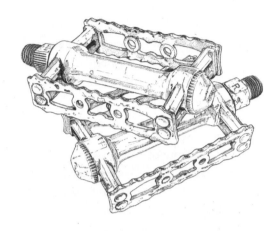

CHAPTER 13

The Pedals

Midway through Turkey Jen and I had been having relationship
issues. What others might call problems with 'distance'.

'Pedal on the downhill,' I shouted at her.

Jen stopped, climbed off her SADDLE and threw her bike into
the scrub. It lay on its side with one of the Pedals wedged into
the dust.

Grit in the bearings, I thought. *Ongoing maintenance may be
required.*

'I don't want to cycle to India.'

'What?'

'I want to rest.'

'Well maybe, you know, after we've—'

'Now.'

'What if we—'

'What about my birthday?'

'But what—'

'Now.'

It was less of a conversation, more a clay pigeon shoot.

That night we stayed in the World Heritage Site of Cappadocia. We slept without touching on a bed with a sequinned satin cover, in a room with fake stone walls.

The Pedals transmit power to the CRANKS, the levers that power the front CHAIN WHEELS and thence the CHAIN. Of the total force transmitted to a Pedal, only that part which is perpendicular, at right angles to the CRANK, is turned into driving motion. The Pedal maintains this right angle as the CRANK is turned because of the ball bearings between the cone and the cup at the ends of the spindle, or axle, that runs through the Pedal. If dust or dirt gets inside it can rub away at the bearings and cause pitting. This can lead to grittiness or grinding in the Pedals, reducing the efficiency of the cyclist, reducing *her* mileage and preventing *them* both touching in a sequinned satin bed with fake stone walls.

> I would spread the cloths under your feet:
> But I, being poor, have only my dreams;
> I have spread my dreams under your feet;
> Tread softly because you tread on my dreams.

These words by Yeats, composed on the privacy and tenderness of dreams, have been replayed tens of thousands of times in cross-stitch samplers across the Western world. When Jen and I awoke in our satin bed she did not have the privacy and tenderness of dreams on her mind. She wanted to lie around and maybe open a few packets of crisps. This, I admitted, gazing nervously at our bikes, was perfectly acceptable.

Cappadocia is a strange landscape of tall rock pillars and geological aberrations described in the tourist brochures as 'fairy chimneys'. Here, for once, we weren't treated as curiosities. The man at the adjacent table of the local cafe welcomed us in English and asked us where we were from. Was this genuine friendliness or did he want to take us on a tour? Where, I wondered, in this fairy landscape, did the hospitality of Anatolia end and the hospitality industry begin?

We climbed to the top of Uchisar's Castle, which had plummeting views over the gorges, and watched silver coaches progress from one side of the valley to the other, zigzagging like metallic beetles up the hairpins. We, and the coaches of tourists alongside us, clicked away with our cameras and phones, devouring the landscape. A storm brewed behind the castle, and the billowing clouds and the pink light and the stripes of candy-coloured rock had a Disney quality. Underneath, we explored the caves of the fortress, with their plastic water bottles and fag butts and the smell of piss.

The act of pedalling involves revolving two CRANKS out of phase with each other. If we were to do this without the support of the bicycle we would find ourselves, as the biomechanic Steven Vogel has pointed out, 'without a leg to stand on'. When walking, running, power-walking, hopping or skipping, our legs do not move in circles, but by unearthing us and replanting us into a different way of being (see TYRES), cycling echoes the fall of all that we once thought certain: the schools, the government buildings, the churches, all flashing past as we continue on the way to somewhere that we hope is the actual destination.

Christian pilgrimages across Europe in the thirteenth and fourteenth centuries created a network of charitable hospices linked by the first mass-produced guidebooks, and by the fifteenth century you could book tours from Venice to Jerusalem. Not long afterwards the aristocracy were seeking betterment in their grand tours of Renaissance Italy. By the eighteenth century the middle class were in on the act, making their buck off the backs of the Industrial Revolution. This theme of self-improvement, of physical and mental nourishment, led to the development of the spa town and later the British seaside resort. What rail travel did for the burgeoning seaside towns, cheap air flights has done for overseas beaches. Tourists want more. More destinations and more experiences, just as long as the comforts of home can be retained. Hence air con and coach trips to visit peasants with flush toilets, hence the theme park, hence cowboys and Indians, hence Aladdin and his genie and the hot-dog stand.

The sage is pervasive across literary culture, producing 'how-to' guides on living in the wild, building tree houses, living in log cabins, rediscovering the lines of the landscape. Such books gaze down with a righteous and ever-discerning eye at the indignities of mass tourism, much like middle-aged men writing metaphorical books on philosophy and cycling. It is no longer possible for a certain kind of cyclist to ride off into the countryside without being aware of themselves and their journeys in an increasingly scrutinised way. But the delight of being on a bike, indeed of any exercise, is that it quickly shakes off any self-awareness. It doesn't matter if you're cycling in a woollen jersey branded as a 'cycling experience' or an old T-shirt gnarled in the laundry run, when you sweat you sweat; when you punish yourself up a hill it hurts; when you careen down the other side, the wind whipping at your face like a birch tree, it still snaps you back into your body, into your white-knuckle hands. And then none of the photo taking, image enhancing or suave theorising matters. These are the experiences that wipe the mind clean, that give us a place to return home from.

*

Postmodern critics will tell you that we live in a postmodern age, when growth, not just of economies but of popular culture and imagery, is accelerating so fast it can't be tracked. In the previous 'modern' era the threads of history were easier to trace; the scientific, academic and institutional bodies of the eighteenth, nineteenth and early twentieth centuries, seemed to be set in stone with their own unspoken codes and clauses. These rules didn't just apply to the institutions but to the culture that surrounded them. 'High' art, as represented by opera, classical music, painting and sculpture, was differentiated from 'low' art – music hall, pop and advertising. But as Western economies went into overdrive and demand for a wider variety of culture and imagery increased, so those seemingly impregnable boundaries collapsed. It became harder and harder to spot what was high art and what was low. Which had more cultural value, the *Mona Lisa* or the mass-produced poster?

Meanwhile the old institutions were being dismantled brick by brick, unmortared by business and the reflexive cynicism of a more liberal youth. Into this postmodern building site the postmodern philosophers trooped, French intellectuals with surnames like hammer drills (Foucault, Derrida, Barthes, Baudrillard) swiping at the plaster walls with a crowbar. They 'deconstructed' this already fragmenting culture with a Marxist heft, reimagining postmodern man as a sucker for pop-opera-adbreak-Disney-sponsored-leisuretime-social-networking, where anything was up for grabs and meaning tumbled over itself in a hyphenated conveyor belt into the maw of money. The problem being that postmodern philosophy was also part of that rush, analysing, fragmenting and tearing itself apart with no coherent picture of where we might be heading. No direction home.

*

On the day of Jen's birthday we went for a cowboy ride. I was told to 'hug' my horse as we were led between the fairy chimneys by a young man in a lopsided Stetson who clearly didn't want to be there. Fifteen minutes into the ride, perhaps because I wasn't hugging my horse hard enough, it galloped ahead of the group and, though I pulled back on the reins, charged over a hillock, where it bucked me off onto my side. The guide looked down, much like an ice-cream vendor might look at a 99 that has slipped off its cone, regrettable but replaceable. Jen helped me limp back to the hotel, and we spent her birthday side by side under a tartan blanket, nibbling at baklava and staring at the stars from our cave balcony, wondering at the phalluses of fairy chimneys in the valley below.

According to French philosopher Jean Baudrillard we live in a time of reality confusion. The division between reality and its reflection is becoming less and less clear. Television, film, screen images and theme park entrances seem brighter, more glamorous, more appealing, more 'hyperreal', than the reality they once proposed to reflect. Baudrillard suggests that we are so saturated with images and stimulation that we have moved beyond desiring reality and now seek only the stimulation itself.

One way to avoid the relentless imagery of the modern or postmodern age is to take a side road, detour into a more intuitive and physical relationship with what we find around us, unmediated by mass tourism and the unkindness of money. Once the road has been decided, a bike ride does not offer multiple options. It skirts around the runways, the coach excursions, the glossy brochures, and allows us to meet people by the side of the road leading their unspectacular lives. I'm under no illusion that I'm leading a more 'authentic' life when I stay overnight in someone's farmhouse or a family's concrete yard, but I am reaching for more than the remote control.

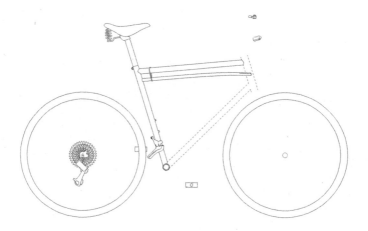

CHAPTER 14

The Wheels

A bike Wheel can carry a hundred times its own weight. It accumulates this strength piece by piece, each spoke pulling against its neighbour in a back and forth like a football chant locked down by a music teacher. If a single spoke weakens it distorts all the others in a domino of militancy. Slowly and painfully the Wheel begins to warp, taking on the buckled shape of a potato crisp. Not good for riding. Not good for cyclists attuned to the slightest rub of brake pads on a metal rim.

And this is why a bike mechanic must, *must*, true a Wheel that has begun to waver, whose spokes have become misaligned. These were my thoughts on the high passes, the ferocious ups and downs, the roadworks of central Turkey, just before we rolled into Malatya and a backstreet repair shop near its bazaar.

The mechanic flipped over the bikes and spun the Wheels between his fingers. After a few revolutions he'd determined that

Jen's, through sheer lack of neuroses, had remained unscathed. But mine were devilishly untrue.

He put the thumb of one hand a hair's breath away from the metal rim and spun. Using a tool that resembled a silver moth, he tightened the nut at the base of a spoke, its nipple, and spun again, and spun again, judging the tiny lateral movements of the metal rim, in and out, with his thumbnail. Periodically he would pull at the spokes and listen to the note they made, and then, with a movement uncannily like a harpist's, grip adjacent struts with both hands and bend them in and out, a process known as stress relieving that adjusts the final line of the metal. When this had been repeated, and we had drunk our *cai*, he gave the Wheel one last spin, his eyes right beside his thumbnail as the rim spun round and round and round.

To calculate the linear speed of a bike Wheel, you also need to think about its tangential velocity, the speed of the Wheel at a tangent to its circumference – the merry-go-round as you step off it. This tangential velocity will be greatest at the rim and will steadily decrease as you move towards the axle at the centre, where effectively it is not moving at all.

Malatya is on the fringes of Zoroastrianism, a belief system which originated in Persia over three thousand years ago, which preceded Christianity and Islam, and which, despite constant threats and persecution, is surviving, just, in the desert heartlands of Iran. For us, cycling through Anatolia, there was no obvious evidence of Zoroastrianism, stripped away by recurrent Christian and Islamic invasions. But two and a half thousand years ago, during the Achaemenid empire, it was the predominant religion as far west as Anatolia and as far east as central Asia. In the West it is mainly known through the iconography of masonic emblems and New Age pendants. Yet it retains a quiet congregation of active worshippers around the world, émigrés from Iran and an Indian branch known as the Parsis. It influenced Judaism,

Christianity and Islam, and was instrumental, if you look closely enough, in the evolution of the rational moral philosophy of the West. To travel from Turkey to Iran and on to India is to traverse the geography of an ancient religion that continues to engage us today.

That man is caught up in a cosmic circle of which he is both humble part but also instigator is central to the Zoroastrian universe. Some time between 1000 and 2000 BCE its prophet, Zarathustra, received the word of the Zoroastrian god, Ahura Mazda, as recorded in the Gathas, its holy hymns. The Greek version of Zarathustra, Zoroaster, stuck in the West, and it is as Zoroastrianism that the religion is known, though in Persia followers still refer to themselves as Zarathushti. The Gathas record that Ahura Mazda created a perfectly ordered reality, only to find it corrupted by the demonic Angra Mainyu. To defeat his evil and chaotic influence, Ahura Mazda created the material universe and all it contained, including earth and man. Angra Mainyu entered the material world through a hole in its flat topography, bringing death, darkness, destruction and cyclist-defeating mountains. It was all looking pretty grim until the arrival of the prophet Zoroaster, who, by recording the vision of Ahura Mazda and enlisting man's support, turned a corner in the cosmic battle against evil and tipped the circle back towards the perfect goodness of Ahura Mazda's original creation.

Man helps to drive the wheel of a cosmic battle, where first evil, then good, triumphs, and the universe reinstates itself to a perfectly ordered beauty. There is not, as in Christian and Islamic judgements, a consuming conflagration followed by eternal life, nor a recurring cycle of death and rebirth, as in Hindu and Buddhist belief, but instead a return to purification. The timeline of Zoroastrian history is both circular *and* linear; there is a revolving struggle between good and evil and a more straightforward trajectory towards a final resolution. Man is given a free choice – to be a part of this history or not. He can either contribute towards the onward good or backpedal into evil and darkness. In this way the story of existence is reimagined as a human-powered vehicle rather than the pure inheritance of fate or the gods.

Zoroastrianism had a profound effect on the Western understanding of good and evil, and of free will, man's autonomous choice. It emerged as a powerful force at the same time as the ancient Veda, the religious texts that form the basis of Indian Hinduism, and in so doing formed an underpinning bridge between the religious and philosophical thinking of the West and East. Hindus and Zoroastrians come from the same Indo-Aryan tribes in central Asia and eastern Europe, migrating south-west into Iran towards Zoroastrianism and south-east into India towards what we now call Hinduism. The perfect moral order of Zoroastrianism, known as Arta, is reflected in the Rta of Hinduism; the chanted rituals or *manthras* of Zoroastrianism reflect the mantras of Hinduism; the woven braid worn around the waist, known as the *kushti* in Zoroastrianism, mirrors the braided wrist bracelet known as the *kalava* in Hinduism. But there are also clear differences. And these differences stalk the imaginary border between what we think of as the contemporary religions of the West and those of the East.

Zoroastrianism is often described as the first monotheistic world religion. It was certainly the first to set aside the 'pagan' gods of its Indo-Aryan past and follow a single deity. Ahura Mazda has his semi-deities or emissaries, and there is the devil figure, Angra Mainyu, but essentially it is a faith centred around a single divine power – unlike most forms of Hinduism, in which there are many (see HEADSET).

Before Zoroastrianism, before even the Indo-Aryan culture that preceded it, there was the Wheel, perhaps a potter's turntable five thousand years ago in Persia or perhaps in neighbouring Mesopotamia (modern Iraq). A thousand years later the first wheeled vehicles were constructed from felled tree trunks. But the real innovation was the axle, the development of a single central turning point, for which there is no obvious comparison in the natural world. It was a conceptual leap that recognised the need for a discontinuity between the centre of the Wheel and the vehicle it was carrying, a meeting point we now call the bearing. The next major advance was the CRANK, a human-powered lever for maintaining the motion of a Wheel, an innovation only transported into Europe from the East during the Middle Ages (see BELL).

We cannot fully rotate our limbs; as the biomechanic Steven Vogel has pointed out, our ability to turn the push and pull of muscle power into a circular revolution is an advance that transcends our very identity. Step changes like this carry their own conceptual momentum, a philosophical heft. The advent of the spinning wheel in thirteenth-century Europe, with its efficiency in binding wool, linen and cotton fibres, meant that the cost of cloth, especially linen, dropped considerably. The resulting plentiful linen rags, remaining from old clothes, made the vast quantities of paper demanded by the new presses of Gutenberg. The subsequent spread of books had an impact on literacy, education and the social and humanitarian changes of the Renaissance. This is another way of saying that the history of ideas is a human-powered vehicle.

When electrical power first entered the domestic sphere, we turned the circular dials on radios, telephones, clocks, television sets and hi-fis. With the advent of digital technology, we now use our fingers to push or touch. The change from analogue to binary systems has changed the way we physically reach towards the world in subtle but telling ways. Is the bicycle a throwback to the analogue era? In fact, the bicycle's motion contains both the analogue turn of the Wheel and the later binary click of the GEARS, a circular and a linear movement that is altogether Zoroastrian in its miniature cosmos.

From Malatya we rode through the mountainous Kurdish border with Iran down into the desert plains and on to the city of Orumiyeh. Jen did not have a hijab, the modest clothing demanded by sharia law, and had been making do with a long-sleeved shirt and a flowery Turkish scarf wrapped around her head. We peered from our hotel room at the strangely subdued citizens outside, the women in various lengths of black cloth. After being stopped by the police and asked for our passports, we shuffled around the markets until Jen found a new headscarf and a knee-length beige jacket that made her look like Columbo, the 1970s TV detective. We then exchanged 240 euros for 3,000,000 Iranian rials. Each note featured the leader of the Iranian revolution, Ayatollah Khomeini, staring at us, with the authority of a religious leader who was quite prepared to stone dissenters to death. After the revolution of 1979 it was announced that Khomeini's rule would have divine authority – 'the commandments of the ruling jurist ... are like the commandments of God'.

Two thousand years before this the divine rulers of Iran had claimed the authority of Ahura Mazda but with a more equable rule. Carvings from the Sassanian period (CE 224–651) show its kings accepting divine power in the form of a ring; 'kingship and religious teaching are two gems set in the same ring'. Zoroastrianism was for the most part tolerant of other religions. However, Islamic rule in Iran judges Zoroastrianism to be not 'of the book', without the written history of Judaism and Christianity, and without reference in the Koran.

When and Jen and I left Orumiyeh we made what we later recognised as a wrong turn. Instead of heading into the back roads of the frontier region bordering Iraq, known as Kordistan, we headed south-east across the vast central plains of Iran, along its major highways. On our first day we found ourselves on a four-lane transit system to Tehran. We spent a lot of time in Iran thinking about that wrong turn as the diesel trucks bullied us into a non-existent hard shoulder, flashing their exhausts like dirty petticoats. There were few hills in these desert plains and theoretically we might have been able to take advantage of solid-bodied Wheels to maintain a flowing aerodynamic ride across the desert. But we were carrying ridiculous amounts of luggage over our Wheels. And that is the real advantage of spokes, the strength of their see-through engineering.

A bicycle Wheel relies on internal tension. Its spokes are slotted through the holes in the outer edge of the central hub and connected to pre-drilled holes in the metal rim. Before they are tightened these wires look like a bloated spider web. Tightening the nipples, one after the other, gives the Wheel an elasticity and internal tension that relies not on any one spoke but on the balance between them, pulling against each other and the surrounding rim. Master wheel builders will tell you that changing the tension in any one spoke means the whole 'map' has changed, and the process of spoke tightening and balancing must begin again. The final spoked Wheel flashes like a geometric jewel. What this brings is strength. Stamina in perpetuity. A tensioned balanced bicycle Wheel is a captured spring. Its stillness is an indication of its tightly bound power, released in the movement of cycling.

When the Aryo-Indian people moved into the central plains of Iran thousands of years ago, taking Zoroastrianism with them, they were at the midpoint of their world. The history of the universe, the great turning battle between good and evil, pivoted around this *axis mundi* and was powered by the creed of Zoroastrianism. To retrieve the ordered paradise of Ahura

Mazda from the evil and chaotic Angra Mainyu, man had to intervene through his 'good thoughts, good words and deeds'. And it was this continual tension between good and evil, between human and divine action, that moved history forward and gave Zoroastrians a moral purpose. To hold the universe in 'right measure' both ruler and citizen had to work for an explicit good. It wasn't just what you did or how you acted that was important, it was what you thought. Ideas themselves began to acquire a moral value, generalised as human rights and human wrongs.

The relentless reinforcement of thought and behaviour in Zoroastrianism has its contemporary parallel with the cure-all psychology of the twenty-first century, CBT – cognitive behavioural therapy – a treatment for depression and anxiety and a multitude of other mental disorders. CBT addresses the links between what we think and how we behave, the way that distorted, often negative, patterns of thinking can detrimentally change the way we live our lives. But unlike CBT the Zoroastrian exhortation to 'good thought, good word, good deed' has an explicitly environmental and cosmological purpose, a consequence not just for the individual but for the whole universe; not only do good thoughts affect your life but they contribute to the wellbeing of others and the very land on which you stand. CBT's target of restoring neutral 'happiness' within a given population mean is very different from the Zoroastrian sense of happiness, *shiyati*, a more encompassing and evolving notion of human experience that includes the individual, community and natural world. Aristotle, himself much influenced by Zoroastrianism, developed his own conception of this, *eudaimonia* – human flourishing, a sense of striving and changing, not towards an absolute emotional mean, rather fulfilling a potential, a pattern of natural growth, like a tree stretching out its branches towards the canopy, its roots towards the water table, so that there is a deepening of meaning, purpose and moral clarity.

South of Tabriz we arrived in the small town of Ziaabad, wondering where the hell to go next as icy rain pelted the backs of our necks. A yellow taxi pulled up and Mr Karim popped his head out of the window and offered to put us up. There were two bedrooms, four factory machinists and a couple of nervous cyclists from England. But all of our flatmates, including the sizeable Mr Mustapha, an ex-wrestler, couldn't have been more affable. Our damp jackets were placed in front of the single heater and we ate quietly together as a mouse ran across the floor. Mr Mustapha told us he had had an addiction problem with marijuana but now was in a twelve-step recovery programme. The next morning, as he cooked us an omelette, Mr Mustapha became increasingly preoccupied with our lack of 'God' and was keen to reiterate the benefit of the twelve-step programme. As far as we could gather, the four machinists were all in the drug rehabilitation programme and Mr Karim was their mentor, in a halfway house. This is the magic of bike touring, confounding your expectations of people, and their kindness, again and again and again.

The notion that Iran is a threatening country, constructed from propaganda within and without, is a nonsense thoroughly disproved by its people. And providing you don't openly criticise the regime or flout sharia law, the state is unlikely to be interested. What cannot be avoided is religion. If you're a woman in Iran you have to choose what you wear on the basis of Islamic law. And if you're Iranian, questions of God and belief and religion cannot be avoided.

We tried to get back to the snow-tipped hills of Kordistan, but the narrowing roads, dwindling hard shoulders and rumbling lorries forced us to return to the main drag. One of the rumbling trucks stopped. The driver jumped out of his cab and pressed a silver ring into my hand and some prayer beads into Jen's, and then, putting his palm to his chest in the familiar sign of Islamic blessing, returned to his seat and drove away. The next day as we were climbing across a high plateau, snowflakes melting on our cheekbones, the same driver stopped on the other side of the road, dodged between the cars and gave us a carrier bag containing two hot meals, drinks, an Iranian route map, a handwritten list of local hotels and his own smiling photograph with his name on the back. He shook our hands, accepted our thanks and then he was gone.

From the moonscapes near Saveh, we cycled into Qom, one of the most sacred Islamic cities of Iran. Its shrine is built around the tomb of the sister of the Eighth Imam, a descendant of the prophet Muhammad, Fatima al Massouma. Qom is also the home of clerical training in Iran and where Ayatollah Khomeini studied Greek philosophy. The country has always had a fondness for Greek classical ideas, which stems from when Alexander the Great conquered the Zoroastrian empire in the third century BCE. When the Neoplatonic followers of Plato and Aristotle were kicked out of their academy in Athens in the sixth century CE by the newly Christianised Emperor Justinian I, they sought shelter in the city of Gundeshapur in Iran, these ideas returning to Europe only during the Renaissance. The Iranian Islamic state, the perceived bad boy of the Middle East, has at its foundational roots the philosophies that gave an impetus to secular Western thinking. There is no guidance in the Koran to account for Khomeini's declaration that the 'most learned cleric' should run the country other than Plato's *Republic*, where the ideal state is run by the 'wisest philosopher'.

However, Qom's Islamic orthodoxy is plain, its women shrouded from head to foot in the hijab, a single slit in the niqab – a full veil. The shrine of Fatima al Massouma, at the centre of Qom, requires all women to wear a chador, a head and neck

scarf that leaves only the face exposed, and we were directed to a
booth where Jen could borrow one.

'Muslim?' asked the official behind the desk.

'No,' said Jen

'Christian?' he asked hopefully.

'No.'

He persevered, 'Roman Catholic?'

'No.'

'So?'

'Nothing,' Jen said.

'No God?'

'No.'

The attendant fumbled for an old Formica telephone and
spent some time arguing with a higher power.

'No chador and no entrance,' he said.

Christians and Jews, being of the book, are more holy than
those who have no faith at all. This meant that Jen had to
wait outside like an underage teen while I sneaked around the
tiled mosaics, the silver mirror alcoves and the vast marble
floors. The chanted prayers of the knee-bent crowds echoed
through speakers, as others wandered through the open
spaces, pressing their cheeks and the palms of their hands
against wooden doors.

Islamic decoration has no human images, which are
considered idolatry. But what Islamic art lacks in figures it makes
up for with repetition. An Islamic mosaic is a dance of tessellated
uniformity, with no particular part or focus leaping out. The
individual reaches towards the wider whole, the infinite, with the
implication being that this is a step towards the divine, towards
Allah.

Coming out of the mosque I found Jen in a state of non-
transcendence. If you ride your bike thousands of miles to one
of Iran's most holy shrines and then your boyfriend parks you

outside while women in niqabs and holy men peer at you it's not going to transport you to a transliminal state.

'Never mind,' I said. 'Let's buy some bread.'

Just down from the shrine there was a bakery with a queue stretching into the road and around the corner. To be specific, there were two queues, one for men and one for women. Dough was slopped out of a mixer, thrown through the arch of a kiln, raked out onto red-hot pebbles, flattened, cooked for five minutes, tossed onto a wire rack, peeled off, the pebbles shaken off, and then folded, still bubbling, into a bag. The man at the head of my queue gave the bread he had been offered to the woman beside him, who had been waiting much longer. And when the two bakers spotted the skinny Englishman, mid-queue, resplendent in end-of-line camping gear, the next platter of bubbling dough was passed over the heads of everyone, men and women, and straight into my jubilant hands.

Jen, however. Jen was furious. She was furious with the whole country, with patriarchy, with me. I tried to find her a veggie meal while she escaped to the hotel room. I came back with a tin of lentils, a tin of baked beans and a chocolate pudding. We sat on the bed eating baked beans and lentils with a camping spoon as the pilgrims spooled in circles outside.

By the time we cycled into the next city, Kashan, the sun was low, the shadows long and soft. Our hotel had old plastered white walls and smooth hidden alcoves, where I hid and completed the songs I'd been making up on the long desert rides.

The next day we followed a single black cat in Kashan's bazaar as it padded through motes of dust captured by sunlight descending through glassless windows. In one alcove, behind some long-unopened gates, we found hundreds of iron bikes lying one upon the other, like a rusting boneyard. The sound of an old man chanting the Koran echoed from a hidden place. Kashan had a glowing textured warmth, a sense of one generation sleeping and waking into another.

The music of Islam, like so much of its formal art and poetry, has a textured, repetitive pattern, a humming reverberating quality that can only be fully appreciated from a distance, in the grain of its tone. A clear melody or linear lyric can be as elusive as the revolving themes of Sufi poetry. My road-worn songs didn't have this elusive quality but they kept spilling out of me.

I had carried the battered Yamaha Junior JR 1 guitar until Jen and I had a bit of a 'conversation' about who was carrying the most weight halfway up a Romanian mountain. From then on I took the two-man tent while Jen cycled ahead with the guitar. It went out of tune occasionally, but strangely none of the strings broke and it survived intact through all the potholes and pitfalls of Turkish road building and the desert plains of Iran.

Pull the spoke of a bicycle Wheel and listen. A low note suggests a low tension, that may be out of synch with those adjacent to it, deforming the shape of the Wheel and the way that the whole TYRE centres and rolls. A Wheel builder alters these peaks and troughs to create a circular uniformity. Guitar strings are not equally tuned in this way but each note does rely on fixed musical intervals, relative note frequencies, to sound more appealing to the human ear. The ancient Greek philosopher Pythagoras recognised the importance of numbers in nature by observing the correspondence between musical intervals and natural numbers. The spoked Wheel, like the fern, like the snowflake, like the arabesque (the symmetry of Islamic depictions of nature), has a regularity that shivers beneath the irregularities of the forces it must bear. The more undulating the road becomes, the more its idiosyncrasies are played through the pre-tensioned precision of a bicycle's Wheels, so what we understand to be a good ride is also the contours of the land playing to us through our bones, like the ridges and indents of a vinyl groove flexing the needle of a record player.

Is it too much of a stretch to believe that the songs I finished in Kashan represented the landscape I was riding through, day in, day out, playing back through my fingers and on to the strings of that knockabout guitar? Religious or non-religious we are all drawn to experiences that are intangibly divine, that are numinous. Some access this through the regularised sacrament of ritual, some through a music underpinned by the innate intervals that make it so pleasing, some through the ebb and flow of a long bicycle ride, with the spoked Wheel, the structured tension at its core.

As we cycled towards the city of Natanz, the guitar bobbing on the back of Jen's bike, I was not daydreaming in diagrammatic forms. I just really, really, really, really, *really* needed a piss. Not an idle, prop-up-the-bike-and-lean-against-a-date-palm kind of piss. More a knock-a-hole-in-the-Hoover-Dam kind of piss.

An hour before, we'd stopped on an escarpment overlooking a desert plain to take some pictures, when a hatchback car pulled over and its driver got out. We waited for him to greet us with the normal offers of fruit and Persian hospitality but he began flapping at the camera.

'No photo!'

He put the thumb and forefinger of one hand around the wrist of the other in the international sign for being handcuffed.

'Oh,' said Jen. And we looked down the road.

It was then that we realised we were cycling towards the Natanz Nuclear Enrichment Plant, home of Iran's contested nuclear programme.

'Do not stop,' said the man. 'Go!'

So we jumped on our bikes and pedalled, energised by the gun turrets of the camouflaged tanks that overlooked the road.

The snipers in their bunkers looked mightily uninterested but I was convinced we were going to be banged up in an Iranian jail for spying. After a delirious piss in a lay-by, well out of sight of the gun turrets, I returned to find my bike had a puncture. As I repaired it another car pulled over and two men emerged with hombre-sized moustaches. The one with enormous arms worked my bicycle pump like he was wringing the neck of a skinny Englishman. We thanked them and sped off towards the nearest hotel.

That night Jen got her hair stuck on some chewing gum no one had bothered to take off the headboard as I lay awake worrying about a pair of boxers I'd left behind in Kashan. 'Farewell, boxer shorts,' I wrote in my diary, 'I shall miss you.' So much for transcending the materiality of existence.

We arrived in the city of Isfahan feeling like burned toast. The endless desert and cloudless skies had scorched us into husks. We hoped that Isfahan would be a good place to rest and forget about cycling. But there in the courtyard of the hostel were *fourteen* touring bikes. Isfahan was the city where tourists got their Iranian visas renewed, and it seemed that all the cyclists on the overland route from Europe to Asia, or vice versa, had converged on the Amir Kabir hostel, chained their bikes in the dusty ten-foot yard like corralled horses and fallen asleep in their rooms.

There was the Irishman who had cycled from Cherbourg to Istanbul on a titanium racing bike with pencil-thin tyres, in *three weeks* (it took us three months). There he'd met a French woman who'd pulled her bike out of a skip, joined him on the road, and they were now travelling together. There was the Lithuanian who was proud of how *low* his daily mileage was. His 'record' was five kilometres. He was carrying a tank of water the size of a domestic fridge. There were a couple of guys from London who were on their way to the 'Stans', the high central plains of Asia, during the winter snows. They didn't have any cold-weather clothes and were the skinniest cyclists we'd seen in ages. There was the Kiwi couple who'd cycled from China across the Stans, and were now en route to Turkey, their tyres sewn up with dental floss. There was the French couple, cycling to New Zealand for the rugby world cup, who'd met a man on the way carrying a surfboard. We sat around talking bike parts as the other travellers made their excuses and left for the sights.

We too locked our bikes to the railings, packed our kit into one pannier bag and took a coach to the ancient desert city of Yazd. From Yazd we went off to find the 'real' desert in a taxi, which provided all the qualities we wanted, sensual sand dunes that played into ripples from the wind, the occasional indentation of a bird's claw or the slithered S of a snake. I sat behind a dune, where all I could hear was a hum. As if all the Wheels of the world, all the bustling roads that had taken us this far, had ground themselves down into sand, into a place deep inside the centre of my head.

The figure of zero was imported into Persia from India. Here the mathematician Muhammad ibn Musa al-Khwarizmi named it *sifr* from the Arabic word meaning empty. With the transport of Islamic scholarship into Spain during the Moorish occupation of the twelfth century (SEE BIKE BELL and TOP TUBE) Al-Kharwizmi's zero was injected, like a non-existent shot in the arm, into the sciences of the European Renaissance. The Venetian form of sifr became *zefiro* which evolved, through its French translation, into zero.

At the very centre of a quick-release Wheel, within the hollow axle of its hub, there is nothing. And that nothing is always moving, on a moving bicycle, with zero tangential velocity. At the centre of our turning world. Our axis mundi. Nothing.

The taxi driver, Harun, made a fire on the dunes from old roots, driftwood from the sea that would never arrive, and we warmed ourselves in the desert cold.

From there we went on to Pir e Sabz or Chak-Chak, a holy Zoroastrian site. After the defeat of the last Zoroastrian king, Yazdegerd III, in CE 651, his daughter Nikbanu was said to have fled here. She was pursued by Arab armies to this remote cliff face, where a cleft was said to have admitted her, before closing against her pursuers. The water that drips down the cave wall is her tears, her grief for the loss of a people. It is a stark setting – a few buildings terraced into the side of a sheer cliff, from which you can see a vast flat desert plain, almost devoid of markers, apart from the outline of the road that carries you here. We, together with coach parties from Yazd, shuffled up the steps, and thence into the cave, where we were given what appeared to be disposable chef's hats. Inside the the cave were two plastic buckets catching the drips from the wall. Kids ran around in circles, LEDs flashing on the soles of their trainers as the digital cameras clicked and clicked and clicked.

'I wish I were back on my bike,' I said to Jen.

'Be in the moment,' she said.

'I am in the moment,' I said, 'and it's two plastic buckets, a disposable chef's hat and kids running around in flashing neon trainers.'

But what I'd dismissed as a 'chef's hat' was the Zoroastrian protection of elemental purity, to prevent contamination of the dripping water and the surrounding fire temple by visiting pilgrims and tourists. This and the *sudreh*, a white cotton shirt worn under clothing, and the *kushti*, a cord worn around the waist, are traditional Zoroastrian dress. What I'd perceived as a tourist sideshow was the remains of the oldest monotheistic religion fighting for its survival. This would have been inadmissible for an Islamic shrine in Qom. Here, in the middle of the desert, wilfully neglected by the Iranian regime, tourism seeped through the sides of Zoroastrian symbolism, its sacred tears splashing into plastic buckets.

Zoroastrianism is very much a faith in action. What a Zoroastrian believes and the world in which they believe it are interlinked by elemental divinities and ritual practices. Fire and water rituals are points of access between the material and immaterial realms. Its archangels and guardian angels are part of the non-material realm but can also appear as water, fire, earth, living beings and plants. It is through the recitation of the holy texts of Zorastriansim that a resonance is found between the two worlds. There is a moral integration with the environment that simply isn't there in Christianity, Judaism and Islam, and is sorely lacking in secular humanism and science. Am I saying we should convert to Zoroastrianism? No, but perhaps we could do with being a bit more Zoroastrian-like, acknowledging the importance of shared physical rituals and symbolic bridges to the natural world.

Cycling has only existed for 150 years, whisking us out of the cities and back into the countryside, but the Enlightenment thinking that made it possible did not provide any structure with which to relate to those natural experiences. The pagan gods had become history, the god of Christianity lowercase, and literal reason drained of human meaning. We retained a yearning to communicate with the natural world but without the *shared* symbolic language to do so. Art and culture fulfilled a role, but there was no shared ritual, no binding sense of congregation between us and our environment. We now appropriate a bit of shamanism here, a bit of druidism there, at the margins of what we rather sniffily call New Age thinking, but we do not share a ritual notion of belonging to the natural world.

I would suggest, however, that we do see aspects of this in cycling. Not as a religion but as a quiet ritual that re-emphasises physical rites as a way to move towards the land we have always been part of but somehow feel estranged from. Is it too much to say that those shared preoccupations about oiling the CHAIN, tuning up the GEARS, the nerdy evaluations of TYRE pressure and BRAKES, that the cyclists in the courtyard of Isfahan discussed were less to do with their technical details, but were a rite of sorts, shared between nationalities, which launch us towards a re-evaluation of our relationship with the natural world. And that all bike rides are, as a cyclist once told me, pilgrimages, not towards an identifiable holy site but towards an older, physical way of meeting with the natural world. Are bikes symbols or are they just Wheels on the hard rails of transport? In an age in which traditional religion, postmodern culture and rational science struggle to give us any sense of meaning or direction, we struggle to create our own folk remedies, patterns of belief that maintain our relationship with the natural world. Might it be that cyclists are reclaiming these connections from the province of the New Age, with the unspoken tread of their Wheels, and in so doing are blurring the divisions between West and East and science and metaphor?

Back in Isfahan, we watched our community unlock their Wheels from the courtyard railings and continue on their individual journeys west and east, east and west. For a time it really had felt like the hostel was a congregation. We shared a sense of purpose that was bigger than us, as if by embarking on these foolish distances we were making something happen; we were transforming the order of things. There is a Parsi Zoroastrian term for the sense of community conjured by ritual prayer, *hambandagi*, meaning 'bondedness'. The Zoroastrian pursuit of 'good thought, good word and good deed' is not just about the end goal, of perfect order and equitable relations in the cosmos, but about the benefits accrued in that pursuit, in mutual co-operation and interdependence. To say that the courtyard in a budget hostel achieved an aura of *hambandagi* is probably a misappropriation of Zoroastrianism. But, for a moment at least, it seemed like we were all moving together around a circular belief system, even though, to all intents and purposes, we were cycling in opposite directions.

The prayer beads given to us by our guardian angel, the lorry driver of northern Iran, had been lifted from Jen's HANDLEBARS. But it didn't matter. We were back on the road. We were returning to the devotion we knew best, mile after mile after mile. On the way to Pasargadae, the remains of the first great Persian and Zoroastrian empire, we found ourselves again narrowing our eyes, seeking out the undulations in the land, the nooks and crannies where we might pitch our tent. And then Hamid arrived in his pick-up truck. A friend had told him there were some travellers on bikes and he'd immediately driven out to find us. He beckoned us from the road to a walled compound, and inside we found a farm courtyard with green trees, a pump for water, a cattle shed and a one-roomed building with a sloping roof that Hamid told us was expressly for putting up passing travellers. It had a sofa and a pull-out bed and a kitchen area. His father had long been inviting wanderers to stay and Hamid had continued this tradition. He showed us a scrapbook of those who had stayed in the room: cyclists, motorcyclists, van drivers. There was a torn photograph of a young woman with a crew cut, the scribbled pen portrait of a German camper, the lonely wandering biro lines of a French hitchhiker; page after page of teenagers, young men and women and wizened parents following an indefinable urge to travel with their passport photos through Hamid's scrapbook. I was moved, not because they had written these things and left these pictures.

But because they were all so *different*, so oddly vulnerable in their individuality. And now our photo had been added, part of a community stretching west and east, and backwards and forwards in time.

Hamid liked to quote Hafez, Sufi poet and mystic beloved of the Persians. 'We are all one under the same sky and sun,' he would say and, 'all our blood runs the same colour.' He asked me to play a song, 'a sad one', and listened subdued as I knelt over my Yamaha Junior guitar and picked out a tune. But then, when I rang up my mum in the UK on his landline, he sprang into jubilant greeting: 'Many happiness to you. Your son is here and playing guitar good. All my love to the peoples of Britain, from my heart.'

There are many nods to Zoroastrianism in Sufi poetry. The Zoroastrian tavern keeper becomes the 'wise man of the Magi', who aids the wayward seeker, the *rend* (translating as drunk or scoundrel), on his road to the divine, into unity with all creation. The metaphorical drunkenness so common in Hafez and Rumi, is an elaboration of the unshackling of the senses, a plea to free oneself from religious orthodoxy and discover an individual connection with the forces of creation, whilst returning once again to the rituals of that religion, the formality of the verse structures, the grounding shape of the poems themselves. This sentiment has a Romantic flight about it but also a yearning sadness, as if man is reaching towards something that is always transient, unnameable, elusive.

The next day Hamid was quiet, gripping the steering wheel of his truck and fixing on the road ahead. Later we helped him take in some of his crops and shared a picnic with the farm workers. Then, with a short handshake, he turned away and went back to his land. We loaded our bikes with the confidence that every folded piece of cloth, every book, every tool had its place in the little scheme of our lives and pulled off once more onto the desert road with the cartwheeling trucks.

The spokes in the lower half of a Wheel are shortened when a load is placed over the axle. However, unlike the wooden spokes in a cart Wheel, they do not gain in compressive tension, rather lose some of the pre-tension that was built into the structure through the initial spoke-tightening process. The rigidity of the whole Wheel is maintained by the tension of the other spokes, which pull the lower spokes back into alignment. This power-packed pre-tensioned engineering is also found in triangulated bridges and planes. The inventor of the spoked wheel, in 1808, was the aeronautical engineer George Cayley, who went on to design the first glider and explored the possibility of powered flight. The Wright brothers were bicycle mechanics long before they started making planes. The innovations that give a bicycle the spring of free-flying movement, its pre-tensioned resilience, are inseparable from the history of human-powered flight. And this feeling of flight, of being transported a breath above the ground, is always there, the implication being that, if not on this ride then the one after, a soaring draught will lift us away from the pin of gravity.

The air was chill as we rode into Pasargadae, the stony remains of Cyrus the Great, built on a plateau of high desert scrub. Cyrus was the pre-eminent king of Persia's Achaemenid empire in the sixth century BCE. Its dominance stretched from Europe to the borders of India, and Zoroastrianism, the religion of Cyrus and his successors, was carried with it. When Cyrus occupied Babylon he freed the Jewish community exiled there. And Zoroastrianism's notions of good and evil, and that every individual must choose between the two, seems to have left an indelible mark on the Jewish texts that followed. It is in the Book of Job, written at the time of Cyrus's invasion of Babylon, that Satan first emerges as a powerful figure, and it is only by the Book of Daniel, in the second century BCE, that heaven and hell become powerful themes. This moral impetus continued to flow through subsequent Jewish and Christian thinking to the extent that two thousand years later the philosopher Friedrich Nietzsche would be impelled to say that Zarathustra had 'created this most portentous of all errors – morality'. But Cyrus, the king who gifted the notion of evil to the West, has also been cited as its first author of universal human rights, the framework by which, in Europe at least, we negotiate our moral obligations without religion. The basis for this claim is the Cyrus Cylinder, a stone scroll discovered in 1879 in the ruined ancient walls of Babylon. This is a kind of conceptual fossil, though it looks more like a partly gnawed cob of corn. Some hail it as the first bill of rights, advocating freedom across culture and creed, others as the propaganda of an invading warlord. It was a later Greek account of Cyrus, the *Cyropedia*, widely read by Renaissance princes in Italy and by the authors of the American constitution, including Benjamin Franklin and Thomas Jefferson, that established his reputation. The more recent magnification of Cyrus most likely comes from the last shah of Persia, Reza Shah Pahlavi, who in the 1970s glorified Iranian culture in the light of its Zoroastrian and mythical past.

As Jen and I wandered between the lengthening shadows we politely declined the invitations of Iranian families and were about to shuffle back to the gates when an unfeasibly broad-shouldered man blocked our way. 'I,' he said, 'am Farhad, Iran's second-strongest man. You *must* stay with me. *You* are my guests.' We politely declined, twice, and eventually he gave us a card for a bodybuilding supplement and went on his way. And that, we thought, was that. But a couple of days later as we were cycling into the next great archaeological crossroads of Iran, Persepolis, we were ambushed again by Farhad, as if he had been waiting in the shadows for the past two days for us to arrive.

'You *must* stay with me,' he persisted.

'We were planning to camp, actually. It's the—'

'No,' he said, as if we weren't quite understanding his Internet-perfect English, 'you *must* stay with me. My family will be upset if you don't.'

'That's very kind, but—'

'Camping is expensive.'

'Well—'

'So you don't trust me?'

'It's not that; it's just—'

'So my family aren't good enough?'

'Oh, ah... It's just...'

But we were already in Farhad's headlock. There was no escaping the hospitality of Iran's second-strongest man. Especially if you're England's third-most-polite couple.

We dutifully cycled down a track to his family home. They were kind, generous and gentle, and Farhad had a strong Persian pride and a clear sense of purpose, but he was also, I think it would be fair to say, a bit of a bully. We were forced to admire photo after photo of him powerlifting, watched a replay of a Skype call with his 'girlfriend', one of 'America's strongest women', and listened to him explain how to get a visa for an Iranian strongman to the UK. We nodded again and again like skinny English people with tired necks.

The next morning Farhad chaperoned us back to Persepolis for his guided tour. Even Farhad's non-stop monologue couldn't prevent us being bowled over by the solid majesty of the place, built on a set of terraces at the foot of the Rahmat mountain, with images of double-headed bulls and sphinxes, otherworldly against the morning moon and blue sky. Farhad's own appreciation of Zoroastrianism fitted the muscular presence and thick carvings of

Persepolis, but his coercion of timid foreign visitors was at odds with the Zoroastrian emphasis on equality. Persepolis's king, Darius, maintained that the way to keep peace in his kingdom was to be a 'friend to right, and not a friend to wrong', to lead a life both straight and true within the circular path of morality that was the backdrop to the Zoroastrian universe.

Back on the road to Shiraz we hoped we'd escaped Farhad, but somewhere on that nameless desert highway we heard once again that neck-tensing yell, 'Jet, Jen, Jet, Jen.' And there again was Iran's second-strongest man, with his car window down, still trying to persuade us to try his bodybuilding products.

I was *never* going to try his bodybuilding products. My body would always be a see-through scaffolding. Here the advantage of cycling alongside him very, very slowly paid off. Both Farhad and the drivers behind became bored and, eventually, hooted onwards, he drove away.

In Shiraz I lost my bike computer, the machine that ticks off the miles using a clicker on the spokes. I never thought it would be possible to grieve for a piece of plastic and electronics, but there Jen was consoling me, her arm around my shoulder. It was as if the bike computer contained the miles we had done, and we would be able to cash them in at a later date at a mystic swap-shop. This did not lessen my still rather distance-focused approach, in which I sounded off the current mileage to Jen at every lay-by, but now all I could do was prod at the map with my finger and gaze at the horizon. I wanted to cycle through Pakistan, while Jen was far from keen. In the end the decision was made for us. Transit visas across the Iran–Pakistan border had been stopped. The race was now to get to Bandar Abbas, the southernmost port of Iran, before our visas ran out, and leave by sea.

On the way we wild-camped in a pomegranate orchard and lay on our backs staring up at the stars through the yellowing ends of the autumn leaves. 'Wild and free feeling,' I wrote in my journal, 'makes me see that the computer is useless, compared to this beauty.' The last full stop dribbles into sleep.

Nietzsche associated Zoroastrianism with the division between good and evil and the later Christian association of evil with much of irrational and sensual experience. But Nietzsche also saw in Zoroastrianism an antidote to this, the mutual dependence between the rational and irrational, between rigorous thought and ragged sensual experience. If rigid moral divisions stopped man becoming the best he could be, a more balanced, turning wheel of morality allowed the *Übermensch* – 'overman' – to flourish into the elite of society. Nietzsche argued that we should all aspire to be this *Übermensch*, a kind of aristocratic superhuman free from the strictures of divisive morality and open to new ways of free thinking and experiencing. Zarathustra was harnessed by Nietzsche as a new humanist voice just as the very tenets of theology, of a philosophy of faith, were being questioned in the West. 'Zarathustra,' said Nietzsche, 'was the first to encounter the fight of the good and evil, the very wheel in the machinery of things, the transport of morality into the metaphysical realm.' But Nietzsche also made Zarathustra into its opposite, into the Übermensch – 'the self-overcoming of the moralist, into me – that is what the name of Zarathustra means in my mouth'.

The arrival of Nietzsche's *Thus Spoke Zarathustra* in the late nineteenth century and its growing hold on the public imagination in the West paralleled advances in cycling technology and the emphasis on superhuman endurance and suffering that came with this. Henri Desgrange, the originator of the Tour de France, was originally a journalist who hoped to boost the sales of his sports newspaper *L'Auto*. He wanted to magnify the victor of the Tour de France into a warrior who overcame adversity through pain, and he sold this idea to his readers in their thousands. Nietzsche's writing didn't create the cycling superhero, but the zeitgeist of that age coalesced around sports cycling and also, unfortunately, around the fascist tendencies of people like Mussolini, who underwent a kind of conversion from socialism to fascism after reading Nietzsche's work. Nietzsche's disrespect for social and moral systems made him particularly vulnerable to hijack by the forces of fascism, who saw in his amorality the justification for the destruction of civil rights and the elevation of the elite – the 'pure' – at the expense of the 'impure'. Bertrand Russell, British pacifist and analytical philosopher, had this to say of Nietzsche: 'I dislike Nietzsche because he likes the contemplation of pain, because he erects conceit into a duty, because the men whom he most admires are conquerors, whose glory is cleverness in causing men to die.'

Away from the pomp of elite sports, everyday cycling has always been anti-intellectual and egalitarian, teaching through experience. Cycling was there at the birth of the socialist and feminist movements and, in Europe at least, has clear working-class roots. These strong communities anchored cycling into society with moral expectations in a way that Nietzsche's free-floating amorality could never bear.

As we cycled through the vast deserts and slept under the star-fizzing skies I began to wonder whether there might be a 'cyclical' definition of morality. Night, winter, shadow have always had a residue of evil, or non-good, associated with them, which is retained in festivals. Celtic Samhain on 1 November between autumn and winter, became Christian All Saints, then All Hallows and then secular Halloween. The goodness associated with day, springtime and light was once the Zoroastrian Nav Ruz – new year – now celebrated in Iran as Nowruz in spring, on 1 March. The morality of elemental change has been hidden from us in plain sight. That the darkness of Halloween has bad spirits and Nav Ruz has the fire-jumping symbols of good light is clear enough, but do we still feel the shiver in our bones of the turning seasons' moral potency? There has always been a grunting, snorting, bloody darkness in winter folk tales and the ceremonies of previous generations, but we have compiled them into anthologies and dressed them in a tinsel that does not feel like the first shake of cold rain on your face. There is a rising, ecstatic joy in mid-summer folk dances, but soon enough we amble into the shade of the gazebo. The elemental sense of morality, of what is viscerally good and bad, requires an altogether different definition, a 'felt' understanding that is so far from us as to be almost absent; a moral force that radiates heat and sucks warmth, a morality that is carried in the charge of the particles around us.

The elements are now just the Lego bricks of our material universe, each with a name and number and a place in the periodic table. But thousands of years ago they carried a moral charge. This wasn't just about the enchantment of the supernatural, a world fierce with mysterious and unknowable spirits, it was a more fundamental conception of morality as something physical, with no division between mind and body and environment. This was the morality of the stabbing cold, a chill so humanly charged it was murderous.

And perhaps, at the limits of cycling, as we career downhill, when we feel the wind spit ice and rain on our eyelids so hard it hurts, we are experiencing something of the moral impetus of the changing seasons. The age-old fear that the sun will no longer rise or the rain no longer fall, that the rivers will not replenish and the fields not fill with fruit now drifts towards us like a statically charged mist. And chasing the seasons on a bicycle, feeling their physical charge ebb and flow as our moral culpability, or lack of it, slaps us in the face, might be better than just shouting at the news.

The road to Bandar Abbas reminded us of the frontier with

Turkey, with steep-sided cliffs that opened into wide-open seamlessly sandy deserts, rather than the pick 'n' mix of rough desert scrub. There was more colour and a loose fold in the dresses of the women, and many of the men wore headscarves. We pushed ourselves faster and faster on the bikes late into the day. I watched the shadows of the spokes, individually perfect in the desert sun, flickering like an old cine film, the Wheels slowly ellipsing, warping into the creatures of sunset.

'Where are we going to camp?' said Jen.

'Uh.'

Jen prodded at the map. 'We've only got twenty minutes till the sun goes.'

I squinted at the departing rays and pointed at a track leading behind a sand dune. 'There!'

We spun off the main drag, hoping to make it past the nearest dune before the next vehicle passed. Unfortunately, we'd been clocked by of all things a police car, which was now chasing us into the desert with lights and sirens blazing in a prime-time cop drama. This was not the subtle disappearing act of wild camping. A loudspeaker on the roof berated us in Farsi.

Jen and I stopped and the police car rolled alongside us.

'Hello, officer.'

'Why are you cycling off into the desert in the dark?'

'We're trying to get to Bandar Abbas.'

'This road does not go to Bandar Abbas.'

Jen and I peered off into the middle distance. 'No. I think you're probably right.'

The officer pointed back to the main road. 'This is the road to Bandar Abbas.'

'Oops. Sorry.'

We followed the police back to the main highway and they allowed us to go on our way. Five minutes later we came to an army checkpoint. It was then that Jen planted her flag.

'We're not camping in the desert.'

'But I want to camp in the desert.'

'We're not camping in the desert.'

'But I want to camp in the desert.'

'We're not camping in the desert.'

In the end we stayed in a small hamlet a few miles from the checkpoint. Despite the random intrusion of two English people into his life, the caretaker of the local mosque, Omid, welcomed us into his tiny home, which he shared with his three children and one of his two wives. They cooked a cornmeal mush in the yard as Jen heated her veggie noodles on the brazier. And then we slept in the only room, while they slept elsewhere, perhaps in the yard under some blankets.

At three in the morning Jen and I had another stinking row. Superficially it was to do with who had more blankets, but it was actually about police-car chases, machismo, hundreds of miles of riding through the desert, long-distance computer loss and not enough veggie noodles. In the morning we wondered if our hosts had heard us. Omid said his goodbyes with an air of quiet desperation as the rich young English people rolled on to the next experience, the next chapter.

We cycled in silence until I demanded Jen hand me her last remaining piece of tissue paper.

'I *require*,' I said with as much dignity as I could muster, 'to use the toilet.'

'I *need* to blow my nose,' said Jen.

My needs pulled rank, and I wandered off behind a sand dune as Jen sat by the side of road with her sandy snot. I returned to discover a packet of paper napkins in a pannier pocket, which we shared. It wasn't a dignified row but it did at least clear the air. And two orifices.

The highway into Bandar had four lanes of trucks. One of them swooped ahead and nearly knocked Jen into the crash barrier. It carried the distinctive blue TATA logo on its side. There was a good chance that the steel in our bikes, and many of those we'd seen in the Middle East, came from Tata foundries. We would see this logo again and again in India. At the heart of the Tata family is the Parsi faith. And at the heart of the Parsi faith is Zoroastrianism. After the defeat of the last Zoroastrian King by Islamic invaders in CE 651 many Zoroastrians fled south to Hormuz, a port on the Persian Gulf next to Bandar Abbas. They would eventually set sail from here some time in the ninth century CE, to become the Parsis of India, retaining Zoroastrianism's beliefs and rituals while assimilating aspects of Hindu and Islamic culture.

When we eventually rolled into the city and found a hotel room, we stripped off, had a shower and lay naked on the bed with the ceiling fan rippling over us. For Jen this represented the end of her hijab, the moral hushing of her body over a thousand miles. For me it represented a moment of stillness. We both fell asleep naked, with our legs dangling off the end of the bed like abandoned string puppets or a budget sex video that had run out of sex.

Evil is in the body, the body is sex and sex is evil. So runs an oversimplification of Augustinian thinking. St Augustine was a fourth-century bishop and philosopher. Before his conversion to Christianity Augustine had been a Manichean, a follower of Mani, a religion which grew alongside Zoroastrianism in the Mesopotamian region of the Persian empire. Mani preached that the teachings of Buddha, Jesus and Zarathustra were incomplete and he was to be the new prophet bringing a more complete understanding of God. His take on morality, though influenced by Zoroastrianism, was much more black and white. He declared that the human body, like all matter, was the product of Satan and therefore inherently evil, whereas the soul was made of light and so the realm of good.

But St Augustine could not accept that the devil was responsible for evil. He believed man had a role to play in his own fate, indeed he had the free will to remain with the devilish material realm of the body or join the goodly mental realm of the soul. The body had been morally engineered, and because it was inextricably linked with the passions of the sexual act, sex itself had a moral dimension. Before the Fall of Man sex was merely mechanical. Following Adam's fall from grace, it became carnal, the body arced in passion away from the ideal realm of the soul. This influenced Roman Catholic and Anglican theology but was most influential with the Puritans of the sixteenth and seventeenth century, who spurned the physical and the sensuous, seeing the body as a vessel of carnal evil. It is perhaps no surprise that the development of capitalism in the West went hand in hand with the rise of the Puritan businessman, for whom the accumulation of finance was to become more important than sensual and worldly pleasure (see BAR BAG).

The boat from Bandar Abbas had fifty cinema seats with a narrow corridor down the middle. Men on the right. Women on the left. The old TV above our heads flickered into life as we moved out of the port. It showed groups of men praying and then a head shot of an Iranian bodybuilder doing neck-stretching exercises. Forward, back, side to side. I nodded in and out of sleep as the ferry rocked: forward, back, side to side. And then I woke to the hypnotic *Songs of Leonard Cohen* playing through the headphones of my phone. The bodybuilder who had been doing neck exercises on the TV was now running on a treadmill, his lips synching around Leonard Cohen's words. 'And you want to travel with her / And you want to travel blind / And you know that you can trust her / For she's touched your perfect body with her mind.'

As the ferry churned through the Straits of Hormuz in the dead of the night, the image on the TV faded, losing the signal, and the bodybuilder on the running machine dematerialised like a ghost.

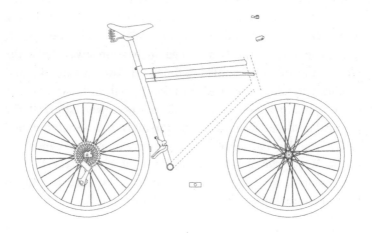

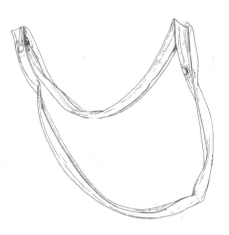

CHAPTER 15

The Inner Tubes

A slow puncture is like a stilted sigh. Down on my knees I pumped my exasperation back into the Inner Tube with a rusty pump and again and again it deflated. South of Shiraz, in the middle of Iran's scrub desert, there were no handy buckets of water and so I had to rely on inflating the tube and then gobbing on dodgy-looking spots and scanning for bubbles. After the third repair I gave up and spent the next hundred kilometres on my knees every half-hour. Later examination revealed three tiny nicks made by the wires that explode from old truck tyres. Puncture maggots. Before I started this long cycling tour I'd been led to believe there were such things as puncture-proof tyres. So-and-so had ridden to Australia with only one puncture. So-and-so had cycled across Africa without so much as a single patch.

Bollocks.

So-and-so had either been cycling on silk or had been super-lucky. No tyre is puncture proof, merely puncture *resistant*.

TYRES, like human beings, wear down. In Isfahan we met an Irish cyclist who'd weathered seventeen punctures in Turkey. He went on to pull out seventy-two thorns from his TYRES (when you have that many, you count them all).

Later, as I was repairing my own Inner Tubes, sitting cross-legged on an Iranian carpet, my thoughts drifted back to an old friend. He'd taken his trusty racer out for a jaunt in the English countryside, got a puncture and then discovered that there were no patches left in his repair kit. Walking his bike home ten miles he was not happy a man. He then discovered his best friend had borrowed his puncture repair kit, used the last patch and replaced the box without telling him. They had a blazing row which preceded them becoming lovers, moving in together and finally getting married. All this caused by the minutest intrusion into the feather bed of air that carries us aloft. Bicycles offer the possibility of simple, direct travel. But when an ordinary puncture thwarts that promise we end up ranting at the wayward vagaries of fate, the bike and ourselves.

The simple answer, of course, is always to carry a new puncture repair kit and stop being such a pansy. Alternatively, many riders now carry a spare Inner Tube, and some even resort to those disposable compressed-gas cylinders for instant inflation. But need the thorn be so vexatious? Could we not learn to love the puncture and cherish those little puncture repair kits, those first-aid boxes; a consistent reminder in a hundred years of cycling of a bygone self-sufficiency?

'Stoical' has come to mean unemotional or indifferent to pain, but the Stoics, a school of Greek philosophy, did not wish to extinguish emotion, rather transform it through calm reasoning. Seneca, a Roman Stoic, and one of its clearest thinkers, put it thus: 'I do not mean to say that the brave man is insensible to these, but that he overcomes them, and in being all else unmoved and calm rises to meet whatever assails him.' Easier said than done, particularly when you have a puncture in the middle of nowhere and it's dusk and you desperately want to find somewhere to put your tent up. But for Seneca this process of transforming emotion and overcoming adversity was not an instantaneous process. It came gradually through accepting the inevitability of misfortune. 'Unimpaired prosperity cannot endure a single blow; but he who has struggled constantly with his ills becomes hardened through suffering.'

I'm not saying here that all cyclists should go around with calluses on the tips of their fingers, just that if we start to accept punctures not as a problem but as an inevitable part of cycling, like oiling a CHAIN, they cease to be such a disturbance. Consumer society has sold us, well me in particular, the idea that we don't have to deal with discomfort, that fate can be bought for a price. Hence puncture-proof tyres, CO_2 gas canisters.

The more punctures I had, the more I repaired, the better I became at repairing them, the less anxious I was about them. Self-sufficiency is one of the magical things about cycling. The modern car demands, with its interlinked electronic components, that you take it to a specialist, who does everything for you and gives you a bill at the end. The car has become emblematic of relinquishing control. But when we are in control we are most self-sufficient and most happy. This is a mighty claim to make for the humble puncture repair kit. But that puncture repair kit only represents what we might be able to do if we embraced the minutiae of discomforts that make up our lives and take control of them, rather than expect someone else to sell us the solutions off the shelf.

Stoicism is not simply a philosophy of endurance or of accepting fate. As with Zoroastrianism (see WHEELS), it shows an optimistic belief in the value of human equality and of accepting and co-operating with the natural environment. It suggests there is a law of morality working within a law of nature that encourages man to work with the grain rather than against it, or suffer a vexatious splinter. Zeno of Citium founded his Stoic school not long after Alexander the Great's defeat of the Persians, and it seems likely that many of the ideas of Zoroastrianism filtered back to Athens along Alexander's imperial highways. The Athens school of Stoicism in turn influenced Seneca, who influenced Christian and Renaissance philosophers and writers such as the British poet Geoffrey Chaucer, who says of his chivalrous knight in *The Canterbury Tales*, 'It is ful fair a man to bere hym evene / For al day meeteth men at unset stevene.' In other words, it is best to have a certain restraint and equanimity because you never know who and what you'll bump into. Or, get over it before you have to get over it.

When I first started cycling vast distances, I was petrified of punctures. I used to hate it when, twenty minutes before dusk and far from a safe place to camp, I felt that jarring bump of metal rim over stone. But having come so far and repaired so many, they started to feel like a familiar scratch. I would jump off the bike, dump the bags, flip the frame over and get on with it, and in fifteen minutes, mostly, I was done. As soon as I accepted that punctures were part of the road, the road itself became less threatening.

Self-sufficiency has been a driving force in the cycling movement, and its power shouldn't be underestimated. 'I really felt the bicycle could be for the world's cities what the spinning wheel was for Gandhi,' said John Dowlin, a 1970s bicycling activist. Gandhi used the emblem of the spinning wheel to suggest his countrymen could create the fabric of their lives; that they could be self-sufficient beyond the machine of the Raj. Similarly, John Dowlin believed that we could create our own way through car-clogged cities and reach for a more self-determined future, an optimistic equality with each other and the natural world. Bold hopes, and it might be trite to force such ideals onto the simple bike and a humble puncture repair kit. But if we don't learn to maintain the transport of our own lives, to own our difficulties, then those tiny problems will start to own us. And that will not help us into an uncertain future.

The ancient Greeks discovered that the arteries of a corpse were empty while its veins were full, and so, a line of Stoic thinking went, the body pumped a 'breath of life' from the lungs and around the body. This was *pneuma*, a mixture of two active elements, air and fire, the hot gas we can feel when we put our hands over our mouths. This, the Stoics reasoned, was the vaporous constituent of the whole universe; it made the body and in a differentiated form the soul or psyche of a human being (from which the concept of the mind and the words psychiatry and psychology come). Stoicism was thus a materialist philosophy. It decreed that mind and body were not separate but intrinsic parts of a universe that was ultimately material. The breath in a blown-up balloon, the ancient Stoic argued, was the stuff of the mind infused into our bodies. The air pumped into an Inner Tube, from this perspective, is an aspect of what constitutes the mind. We are not just riding on bikes; we are riding on the constituents of our own existence. Thought moves in and out of a world that moves within us.

The early Stoics were admirers of Homer, who had a similar, though less analytical way of understanding breath. Like many poets Homer was happy to stretch the meaning of words so that they fitted the passions of a life lived to the full. As Michael Clarke points out in *Flesh and Spirit in the Songs of Homer*, Homeric thought was associated with 'the palpable inhalation of breath, and the half-imagined mingling of breath with blood and bodily fluids, in the soft, warm, flowing substances that make up what is behind the chest wall'. And it seems to me that the cyclist, lost in the hypnotic rhythm of a long ride, propels this same *thumos*, mind flowing in body, breathing in the breathing world.

Pure rubber from the sap of rubber trees is frustratingly sticky when hot, and brittle when cold. It was only when Charles Goodyear mixed it with sulphur in 1839 that it achieved the pliability and elasticity we know today. It is a long chain polymer of many smaller molecules known as monomers, for which the sulphur acts as a bridge, tempering the elasticity between them and improving the overall strength.

The pneumatic or inflatable tyre, made using vulcanised (sulphur-suffused) rubber, was patented by Robert William Thomson in 1845 and used, rather unsuccessfully, on cartwheels before a fellow Scotsman, John Boyd Dunlop, used it more successfully on bikes. Later developments included a removable rubber Inner Tube to allow the better repair of punctures. Natural rubber, in the form of water-based latex, pure and unvulcanised, is still used in some Inner Tubes to minimise the rolling resistance of TYRES, as it is so light and flexible. However, latex easily allows air to pass and even without punctures can require daily reinflation. Most Inner Tubes are made of butyl, a synthetic rubber that loses air over a slower period, requiring inflation every two weeks or so. And this means that even if we repair a puncture, full of optimism that it will remain sealed, there will always be a slow, inevitable, decline.

Aristotle believed that *pneuma* was responsible for locomotion in human sperm and carried the vital essence of life from parent to offspring. And the development of the modern condom or prophylactic mirrors that of the Inner Tube. The invention of vulcanised rubber led to rubber condoms that were the same thickness as a bicycle Inner Tube, with a seam along the side. More modern condoms tend to be made of latex, or a synthetic equivalent, and puncture remains a problem. Even when properly used and without breaking, there is a two to three per cent rate of leakage through the latex. They have been handed out to soldiers for the past hundred years, not just to prevent sexually transmitted diseases, but to stop gun muzzles being spoiled and for the battlefield treatment of sucking chest wounds, making a rudimentary one-way valve.

Following the Iranian revolution of 1979 many countries enforced an economic and trade embargo on the republic, principally America, eventually joined by the UN after concerns about nuclear weapons. Iran then saw a reduction in the import of materials necessary for the manufacture of tyres. The problems of tyre supply and the enormous variation in terrain and climate in Iran, from glacial freeze to blazing desert, mean that there are tens of thousands of poor tyres running over tens of thousands of miles. And when truck tyres go bang, they really go bang. The high pressures needed to support heavy vehicles are made possible by weaving layers of cotton, called plies, underneath the tyre tread, and more recently by using metal-reinforced sheets. A poorly maintained truck tyre can explode with a force of up to twelve tonnes, sending shreds of thin metal wire across the road. Which burrow into bicycle TYRES and our slowly deflating Inner Tubes.

Cyclists often match their cadence, their pedal revolutions per minute, with their breathing. And cycling, one of the most oxygen-demanding forms of exercise, can push lung capacity and breathing capability to the absolute limit. The ticking metronome of a pedalling rhythm is not far off the mantras that regulate breathing in Hindu and Buddhist practices (see FREEWHEEL). In these living philosophies breathing isn't what we do while the mind has a think; it is the thinking, it is the way in which we begin to understand the world in a different way. Our breathing develops and alters at the same time as our development of words during infancy. All those plosives and diphthongs are exquisitely formed using breath control.

To cycle on pneumatic TYRES is to breathe at our fullest on the transport of a captured breath. What could be more expansive? And yet offer the possibility of being so deflating?

'Aha,' I said to Jen as I sat cross-legged on an Iranian carpet in a mud house in the middle of the desert in the middle of the night, pulling out the splinter of an exploded truck tyre, 'we're rolling.'

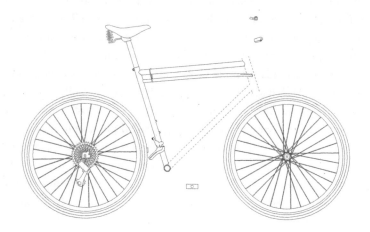

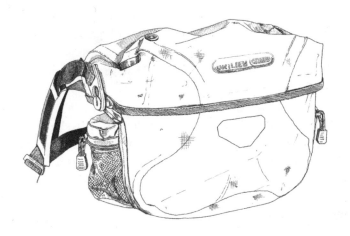

CHAPTER 16

The Bar Bag

I dived into a swimming pool on the roof of an apartment block in Sharjah in the United Arab Emirates. My arms, having been rigidly attached to the HANDLEBARS for thousands of miles, were finally released in an underwater cranking version of revolving legs. And I noticed how I could see my breath, great galumphing bubbles pouring out of me, the invisible becoming material before my eyes.

Coming off the ferry from Iran, we'd been told to leave Billy and Bertle and all our baggage in a kind of holding bay, while we went to a waiting area and our passports were taken. We waited there, without our ID, without our bikes, in what was to be the first of many airlocked purgatories in the Emirates. I sneaked back to the bikes to rescue the credit cards we'd stowed in the BAR BAGS attached to the HANDLEBARS.

'They're going to mule our bikes,' I whispered to Jen.

'They're going to do what?'

'Mule them. Smuggle contraband in our luggage.'

'Who would do that?'

'I don't know – mulers. They could stash our panniers with brown and white.'

Jen stared at the ceiling.

At least I have the credit cards, I thought. If we're going to be thrown into a cell then at least we can buy ourselves out. In the Emirates cash, or specifically credit, can buy you anything. Absolutely anything. Except, perhaps, your freedom.

I always associate luggage with the empty third floors of provincial department stores. Unfortunately, you can't travel long distances with only the wind in your hair. You also have to carry stuff. Materiality. And, though some would have you believe otherwise, you also need money, or its Machiavellian cousin the credit card. But where are we to keep it all, deep in our pannier bags or on our bodies? One Japanese cyclist I met kept $200 underneath the insoles of his trainers, figuring that most muggers would draw the line at stealing someone's footwear. As the songwriter Tracy Chapman once said, 'All That You Have is Your Sole.' But many touring cyclists also use a Bar Bag, essentially a safety deposit box attached to the HANDLEBARS. Our Bar Bags had solid frames built into them so they could be clipped onto the HANDLEBARS and removed and carried around like handbags. During these times, with the Bar Bag dangling on a strap around our necks, wobbling about on our flat-soled cycling shoes, we looked like two lost penitents searching for a place to dump our car batteries. The main reason cyclists use Bar Bags is because it makes them look too ridiculous to mug.

It is a strange fact that while cash exists to buy *things*, it isn't in fact *anything*, being merely a promise of a material reward. Money is another frontier in the stuff–ideas trade-off we call metaphysics which has mostly been co-opted into economics.

The major exception being Marx, who trampled all over it with his hobnailed dialectics (see SEAT POST). In the modern or postmodern world there is no escaping money. Capitalism does not so much demand your attention, as co-opt it and then try to sell it on to the highest bidder.

Despite the increasing suspicion that our passports would be confiscated and we wouldn't cycle again, the customs officer ushered us and our bikes out of the port and we found ourselves on a silent Scalextric set. If the cars and trucks of Iran had guffed and roared and beeped and honked amid a cacophony of jaywalking Iranians, then the traffic of Sharjah whirred along in perfect solitude, pedestrians and bikes entirely absent. Its only witnesses were the floppy-fringed palm trees, planted at intervals like so many stage props. Pavements and hard shoulders were incidental, and there was literally nowhere to cycle. So when we let ourselves into Rachel's flat, a cousin of a friend, who was living in Sharjah, we locked our bikes to her balcony railings and that was that.

After snooping around the apartment block, I found a door off an anonymous corridor. RESIDENTS ONLY, a sign said. NOT FOR GUESTS OR FRIENDS.

'Don't worry,' said the Indian man sloshing past with a mop, 'it doesn't apply to Europeans.'

On the other side was a rooftop swimming pool, and I did my daily lengths there. Holding my breath. Breathing. Holding my breath.

The journalist Jim Krane, in his book on Dubai, reports a conversation with an Emirati woman. 'Before,' she says, 'life had a taste, now nothing makes you happy ... children have so many things in the house, but they are bored... And there's too much building, building, building, building. It's like someone sleeping on your chest. There's no air.'

The first taxi driver Jen and I asked to take us downtown said, 'I don't know where anything is, so I can't take you unless you show me.' When we eventually found someone who knew the way to Dubai Mall, the world's largest shopping mall, we discovered inside it the world's biggest fish tank, which contained tiger sharks, manta rays and a selection of penguins, seals and crocodiles. When this aquarium was first made the larger sharks ate the smaller sharks, and 10 per cent of the shark population was lost. Not a bad cut for Dubai. We wobbled through the mall with our Bar Bags like drunks in a hall of mirrors. The sharks and the scuba divers circumnavigated the tank as we gawped at them and they gawped at us, and the shoppers drifted past like jellyfish. I bought a takeaway that came with a silver plastic fork. It snapped in half when I prodded at the chicken.

From the mall we sloped across the bone-dry plazas to the Burj Khalifa, the tallest man-made structure in the world. The sky was a perfect blue, the moon a perfect ice, and the Burj a crystalline needle injecting the heavens. But where was everyone? No sightseers. Nothing. The Burj Khalifa is so tall that you can watch the sun set twice, first at ground level, and then up top after a quick elevator ride. The thousands of migrants who built it are among the poorest and most neglected in these city states, Indian and Pakistani men who live in labour camps, many of them trapped in loan-shark agreements that paid for their travel to Dubai.

The Burj Khalifa's 2010 inauguration was held back by the credit crunch, the knock-on effect of unpaid US housing loans. So great was its impact that Dubai had to be bailed out by its oil-rich cousin Abu Dhabi. The caveat was that the Burj, once called the Burj Dubai, had to be renamed in honour of Abu Dhabi's leader, Sheikh Khalifa.

A hundred years ago Dubai was a sleepy silted-up-creek town, with single-storey mud buildings and a coral fort where the sheikh lived. Life expectancy was low and its inhabitants would daub kohl on their eyelashes to protect themselves from the sand glare and the cataracts that were their only birthright. Yet within a few generations many of them were millionaires. Dubai's population rose from a few thousand to two and a half million, with the most diverse ethnic mix of anywhere on the planet. The rivers of money and the almost unlimited wellspring of credit that generates them did not come from the high Hajar Mountains behind the city but from the shipping lanes that splay out from its creek, reaching back through history to England and London.

The East India Company was a profiteering arm of the British state, which by the 1800s had recognised the strategic importance of the Gulf coast, lying a few hundred miles from India. The company forced its sheikhs to sign a treaty that gave British control over the area that then became known as the Trucial States, a colonial outpost of Britain that lasted until 1971, when they gained independence as the United Arab Emirates. The stability of the Trucial States allowed for the development of the port cities that now make up the Emirates but also for their unfettered growth, helped along by a few barrels of oil.

At the beginning of the nineteenth century the oil hadn't been discovered and the majority of Emirati trade was based on pearl diving. Divers would sink to the seabed wearing a nose clip, with a leather sack and a rock tied to their leg. These exploits are translated in Sufi verse as the singular search for a wider metaphysical truth (see TOP TUBE). But Dubai's pearls were as vulnerable to shifts in global trade as any other commodity. The Great Depression of the 1930s drove down prices at the same time as the discovery in Japan that pearls could be artificially created. The Pearl Crash, still within the living memory of some Emiratis, resulted in a level of poverty and famine unthinkable today, with people subsisting on fried locusts. Sheikh Rashid dredged Dubai creek in 1954 and pumped up the city using all that capitalism and self-interest could offer: tourism, real estate, manufacturing and global trade. The creek was too small to contain this, and by 1981 Jebel Ali port had been created, the world's largest man-made harbour, dredged through the Gulf's coral reefs. The pearls soon disappeared, along with the oyster beds, and the skyscrapers grew tall capturing gold in their glass panels.

After a month we moved from the city state of Sharjah to the middle of Dubai. If Rachel's apartment block had seemed reasonably large then Cluster Block C was mammoth, forty floors in total. I discovered the day we moved in that the money we'd wired to Canada to pay a shipping company in France to get us on a container ship out of Dubai had been blocked.

'Why the hell can't we just leave?' I shouted at Jen.

'Because we refuse to fly?'

As I swam in the empty rooftop pool of Cluster Block C I became more and more aware of the light, as if only here, in this postage stamp of water, could I understand the sky. The evening light was thinner, softer, graduating to a whitish gold that retreated up the skyscrapers like it was being put to bed by a lengthening sheet of shadow.

Usury, the process of making unethical loans which enrich the lender through interest (*riba* in Arabic) is condemned by Islamic law. The prophet Muhammad explained that finance had to have some kind of physical tether, that money was purely the medium not the means to make more money. Islam itself is an *ummah*, a community of believers, not a marketplace, and when terrorist jihadis attack the capitalist West, they often use this religious pretext. Yet Islamic states obviously tolerate capitalism, otherwise places like Dubai could not exist. Dubai's financial bust in 2009 was partly based on its inability to pay back an Islamic bond, a device structured to give returns to both parties without breaking sharia law. The disconnect between physical and immaterial worlds that we understand metaphysically as the separation of body and mind is played out in international finance as a card trick of digits, where the numbers flickering across computer screens appear to be as disembodied as the ghosts that power Descartes's machines (see BOTTOM BRACKET). But there *is* always a material outcome. Rapacious, ever-expanding economic growth borrows from the future to accelerate the present. But nature does not have the capacity to await the return of its credit. Its resources, its raw materials, return only over decades, centuries, millennia. What appears to be a never-ending gift – taller skyscrapers, cheaper goods, cut-price travel, turns out to be the grubby robbery of generations that come after.

But guess what, the bicycle is a sit-down protest. You travel by your own sweat, and not the promise of someone else's payday. You carry only as much as you need, and eventually all commodities, including the bike itself, cease to have any meaning beyond the experience. And then the cheapest food tastes rich and the dustiest water priceless. You trade the credit of the future for the experience of the present. And the only payback is your racing heart.

But it's not going to change the world, is it? It's not going to scuttle the Burj Khalifa and send the stock exchanges reeling? No. But it does offer a glimpse, a chink, a wink of light through the cataracts. Cycling is an expression of self-interest, but one that wrenches interest from the self and sets its gaze outward, that pays us back further than we can see.

On Christmas Eve we tried to saunter onto a beach that cost sixty dollars to lie on, but I was marked out by my old carrier bag and pointed back the way we'd come. We found a different way in through a beachside hotel and ended up in a circular thatched bar, the type forever associated with Hawaiian movies, and there ordered gin and tonics and a bowl of peanuts, and got slightly drunk watching a tractor go back and forth, heaping sand higher up the shore. From there we stumbled out onto the non-paying part of the beach, but the sliver of shadow we thought we'd co-opted belonged to another hotel and we were moved on again. I wobbled, still drunk, into the water, closed my eyes, and floated face down in the salt water. Holding my breath. Breathing. Holding my breath.

A hundred thousand years before this, the planet was caught in its Glacial period, an ice sheet thickening across Canada and northern Europe. The trapping of water meant that what we could see in the Gulf, the bobbing dhows and container ships, would have been mostly dry land. And the higher northern ice pack altered ocean flows and weather systems so much that the Gulf, thirty thousand years ago, would have been fertile grasslands rather than desert (Dubai creek is the remains of a river channel that ran through these grasslands). The first humans migrating out of Africa could well have paused at this fertile fork in the road, before moving on and diversifying into the different ethnic groups of the Middle East, Europe, India, China and Australia. Seen against the larger tides of history the Gulf is an ongoing port for the very flow of humanity. Its abundance at a time when human beings were first telling stories about themselves has led some to suggest that the Gulf *is* the Garden of Eden. That it is 'Paradise Lost'. The two rivers that empty into it, the Tigris and the Euphrates, are mentioned in the book of Genesis. The flood of Noah's Ark, can be reread, with the revisionist's eye, as the story of the Gulf's returning sea levels five thousand years ago, at the end of the last glacial melt. Above this once fertile land we now have one of the busiest shipping lanes in the world, below it, the lake of oil that fuels those boats and the diminishing diversity of a paradise lost. Homo sapiens didn't invent paradox. But they manufactured it. Big time.

A few bike paths have now been built out from Dubai, one follows an old camel racing track, another loops into the dunes and back into the city. For many years bikes were merely the transport of 'bachelors' (the single migrant workers escaping the unseen labour camps of Dubai). Now some young Emiratis are taking up cycling, riding out into the no man's land on the smooth tarmac and back again in time for sunset.

The Empty Quarter makes up the world's largest single continuous desert and encompasses parts of Saudi Arabia, the United Arab Emirates, Yemen and Oman. It is an area of barren lifelessness marked only by swells of sand. Wilfred Thesiger, an ex-army officer who traversed the Empty Quarter with Bedouin guides in the 1940s, found no shade, no food and little water. What he did find was the unstinting solidarity of the Bedouin and the expansive experience of travelling through the desert. It's an easy and perhaps glib comparison to make, but what the Emiratis, and we, have lost in materialism is the immaterial sustenance of nothing. Emirati men do still engage in *al-taghrooda*, an antiphonal poetry used on long camel rides, where groups in one part of a camel caravan improvised chanted lines that would once be repeated back and forth along the line. It provides a rhythmic pattern to help the group to walk in time but also has a role in social bonding, in bringing the community together, and is now sung at weddings and tribal gatherings. Like the chants and dances of Sufism (see TOP TUBE) and the *hambandagi* of Zoroastrianism (see WHEELS), its cohesion comes from a shared ritual, a travelling sense of belonging, where your identity is not kept in the material of your luggage but in the way that you carry it.

*

On Christmas Day our Indian visas arrived and our ship tickets were confirmed. We spent New Year's Eve in an Irish bar run by Filipino bartenders who handed out leprechaun hats to English businessmen shouting, 'Aby newb ear, motherfucker.'

At 5 a.m. we rolled out our fully laden bikes from the elevator of Cluster Block C and heaved them into the back of a pick-up to be driven to Jebel Ali port outside the city. Jebel Ali is owned by the Emirati group Dubai Ports World, which bought the British company P&O and now has container ship terminals in forty countries across six continents. The world of Dubai is not just being built into the ocean (and a map of the world is being dredged up from the seabed for this very purpose); it is being exported across the planet by 100,000-tonne container ships.

At customs we discovered that when we'd first arrived in Sharjah, two months previously, we hadn't actually been given a visa for the Emirates, just a stamped date in our passports. We'd always been living on borrowed time. The port agent smoothed things over for us, and then our bikes were loaded into a Land Rover and driven the last fifteen kilometres to the harbourside.

It is hard to convey the enormousness of container-ship docks, a size differential only magnified by the dockers themselves, tiny figurines in a Bond film. The bikes were taken out of the Land Rover and then, after some chin stroking by the crew of the CMA CGM *Coral*, attached to the hook of an onboard crane that dangled over the side of the hull. It was oddly moving seeing Billy and Bertle fly through the air, free of their respective owners, triangles and circles made explicit by the blue sky.

When I eventually leaned my head against the wall of our cabin I could feel the chug of the generators through my skull, as if that vibration was a continuation of all the roads that had gone before us, all the worry, all the scribbled bits of paper, all the potholes. And it was only now, setting off in this biggest of bathtubs, that I could stop holding my breath. And breathe.

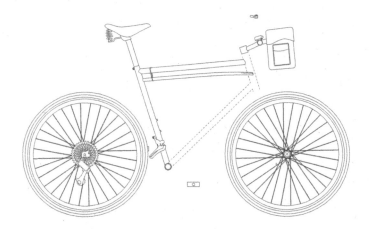

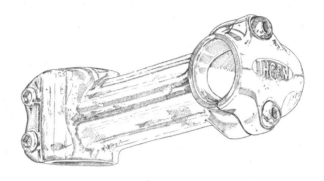

CHAPTER 17

The Stem

Heeeewwwge metal boxes whirred past our porthole on horizontal gantries. The steel container would lurch disconcertingly as the pulleys came to a halt and then disappear down into the hold as a tiny man in a high-vis jacket and a hard hat gave weary directions with his tiny hands – 'Left a bit, right a bit' – like he was trying to help park an oversized van in a multistorey car park. When one container was finished with, the crane would go back and hook up the next from the flatbed lorries that arrived one after the other. The CMA CGM *Coral* was simply the next link in the supply chain of lorries that had been overtaking us all across Europe, Turkey and Iran. It occurred to me that we'd always been racing these material rapids, and not following the metaphysical 'rivers of solitude to the boundless sea', even if my reading of Rumi would have me believe otherwise. In the ship's mess I found a set of fairy lights draped over a plastic Christmas tree with the plug pulled out.

The East India Company's trade with India along these highways, using the ports of the Gulf as a stopping-off point (see BAR BAG), led to the company not just profiting from the subcontinent, but ruling it with its own private armies. The soldiers who travelled with the company often 'took' Indian wives, due to the lack of European women in the country, and their offspring (sometimes known as Anglo-Indians) began to form a distinct cultural group. By the time of crown rule in India in 1858 Anglo-Indians were a significant community, often marrying each other, holding posts in the Raj administration and separating themselves from the rest of the population. One of the ancestors of my biological father was a British policeman, involved in the Indian uprising against the British at the beginning of the 1900s. He was shot during the struggle, and his white daughter ended up in an Indian orphanage. She married an Anglo-Indian and their children were my immediate forebears. Another ancestral line leads back to Lord Reading, Viceroy of India, the man who put Mahatma Gandhi in jail. When Indian self-rule finally did arrive in 1947, many of the 800,000 Anglo-Indians emigrated to England, bringing their families, and my bundle of genes, with them. I am not Indian, but I am, like so many people in the UK, part Indian; as much as I am part French, part Scottish or part cyclist. To travel anywhere is to arrive at an aspect of who you are or the kind of person you unconsciously imagine yourself to be.

It was four in the morning, and Jen and I peered out the window as a tug nudged us away from the dockside. We awoke five hours later to discover that the gym cycling machine wasn't working and the ping-pong table had no net. The true meaning of cabin fever is not being confined in a wooden shack in a forest, but the nervous sweat of being banged up in a 50,000-tonne ship with too many cups of coffee. I summoned my deepest reserves of

British assertiveness and rang JK, the first officer, from the empty mess.

'Could we possibly ... you know ... go outside and look at the sea?'

'Yes,' he said with the groggy yawn of a man who has been piloting 50,000 tonnes of metal through one of the busiest shipping channels in the world, 'But wear hats.'

The further we went from steerage, away from the ship's engines, the quieter the boat became. Over the railings the sea was surprisingly close, as if all those containers were pushing the deck closer to it. With nothing else to do I spent some time admiring its textures. We went through a smooth syrupy patch of green algae where the wash of white water against the hull had the lime tinge of fizzy pop. Then it chopped into a darker blue with more depth, while at the stern there was an unravelling carpet of calm water, which gave a certain dignity to the passage of the ship. From our cabin we would watch the sun go down behind cirrus clouds and a leaping pod of dolphins, but this was merely the background to the main attraction, a white van parked atop a stack of metal containers, apparently flying through the sky.

At dinner I noticed the rings on the surface of the mineral water were made not by the rocking motion of the boat but by the vibration of the engine.

'The next time you pick up a bottle of water and put it to your ear this is what you will hear,' I said to Jen: 'the engines of a container ship.'

'Eat your smoked salmon,' said Jen and popped a gobful of veg in her mouth.

That evening we stepped onto the balcony outside our cabin. The darkness was indecipherable and a gathering wind shook us. But unlike Dubai, the night here was infinite, the dusting of stars leaping from the horizon like talcum powder beaten off a drum skin. Once again we were insignificant beings, of only limited definition, in a limitless sky. The sea had been redacted into mystery.

My nan, my dad's mother, used to scoop the bubbles off the top of her cup of tea with a silver spoon, saying that the more of them you could stick in your mouth the richer you would become. Nan, a white woman from Birmingham, married Barney, an Indian man who had come to Britain to work for the National Coal Board. They had four sons together, my uncles, before they separated. Then she met a white Brummie, and my dad was born. And so my childhood always had the presence of those uncles, half Indian by birth, British by design. And India has always lived in my memory like this, as a half-known family.

The next day we were interrupted in our pacing up and down the ship's staircase by Nikolai, the Ukrainian chief officer.

'Two things,' he said. 'First you mustn't wake First Officer JK when he's asleep, and secondly –' he smiled like he was opening the partition on a TV quiz show '– it's time for the tour!'

In the ship's office he showed us the computer-operated ballast system. Depending on the distribution and number of containers, various valves could be opened between different ballast compartments and water shared between them to balance out any toppling asymmetry. Water not only supported the movement of the container ship, it was locked inside it by a touch screen that looked like a circuit diagram. Back on deck, Nikolai pointed out the refrigerated containers. They would be filled up with produce in India and then returned to suppliers in Europe. He and the crew might be told if they were carrying toxic chemicals, but for the most part the towering stacks of steel boxes were as much a mystery to them as they were to us.

The advent of steam-propelled ships meant the advent of the shipping timetable; the once wayward voyages of wind-driven clippers could now be plugged into factory deadlines. By the 1960s the container had become a standard unit of cargo, exponentially increasing trade around the world. This didn't just allow merchandise to be shipped faster and more efficiently, it changed the way in which labour could be exploited to drive down prices. Workers making trainers in one country could immediately be laid off and their cheaper counterparts hired. All the raw materials to make those trainers could then be shipped to the new destination with a quick flip of a spreadsheet. Whole factories could be disassembled, loaded into boxes, and transported to places where sweat was cheaper.

But something less tangible was also happening. As the maritime photographer Allan Sekula pointed out, there was a sealing off of the physical experience. Goods that once *whiffed* – tuna, hemp, spices, bird guano – were being locked into spaces that could not be seen or smelled. Harbours became enormous accelerated turning basins rebuilt outside the river and coastal cities they once occupied. The old port of Bristol, the setting for Robert Louis Stevenson's *Treasure Island*, was long ago backfilled, and now its shipping goes to Avonmouth, ten miles away. The stuff we eat, consume, dispose of, has become invisible. The shipping news, a once-regular feature of newspapers, dematerialised, replaced by tables of stocks and shares. In 1971 in his preface to the reference guide *Jane's Freight Containers*, R. P. Holubowicz explained that 'the container must be viewed as a vehicle of transportation and the ship itself only as an underlying carrier, or perhaps, more vividly, as merely a form of locomotion for the container'. The ship had become as empty as the Cartesian body, the captain as distant as the rational mind (see BOTTOM BRACKET).

To understand the processes of a working living philosophy today, we have to understand the economic and social forces in which we all live, the hidden highways that are transforming how we understand the world, even as we seek to accumulate knowledge of it, box by sealed box.

The division of west and east is not just an illusion of geography, it's also a trick of history. When Columbus famously sighted a group of islands off the coast of the Americas in 1492, he christened them the Indies, thinking he had found a western passage to the islands off the coast of Asia. The Spaniards, to differentiate this archipelago from their territories in India, renamed them the West Indies. My mother arrived in England from Trinidad as a sixteen-year-old aboard the steam liner *Golfito*, on the Southampton–Avonmouth–West Indies service, to have a British education. She was born and raised in Trinidad, and although from a privileged white European enclave, grew up alongside the cultural diaspora of the Afro-Caribbean and Asian Indian communities.

Afro-Caribbean Trinidadians are descendants of slaves brought to the island from Africa, a leg of the slave triangle that had Bristol as its apex. After the abolition of slavery in the West Indies, a system of indentured labour was created, by which workers from India signed up for stints of five years, in return for miserable wages, poor conditions and contracts that many couldn't understand. During the nineteenth century 150,000 people travelled from India to the island. Many stayed and developed a distinct Caribbean Hindu-infused culture, one that swirled around my mother and her siblings. And so the partition of west and east that I see in myself becomes ever more mixed. We live in times of such ethnic haze that to strike a flag anywhere is like drawing a line in water.

*

Most modern bikes have HANDLEBARS connected to the steering mechanism by means of an intervening tube of metal, the Stem, which appears to be nothing more than a join, or branch, in the overall make-up of the frame. As with so much of bike geometry, small differences in reach and angular rise control the overall position and comfort of the rider's upper arms and torso. In true Jet McDonald style, I bought five different Stems and then returned them, one after the other, until I found one that suited my variation of the sit-up-and-beg riding style, a slightly more hunched apologise-and-try-to-be-more-assertive head-down approach. Manufactured somewhere in Asia, the Stem was likely transported to the UK in an anonymous container much like the ones on the CMA CGM *Coral*. One thousand five hundred bikes can be packed in a single forty-foot container with the HANDLEBARS turned sideways and the PEDALS removed. Boxed in this way they are just capital. It is only when the HANDLEBARS are straightened and the PEDALS screwed on that the wonder button is pushed.

Having shown us around the cargo area, Nikolai took us right to the prow of the boat. We peered over the front and saw a pod of dolphins jumping about the keel. Nikolai said they built up speed here where the ship pushed the water in front of the hull. We watched the dolphins peel away one by one, until the last remained, sweeping and curving and jumping in front of the massive container ship, until it too dived into the ocean, and was gone.

Nikolai told us that every now and then a whale would 'commit suicide' by jumping in front of a ship's keel. Could this be possible? What is the moral context of a whale's decision-making? Clearly the sea still had its shadows, despite the freighters that so lightly travelled its surface. Nikolai said it was good luck that we'd seen the dolphins. I scanned the horizon for hopeless whales.

He told us that in its thirty-day voyage the CMA CGM *Coral* would take on one hundred and eighty tonnes of dirty 'bunker oil' at a cost of a million dollars. Its remains covered the decks in a black soot. Nikolai talked about the different nationalities on board: how Ukrainian ratings were 'more likely to get drunk and fight than the Filipinos, who expected more money than Chinese but were better workers and spoke better English'. The same day everyone crammed into a lifeboat in an abandon-ship drill. The eastern European officers on one side, the Filipino crew on the other and us, the incongruous tourists, in the middle, all blinged up in our crimson life jackets. Here, finally, everyone talked to each other, packed like mackerel in tomato sauce.

The next day we woke to find the CMA CGM *Coral* navigating down a mangrove estuary towards Karachi in Pakistan. There was no question of us being allowed to disembark for a quick look-see. The port agent had sent word to the captain that 'three white guys' had been shot dead on a visit 'just because they were white'. Instead we found ourselves on the bridge watching the helmsman follow the pilot's and captain's instructions, using a joystick small enough to be controlled with the tip of an index finger, like he was conducting a brass band by rolling the tip of a biro. Back in our cabin we watched as the ship loaded and unloaded containers to and from Karachi with markings like 'Noah' and 'Eco container with Bamboo Flooring'. This was all I would see of the country I had wanted to cycle across. We took to running up and down the stairs.

Joseph Conrad, Polish-Ukrainian and British sailor and writer, had this to say of the ship at sea: 'Round her the abysses of sky and sea met in an unattainable frontier. A great circular solitude moved with her, ever changing and ever the same, always monotonous and always imposing.' The ship itself was 'alive with the lives of those who trod her decks; like that earth that had given her up to the sea'.

At the beginning of our passage I imagined the ship would become a part of who I was, that I might even be inducted into 'sea life', whatever that is. But here I was sitting on the floor, pointing a handheld GPS at the ceiling, trying to figure out where exactly we were off the coast of Pakistan. We ate alone in the mess that night, as we had when we'd first embarked on the CMA CGM *Coral*, sucking on prawns with eyes like bloated ink spots.

Direct British rule replaced the East India Company after the Indian revolt of 1857. There followed a slightly more nuanced understanding of Hindu philosophy, mainly through the work of German philosophers studying and translating ancient Sanskrit texts. But Hinduism continued to be thought of as irrational, unduly imaginative and inordinately passionate – a 'dream like knowledge' (James Mill, father of John Stuart Mill, the liberal philosopher). Its vastly different philosophies had value but required the imposition of Western reason, and by inference British rule, to maintain their civility. At the end of the nineteenth century a British Government official, Albert Lyall, would say of Indian beliefs, 'We can scarcely comprehend an ancient religion, which is a mere troubled sea, without shore or visible horizon, driven to and fro by minds of boundless credulity and grotesque invention.' For British bureaucrats, India, like the oceans, could only be safely subdued by global trade and imperial bureaucracy. In 1906 the viceroy, George Curzon, rejoiced in the 'dawn of an intellectual enlightenment' gifted to the country by UK rule, forgetting that India had been pursuing its own awakening for well over three thousand years.

Religious and political philosophies around the world have needed to accommodate the irresistible rise of capitalism. For Tata, the India-based manufacturer and telecommunications giant, this has meant ethical allowances for employees and the environment based on Zoroastrian ideas of equanimity and harmony, while also knocking out the cheapest car on the planet and belching out considerable amount of drudge and pollutants. Old British colonial firms like Booker, one of the world's largest food producers and distributors, latterly pursued Fabian social ideals, which led its chairman Jock Campbell to announce in the 1930s, 'people are more important than ships, shops and sugar estates'. These attempts by major employers to create 'managed capitalism' echoed the rise of state-managed industry well into the 1980s (1990s in India), when the free-market principle became dominant and swung its wrecking ball into workers' rights. That Western and Eastern philosophies and the ethical values that emerged from them have been changed by and go on to change the considerations of capitalism shows that the flow of ideas and global trade cannot be disentangled in the modern world. And the reality of these changes was now materially present to us, swinging past the porthole on thick iron chains, Tata containers hanging from crane towers that looked like Apollo rocket gantries. And there, beyond these boxes, India, looking very much like the concrete slab we'd left behind in Dubai.

Nhava Sheva is the freight port that lies opposite Mumbai, and is owned and run by Dubai Ports World (see BAR BAG). It was dark when we arrived there. Cycling during the night didn't take our fancy. Maybe the captain would let us stay another evening? But the port agent for Nhava Sheva, an unpleasant man with a swarthy moustache, demanded our passports without meeting our gaze and then said we had to leave now or pay the custom officers 'overtime'. This was to be our first encounter with baksheesh, related to the Sanskrit word *bhaksati* – 'he enjoys' – a tip that magically transforms into a bribe.

'OK,' we said. 'We'll leave now.'

'You must now pay three thousand two hundred rupees,' he said, 'to have your bags sealed.'

The captain looked on blankly as we handed over a stack of rupees. And it was then that Felix appeared, an Aussie bike tourist, who bounded up the gangplank with his bike on his shoulder, having just cycled five thousand kilometres from Nepal through India.

'How ya doin?' he said breezily.

And then, in a clear breach of customs protocol, he carried our bikes down the gangplank, confusing both crew and dockers. We only met him for about ten minutes but in those six hundred seconds he made me want to shrug off a lifetime of wet winters, twelve thousand miles of sit-up-and-beg cycling, one month of hanging around in Dubai, one week in a container ship, and go riding through India with all my shirt buttons undone. Well the top two anyway.

We then bundled after the port agent, flung ourselves and our luggage onto our bikes and chased a car through a series of army checkpoints till we arrived at a ramshackle 'customs' office. There was no framed photograph of the Indian prime minister nailed to the wall, rather a Ganesha statue, the elephant-headed god with many arms, known as the overcomer of obstacles. This particular Ganesha seemed like he was waving us on with one hand while telling us to get back on the boat with several others. In the adjoining room our pannier bags, even our bikes, were 'sealed' with bits of string and a piece of card stuck to the tie with hot wax. An army officer with henna hair ogled us, while the other officials played with the GEARS and the bikes' back lights. Somewhere money exchanged hands. Then we, our bikes and our bags were rammed into a small taxi, driven to the exit to await the exchange of yet more rupees, the raising of the port gates and, finally, *officially*, our arrival in India – in the back of a car.

Shadows of trucks went past as Jen gripped her bike, which was dangling out of the cab. She switched on its back light as a bus with no headlamps swerved towards us. We saw the outlines of tin roofs, a family sitting around a fire in the middle of the street and a man peeing in the gutter, then arrived at a mud track to the Uran Plaza Hotel that the locals told us wasn't passable by bikes after the recent heavy rains. So we got back into the taxi, bumped along for another twenty minutes with Jen's front forks bashing my knees, then were finally deposited at the hotel like so much scrap metal. The taxi driver demanded another five hundred rupees and we were left beneath the shadow of a palm tree, listening to the waves roll on the beach, our customs cards fluttering on the bikes like lost luggage tickets.

'Hey, rocket boy,' said Jen, 'we made it to India.'

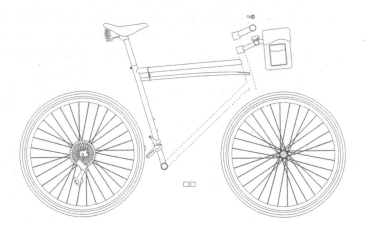

CHAPTER 18

The Headset

The Uran Plaza Hotel stands on the shoreline across from Mumbai next to an overgrown tennis court, some sun loungers and a few empty hammocks. Behind its rooms there are fields of cracked earth grazed by sleepy cows. I remember the crash of waves, crows picking up scraps from the palm-tree shadows and a dog barking. I had a sip of tea. And it was the taste of this that sent me reeling. Tears running down my face and onto my hands. The taste of home transported in tea leaves all the way from India. It was as if I'd found, in this quiet place next to the sea, that I was back where I started.

I wrote in my diary, 'However far we travel and however far we go, we're always left with who we are. I feel like I've washed up on a strange shore, only to find myself not looking at that shore, but at my own hands.'

Jen gave me a hug. She reminded me that I always set myself tasks and then had an emotional crash when they were done. I'd thought about the trip for so long, 'held it together' over so many miles and ups and downs, that now here I was falling apart in the sleepy afternoon.

We walked along the beach, a tidal flat of grey sand where families were out on a Sunday stroll, a line of bright shirts and saris slowly moving towards us like the edge of a burning identity card. India, now, arriving at me.

It is at this point that we must climb the foothills of Indian philosophy, an experience not unlike gazing up at a mountain range and wondering where one set of peaks ends and the next begins, as the singular sun sets behind them. A somewhat daunting experience but easily surmountable with the correct set of GEARS.

Around 1500 BCE the Aryans of central Asia moved into the Indus Valley, a river basin that extends from Afghanistan through Pakistan into northern India. These groups brought their own class divisions to the caste and tribal systems of the civilisations already living there. It was in this mixing of cultures that Hinduism was forged – or the many philosophies and beliefs 'we' now call Hinduism, Hindu meaning 'from the Indus river'.

And it was at this time that the foundational texts of Hinduism, the Vedas, took shape, chanted hymns passed down from teacher to pupil and finally recorded in written form in Sanskrit. They contain references to Hindu deities, with instructions on their worship, but also information on agriculture, social order, medicine, astronomy, music, as well as philosophical meditations on the nature of creation and the self. It was long thought in Europe that the Vedas were nothing more than a rattle bag of myths and pagan liturgies. In fact, they contain the symbolic blueprint for an evolving theory of selfhood, a metaphysical road map that influenced the people of India and their neighbours for thousands of years. From the original four volumes there followed a series of commentaries that discussed the practices and questions raised by these primary sources. From these three commentaries other subsidiary texts flourished, in a branching and spreading debate, powered by a process of argument and counterargument. This rich seam of discussion developed alongside physical practices, rituals and meditations believed to contribute as much to intuitive understanding as the formal reasoning we associate with philosophy in the West. But such a branching of ideas does not mean that Indian belief lacked a clear viewpoint or viewpoints.

There are six main schools of Indian philosophy, known as Darsanas, meaning ways of 'seeing'. Of these, the Advaita Vedanta has become the main, or orthodox, Hindu philosophy we know today. Some familiar non-orthodox schools, traditions which do not accept the authority of the Vedic texts, are Buddhism and Jainism. All of these were involved in an ongoing dialogue with one another, a conversation that was itself influenced by the invading cultures that poured through India: the Greek invasions of Alexander the Great in 300 BCE, the Zoroastrian Parsis escaping from Persia, Muslim rule from CE 800 to 1800, and finally the British Raj, followed by Indian partition and independence in 1947.

To characterise Indian philosophy as an inward-looking pastiche of cartoon-like gods, as Western philosophy has tended to do, is to ignore its breadth, its discursiveness and its responsiveness to external ideas and cultures. In the traditions of Indian philosophy the division between how we understand the world and what we understand is not only limited to intellectual argument. Practical methods for gaining insight are equally relevant. Sexuality, meditation and ritual all still have a role to play. Wisdom in Sanskrit is *prajna*, and *prajna* values intuition and personal experience alongside objective analysis and empirical evidence. The complex, intertwining strands of ancient Hinduism do not attempt to frame themselves as a coherent tradition, rather they are a varied response to a shared predicament: what is the self, what is a person, and how does that person fit into the universe?

Our difficulty with Indian philosophy isn't just about dividing the logical reason of the West from the irrational intuition of the East, it's about our inability to tolerate the two together. Indian philosophy is run through with arguments based on both reason and intuitive experience. Contemporary Western culture fails to allow a forum where both can co-exist. All too often Indian philosophy is seen as archaic dogma or unexamined spiritual salvation. But Indian philosophy is far more contradictory and provocative than that; it is as mad, bad, joyful, transcendent and gutter-rich as the country itself.

Wherever you go in India you come across statues of the Devas, its deities, but it would be wrong to characterise these as gods in the Western sense. They do not have the sealed-off identities and roles of the Greek gods, nor are they pure levers of creation as in the faiths of Islam and Christianity. Indian Devas, like Ganesha, are metaphorical and figurative representations of underlying philosophical and ethical principles, their roles and representations diffusely bleeding into one another. Some Hindus do worship Devas in a way akin to gods, but many others use their names and iconographies in familiar ritual practice, a structured ordering of the universe that has more meaning of itself than the names being incanted.

The original Veda, the Rg Veda, contains 1028 hymns. It is a mixture of incomplete myths, allegorical tales and paradoxical streams of consciousness. The Vedic hymns are best thought of as an adventure in metaphor, where concepts took on symbolic form at a time when ideas, poetry and nature commingled – before mind and matter was wrenched apart in the West by thinkers like St Augustine or Descartes. The ancient seers who originated them were not prophets or emissaries of the gods, rather guardians of a timeless truth, who saw around them a living philosophy.

As we walked along the mud beach outside the hotel we stumbled upon a shipping container, washed up and crushed on a lip of sand. Its singular boxyness was utterly lopsided and, given the backdrop of strolling families and cricket games on the shore, somehow less important. I prodded at it with a stick.

By arriving in India I hoped I might arrive at a more definitive version of myself. Instead I found the one I'd left behind, a middle-aged man carrying far too many bike tools. A more integrated way of understanding our individual identity, or self, is as a singular expression of a much wider whole. This is the Atman of Hindu philosophy, an individual representation of Brahman, the principle that underlies everything in the universe. Atman is an expression of Brahman and Brahman is Atman. These ideas don't make much sense when you examine them and much more sense when you don't. Concepts like Atman and Brahman are easier to circle, to catch from the corner of your eye, as relayed in this conversation between teacher and pupil:

> 'Fetch me a fruit of the Nyagrodha [banyan] tree.'
> 'Here is one, Sir.'
> 'Break it.'
> 'It is broken, Sir.'
> 'What do you see there?'
> 'These seeds, almost infinitesimal.'
> 'Break one of them.'
> 'It is broken, Sir.'
> 'What do you see there?'
> 'Not anything, Sir.'
> 'My son, that subtle essence which you do not perceive there, of that very essence this great Nyagrodha tree exists. Believe it, my son. That which is the subtle essence, in it all that exists has its self. It is the True. It is the Self, and thou, O Svetaketu, art it.'

> (from the *Changdogya Upanishad* trans. Friedrich Max Müller 1879)

In other words Atman, the finest essence, is not only the seed but also the pupil and all nature. It allows our individual identity, whilst underpinning everything.

In Hinduism to reach a state of the most profound understanding, of Atman-within-Brahman, is to be released from the narrow vein of the self into limitless universality. But to recognise this singular essence within a wider unity requires more than allegorical or metaphorical explanation. You have to experience it. You have to taste it. And that's where meditative practices enter into Indian philosophy. To appreciate the underlying order of the universe, and your position in that order, it is not sufficient to think about it, you have to alter the way that you think – approach the world in an entirely different way. Brahman is essentially ineffable. To explain Brahman is to categorise and define with terms that Brahman itself outgrows. The concept cannot be sealed like a container. It can only be suggested within a state that recognises the hived-off self, which we call the mind, for what it truly is – boundary-less. Brahman, in other words, can only be fully known within the contentious state of transcendence. And transcendence, in its Indian use, is best explained not through sentences like this, but in physical processes like meditation, or physical 'flow' states, like the bicycle ride, where knowledge is imparted in the incantation of breathing and pedalling, a state reinforced by a cyclist's sense of elevation above the landscape while being pulled back to the ground, a reaching towards Brahman while always being centred towards Atman.

The Headset is the part of the bicycle that integrates the STEM with the forks of the front WHEEL, so that the HANDLEBARS can move smoothly and evenly, and turn the front WHEEL. It consists of two large bearings, circular rings of tiny metal rollers, that fit into the HEAD TUBE of a bike frame, and into which the forks of the bike are inserted. For the mechanism to fit snugly there are a series of cups and spacers that fit one upon the other, into a Russian doll of rings. In most modern bikes the Headset is threadless – all the components are held together under a downward pressure rather than screwed into the frame itself. While it is the STEM that does the hard work of clamping the steering tube and front forks to the HANDLEBARS, it is the Headset that keeps the steering smooth, focusing the rider on the straight and narrow, or wide and infinite, with the minimum of fuss.

In contrast to the labour of the BOTTOM BRACKET, which manages a constantly driving radial force, the Headset experiences a variable downward thrust, and minimal sideways excitement. Its role is to smooth out these forces while allowing the subtle changes of movement that mean that the bike can be evenly steered by the HANDLEBARS. If the BOTTOM BRACKET is all about power transfer, the Headset is all about direction. Most modern Headsets can be taken apart, so the ball bearings can be cleaned and greased and, if necessary, replaced. If, as I have argued, the BOTTOM BRACKET represents the point where mind and body meet, but are unfathomably separated, then the Headset represents the point where mind and body can achieve a transparent integration, if not always equilibrium.

Bikes have always had a thronely quality about them, the rider sitting atop the SADDLE, above the grot of the road. And there is something undeniably royal about a good quality Headset. Its seamless integration suggests as much, with the crown race, sitting on the forks, abutting the bearing race above it. And manufacturers have always played to this with all the bling they can muster. You can get Headsets in ruby red, emerald green and sapphire white. The Chris King company is the originator of some of the best known and highly engineered Headsets in the world. If you're rocking a Chris King then you're probably A) loaded and B) a king.

If Atman and Brahman underpin the order of the Indian universe, then class and the caste system divide it: inherited serfdom for the lower castes and priestly privilege for Brahmins. The final irony of the Raj is that Britain found in the caste system a parallel to its own class system, and sought to reinforce the divisions as a way to maintain its colonial power. The discrepancy between the philosophical unity of Hinduism and its social divisiveness is everywhere in India, from the rule of Ganesha in the customs office to life and death in the gutter, to lattes and laptops in the coffee shop.

Further along the beach, and just along from the shipping container, a boy asked us for a photo. We stood alongside his extended family, our arms rigidly by our sides, gazing across the water at Mumbai, still invisible to us, as I began to wonder where we had landed. It was only when we navigated our way up the mud flats to Uran town, that – BAM – India arrived. Or the version which would occupy us for the next two months: Hindu temples with peeling gold paint, Christian churches painted yellow and purple, crumbling houses with corrugated roofs, endless litter, a man rolling a sign with a wheel on the bottom advertising rat poison, boys with no trousers squatting by the side of the road, one goat pissing on another goat taking a piss, stray dogs screwing, an argument with a rickshaw driver about the price, which seemed to mean nothing and everything to both of us, a glimpse through the palm trees to a chemical factory spewing orange smoke.

Back on the shore we found a concrete slab covered with ashes and flowers, and a jetty going out into the ocean. I thought it was a picnic spot. Jen thought it was where ashes could be scattered. 'But,' I wondered out loud, 'aren't ashes meant to be shared with the sacred rivers?' We were only a ferry ride from Mumbai but thousands of miles from any real understanding of India.

In the morning we discovered a chirruping bird in the rafters of our room. It stayed there despite our attempts to flush it out through a hole in the eaves, locked into an argument with the slowing turning fan in the centre of the ceiling. In the afternoon I watched fishermen float past on flat wooden rafts, using a pole to push them along, inch by inch.

To install a Headset so that all the components are perfectly aligned, and the HANDLEBARS turn evenly and smoothly, every part has to sit level on the part below. There are specialist tools that seat the Headset into the HEAD TUBE. If you don't have these tools then you might end up using a mallet, a scrap of wood and some heavy whacks. If, amid the grunting and thwacking, a Headset lands unequally on the bevels on which it rests, then this is a recipe for misalignment. Which in turn could lead to brinelling, small indentations in the ball bearings that accelerate other forms of wear such as spalling, and even (string section goes up an octave) galling. It'd been so long since we'd actually ridden our bikes, the possibility of brinelling seemed unlikely. But what about false brinelling. Oh yes, such dark forces exist. When components are transported over long distances they rub and fret with one another producing a kind of polishing. Little pearls of imperfection. The only way to make false brinelling go away is to use those parts normally. In other words, ride your bike.

The evening shadows cast by our D-locked bikes rippled over the sand and sedge.

'Jen,' I said, 'I think we should ride our bikes.'

'Oh yes, it would be good to have a look around.'

'No, I mean really ride them.'

'Well that's why we brought them here, wasn't it? To have a nose around. After we've been to Mumbai.'

'I don't think I want to go to Mumbai. I want to ride, um, south.'

'But Mumbai is only half an hour away. We ought to at least have a look.'

'It's a bit too close really, don't you think? We should just head south.'

'What do you mean, south?'

'Oh, I don't know ... south.'

'We've only just arrived. Let's just chill.'

'Ah yes, I'd like to *chill*; it's just I'd prefer to chill out, well, you know, a bit more ... south.'

'And when we get to a good beach ... south. We just chill out. Right?'

'Right.' I dabbed my toe in the sand under a hammock.

'No daily quotas. No "We have to be in Goa by next Monday."'

'Of course not. We've just arrived.'

Jen peered at me over the top her sunglasses. 'I have,' she said.

The fishermen pushed themselves out to sea on their rafts. Inch by inch by inch.

To arrive at the self is to arrive at the universe. Every destination is merely another lookout on a landscape that never changes, the individual's essential integration with everything that surrounds them. Mind and body are not separate islands, merely different expressions of an underlying substance. So, rocket boy, the self is the boy but is also the bike and the road, the cup of tea and the bubbles on top, the waves and the sea.

When we rolled our bikes onto the mud flats the following day, the families of the previous day had gone, replaced by oxen and their carts, seen through a morning haze of sea mist. On the other side of the bay was an urgent metropolis, and yet here, ten kilometres from Mumbai, solid wooden wheels were turning so slowly they hardly appeared to move, laying their silvery tracks in the tide like snails.

Later that day we found ourselves cycling along a track to a beach 'lodging' that turned out to be a tumbledown relic of a Portuguese fort, ferns growing out of the walls and cannons lined up as if still waiting to defend it. It only took a few minutes for a teenage boy to pop out from the undergrowth, wanting to talk about cricket, a subject about which I know shamefully little, and about which India would expect me, as an Englishman, to possess ultimate wisdom. Here it was the currency of conversation. The advances and retreats of a player's and a team's misfortunes were the stuff of every street corner, and the knock of a cricket ball a village's wayward clock, marking out the hours in unsteady punctuations. At dusk we rode up one last hill and I began to feel dizzy. I'd forgotten that when you're on a bike you need to eat between meals; that the thing below the neck, the body, needs something to keep the thing above it, the head, vertical. Jen pulled out a bottle of honey and poured it down my throat.

Thwack.

The sound of a cricket ball being knocked for six as the sun set through the startled silhouettes of the trees.

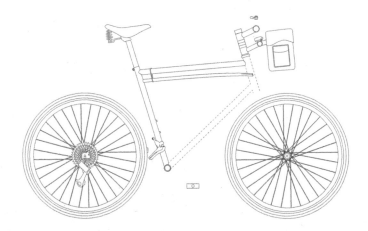

CHAPTER 19

The Star Fangled Washer

Other bike parts do more work, others are more bike-like, but for sheer exuberance combined with humility, nothing beats the Star Fangled Washer. If you want to dumb it down, the part is just a nut, a hole for a bolt, hidden inside the HEAD TUBE. As the bolt is tightened it provides just enough tension, through the bearings of the HEADSET, to keep the HANDLEBARS moving smoothly. Slightly larger than the steerer tube (an extension of a bike's front forks), into which it invisibly sits, the washer takes the shape of a twelve-sided flower. 'When the compression bolt is tightened the "petals" spread slightly and grip the inside of the steerer tube' (Haynes, *The Bike Book*, 5th edition).

At one level this means a bolt has been tightened into a nut and the steering mechanism of a bike tensioned. At another, and this is no doubt what the publisher Haynes intended, with sales of over 150 million technical books around the world, it explains how the lotus petal opens into the 'moksha' of Hindu enlightenment. That the lotus petal, all-encompassing symbol of insight in Eastern philosophy, bears an uncanny resemblance to the Star Fangled Washer suggests it was deliberately put there, hidden in the bones of the bike, by a divine/non-divine/atheist machinist with a biting sense of humour. The Star Fangled Washer may look like a floppy flower, but its sharp-edged metal petals expand and dig into the steel surrounding it, holding it in place like fangs.

First and foremost, the washer is a star, so named for its pointed edges. And the six-pointed star, consisting of two overlapping triangles, in Smarta Hinduism represents the union of the self and the universe, a state of enlightenment that can only be reached by both meditative states and conventional reasoning. The lower three points of the star represent the self; the upper three points represent the wider universe. To know the seamless place of the individual self in the wider universe, the overlapping triangles that make the six points of the star, is to experience Brahman (see HEADSET).

Hinduism suggests that the aspects of the mind which we are familiar with in our waking life, our sensations and emotions, and the thoughts they then evoke, are like unruly horses, to which we are beholden, bucked this way and that. Meditation, among many other physical practices, helps us to focus our attention away from this chatter, and see who we are and how we fit with the pieces that surround us. This is one way in which we can reconcile our unrevealed self, that part of us we carry around like a lonely twist of unread paper, with the wider world, the materiality of bodies and the complexity of relationships. Meditation leads to stillness, the quietening of the senses, in which a new focus is achieved. In a place like India, where the volume and the contrast appear, at least to the Western eye, to be turned up, the stillness of cycling can be grounding, locating a quiet, inner, perspective in the act of movement itself. The stillness I found in India was not in a yoga class but in the chaotic roads we were riding, a living, breathing, physical philosophy.

We rolled along the coast of India from beach to beach, from ferry to ferry, from smart hotel to broken hotel. We ate patties and samosas wrapped up in folded newspapers sewn along each edge. On a high winding road that reminded me of Salisbury Plain an old man offered us a friendly wave and a '*Namaste*.' Then we came across another elder, propping himself up on a stick. He started talking in Hindi, gesturing for money, and when I didn't respond felt the pockets of my shorts. Surely this white man on a bicycle could spare a rupee? As I rode away I could still feel the heat of his hands against my legs, as if he had branded me with my own shame.

We could see the white breakers of the Indian Ocean rolling towards the coast, the corrugated beats of the jungle valleys, and then the flat paddy fields beyond, divided by palm trees and bridges. What had seemed like a jolly good idea, ferry-hopping our way along the coast, slowly turned into heat exhaustion and a drawn-out apology to Jen, conducted on dead-end roads with no food and nowhere to stay. On the hot plains south of Ratnagiri I drank eight pints of water, which just didn't seem to be staying in my body. The telltale sign that I couldn't go any faster was me telling Jen to go faster. Halfway up a hill I keeled over. The journal entry for that day reads, 'Mind says go. Body says no.'

Jen found a beach hut, into which I collapsed with what I thought was malaria but turned out to be flu, vomiting into the cup of a half coconut shell.

'Jet,' said Jen as I blinked through the soft focus of the setting sun, 'you're going to rest. Properly. In Goa. No more riding. No more hills. No more plastic water bottles.'

'Yeh, I just gotta let go.'

'No,' said Jen, 'you just gotta stop.'

The bridge that connects Maharashtra state, south of Mumbai, to Goa was nearly but not quite complete when we arrived. Jen and I peered over its unprotected edge, wondering why they had stopped, and then retraced our steps to the ferry. When we finally made it to the other side we found an elderly American man in a beige safari suit filming buffalo while his wife looked on, bored. There was an English tourist on a Royal Enfield motorbike, taking pictures of Indian women carrying baskets of fish on their heads. We had definitely gone over to the other side. Whether it was into a new state of expanded consciousness or a beachfront parade of knock-off sunglasses, depends on which side of the price tag you're looking at.

To say that Ajoba, the first resort we came to, was surreal, would be to damn surrealism with faint praise. Tangle-haired hippies meditated on their knees as the sun went down, and bare-chested Indian men on mopeds looked on. There was a podgy white guy with two walking poles, trekking along the beach like he had taken a wrong turn at Oslo. I was dozing on a lounger under a palm tree when one of the many paragliders who had been rising and falling above us landed just in front of me. He shot me a 'Yeh, so what?' look, spun around, crossed the lines of his parachute, and then packed it up inside a backpack like a spider sucking in his web. And all the time I could hear the *zither* of angle grinder in the background, putting the finishing touches to a Hindu temple. The bartender told me that in February 50,000 people would arrive at the town to worship the Devas of Vishnu and Lakshmi, and there would be 'bananas everywhere'. I tried to contemplate this as I sucked at the remains of my banana shake, making a spluttering sound like a moped exhaust.

At the end of the nineteenth century Indian philosophy was an afterthought in the West, a magical elaboration of ancient Vedic texts. But perceptions of Hinduism and yoga quickly began to change. Cheap printed booklets appeared, within India itself, which were essentially do-it-yourself handbooks for yoga exercises and breathing techniques. There might be a short piece of theory and then a series of practical instructions on how to use your breath and what situations this might be useful in. Breathing techniques might be described for the purchase of a horse, an elephant, a camel, or the buying of jewellery, anything with a dangerous or risky connotation. In this way meditation slowly but surely began to be separated from its religious and philosophical context.

Swami Vivekananda was an enormously influential figure in the West. He spread Hinduism across Europe and America at the end of the nineteenth century and was instrumental in its acceptance as a world religion. His focus was predominantly on the use of breathing in meditation and not on the physical postures we now associate with yoga, known as hatha yoga, which in his bestselling *Raja Yoga* he described as 'very difficult and cannot be learned in a day, and do not lead to much spiritual growth'. Vivekananda compared the use of the breath to advances in Western science, explaining, for example, 'what moves the steam engine is Prana, acting through steam'. This forged a link between Hinduism and the paranormal and parapsychological cults of Victorian England and America, strange amalgams of science and supernaturalism.

It was not until the 1950s that the yoga we know today was perfected. It began in the 1930s with the scholar and teacher Tirumalai Krishnamacharya, who found in the older writings of hatha yoga a way for Indians to take possession of their own bodies in opposition to the public-school rigidity of the ruling British class. Some British army exercises and the Danish educator Niels Bukh's 'primitive gymnastics' look similar to Krishnamacharya's postures, raising the possibility that they influenced each other, though Krishnamacharya's yoga, and contemporary globalised yoga, clearly have a pedigree with centuries-old asanas or Indian physical poses.

My journal records that the next resort along the coast, Arambol, was 'a long street of tie-dye nothingness where Indians sell hippy shit to hippies'. Which probably reflects my post-flu malaise more than anything else. We were here to see Slav, the Aussie we'd previously met in Iran. He was ambling along the beach in flowery shorts, beaming and wanting to know if we'd like some space cake. I was feeling frazzled and worrying that I was going to catch rabies from a dog that had licked me on the leg. I left him ambling through the waves.

At one of the bars along the beach I talked to a middle-aged man, sharing a meal with his wife and young son. He asked what we were doing there and I recited the countries we'd cycled through.

'Yeh. That's pretty cool,' said Rick. Then he explained that after leaving university he'd cycled around the world for fourteen years and visited 181 countries. He'd ridden the breadth of Canada and from the tip of South America to the north of Alaska, across Russia, central Asia, down the east coast of Africa and then back up the west coast. He'd canoed down the Amazon. He'd kayaked along the coast of Chile to the tip of Patagonia and then around the coast of New Zealand. He'd crewed on sailing boats (he would strip his bike, grease all the vital parts and put them in a carrier bag to stop them rusting from one port to the next). He'd sailed a dinghy around the world. And he'd seen floating islands of plastic rubbish and islands in the Pacific where you could have your own private beach for ever.

'Yeh,' I said, 'that's pretty cool.'

German Heinz Stücke is probably the most travelled cyclist ever. Some people say there are no good melodies left after the

Beatles used them all up. Well there are probably no more miles left after Heinz Stücke cycled them. For forty of his seventy years he's been on the road, covering nearly 400,000 miles by bike and visiting nearly 200 countries. As a young man he left his job as a tool maker in Germany and didn't return because of his aversion to factory work. He spent the first twenty years surviving on hospitality alone. In his later years he sold photos and a booklet he'd made about his trip, before finding sponsorship from cycling companies. He said:

> ... unfortunately, most lives in this automated society are very degrading. You know, you have a job that you repeat and ... just to get the money and to pay for your life ... Listen to this: I am very proud that it is possible, in our interconnected, dependent society, to have a guy who is a one-man enterprise who completely lives on his own wits and does reasonably well ... I can really meditate on my bicycle when I'm riding alone in the bush, you know. And I still have that feeling of progress, because I think it's the motion, the riding into the unknown, and that is what keeps you quite happy. I don't know how to explain it otherwise.

(from an interview on the Travelling Two website)

Anthropocene is a term coined to denote the current geological age, which reflects man's impact on the earth's climate and geology. The suggestion is that it is man who has conjured his own fate; his compulsion to consume has swallowed up the environment he relies on. The determinist view (see HANDLEBARS) suggests we were doomed to this end from the very first moment we picked the low-hanging fruit from the trees. It was only a matter of time before we invented the axe to cut the whole tree down. Technology has always been complicit with man's greed in an overextension of his powers. But bicycles have an odd kind of partnership with man that works in the opposite direction. Bike technology isn't just riding in the opposite direction to the Anthropocene with its tiny challenge to petrol-driven transport; it rides in the opposite direction to the very conception of what the Anthropocene is – that man does unto the environment, not that he *is* the environment.

In the earliest Vedic texts human bodies were symbols of the wider cosmos (see HEADSET), and human beings understood themselves to be kindred parts of the universe. What did it for us was not some genetic imprint of greed but the social construction of capitalism. It is capitalism that devours the other of external reality, the environment and its resources, while leaving the apparently isolated us to profit. This is the hollow core of the Anthropocene, which has also been termed the Capitalocene.

> All progress in capitalist agriculture is a progress in the art of robbing the soil; all progress in increasing the fertility of the soil for a given time, is a progress towards ruining the lasting sources of that fertility.

> (Karl Marx, *Capital*)

> Thus at every step we're reminded that we by no means rule over nature like a conqueror over a foreign people, but that we, with flesh and blood and brain, belong to nature, and exist in its midst, and that all our mastery of it consists in the fact that we have advantage over all other creatures of being able to learn its laws and apply them correctly.

> (Friedrich Engels, 1887)

So, what to do in the face of this vast lever of capital and the destruction it wields? The simplest choice is to just turn away. But denial has a hidden cost. What we do not admit to in our waking hours becomes the ache of our dreams, a yearning that pours through modern culture, a disconnection, an insoluble solute. But if we can begin to endure the changes that are happening around us, if we can recover some kind of kinship with the environment, then we might better be able to bear the pain of its loss.

To return to Swami Vivekananda: 'You must be able to sympathise fully with each particular, then at once jump back to the highest monism.' If capitalism operates at the level of duality, of us and them, of us and it, and much of our grieving for nature operates at the level of monism, where there is only all, then to engage with both, with the forces of capitalism and nature, we need to shift our perspective from one to the other, from near to far, from the hard mechanics of social co-operation to the sensual meditative states that beckon us back into the natural world. Only in this way can we begin to overcome the inertia, the denial, that stops us moving forward.

The powers that be, the state apologists for Western capitalism, would have us believe that salvation comes not through using less but by thinking more, through better technology, through better batteries, through better devices. But that better kind of technology was already here a hundred years ago. And it's rolling past your window. It's thinking less and doing more. It's getting off the rails and out of your head. It's turning wisdom into leg pain and leg pain into waking up. Cycling will never be the Nobel peace prize or a global climate accord but it might help us recognise what it is already being taken from us.

Those who come (back) to cycling as adults often have an epiphany: that there are other ways of moving around than the ring roads dictated to us by the mainstream. The beats and the hippies knew from the very beginning that there are alternative ways of living and that the very best way of experimenting with this is to travel beyond your expectations.

The first round-the-world journey by bicycle was made in 1884 by Thomas Stevens, a thirty-year-old British émigré to America, on a penny farthing. A journalist of the time noted 'that modern mechanical invention, instead of disenchanting the universe, had really afforded the means of exploring its marvels the more surely. Instead of going round the world with a rifle, for the purpose of killing something – or with a bundle of tracts, in order to convert somebody – this bold youth simply went round the globe to see the people who were on it; and since he always had something to show them as interesting as anything that they could show him, he made his way among all nations.'

Cyclists have always been quietly going round the world, discovering a different way of being alive, and they have been doing this without fanfare, without glossy ads, without a great deal of arriving. And they have been saved from the same old formulas and snares of capitalism through doing this. However, there was something about Rick in Arambol and Heinz Stücke the world traveller that didn't sit quite right for me. If escaping the nine to five is the reward of a long-distance bicycle ride then surely the compromise is the friends and family you leave behind. If cycling thousands of miles encourages a certain kind of global openness, then it also leaves behind a more local sense of belonging. It's a gamble that relies on your ability to survive without a more familiar kind of love. A risk mitigated by taking the person with you that you love the most. Or them taking you.

'We're in Goa,' said Jen. 'Let's party!'

'I was kind of thinking,' I said, 'that we might move on to the next beach... Maybe there's a quieter one. I've been feeling a bit washed out and I've—'

'We've finally arrived somewhere we can let our hair down. So why don't we party tonight and then chill out tomorrow. Do some yoga.'

'That's the thing, you see. There's a bit too *much* yoga. I was wondering if there's another beach...'

Jen pushed open the flimsy door of the palm shack and hurried into the night, leaving me to the bikes. Until, with a fear of missing out, I scuttled out after her. Near the shoreline tourists were taking pictures of a drumming circle. Beyond the circle, where the waves gently broke on the sand, toned men did half back bends and lotus headstands, as another group did t'ai chi in silhouetted formation, like synchronised swimmers. There was an air of frustrated wholesomeness about the place, as if its surface peacefulness might suddenly shatter. Or. Perhaps. It was just me.

The next day I tried to take Jen's advice and lazed around on a sun lounger for hours and hours, marvelling at Slav's ability to enjoy this without guilt or regret. What, I asked, was his diagnosis of our continual meandering south along the coast of India.

'You're crazy,' he said.

'And the treatment?'

'Stay put. Swim in the sea.'

But I couldn't. I just couldn't.

'What are you looking for?' Jen asked over a banana pancake.

'A quieter beach. A bit more ... empty.'

'You're looking for the last empty beach in Goa?'

'Yup.'

'Has it ever occurred to you that you might be looking for something that doesn't exist?'

'Well, I won't know until I find it.'

'You won't know it doesn't exist until you find it?'

'Exactly.'

*

The beach road in Goa runs parallel to the main beaches and resorts. It is flat and curving and shady, with whitewashed Catholic churches here and there amid crumbling temples and sacred banyan trees. Its colonial-era Portuguese houses have tiled roofs and high-arched doors and windows, some with a new lick of paint, others with an air of decaying grandeur. It is the kind of place where stories linger in the groves, where magic, whatever that might be, hangs in the air. But as we cycled through its flickering tiger stripes of shade, through its scattering of birdsong, there was also a sense of this being lost, that its living myths were, slowly and achingly, giving up their definition to the future.

Over the next week Jen and I cycled from hippy shack to hippy shack, pounding the beaches like rag 'n' bone estate agents, looking for an elusive corner of paradise that never seemed to arrive. On one beach I ordered a writer's desk so that I could compose work of great merit and meaning outside our hut as I stared at the waves. We returned that evening to find a lopsided piece of broken slate balanced on a bucket.

I had managed to infect Jen with my ever-wandering desolation. At least now I had a partner in my disquiet. It was on this beach that I developed a gooey eye infection, which Andre, a friendly Danish man in the hut next door, tried to cure with some homeopathic drops. He asked me what I'd been up to and how I was feeling and then he put his hand on my shoulder and pipetted some of the invisibly tinctured solution into my eyes. I retired to my hut and burst into tears, great rivers of saline and globs of snot. It was the first time in a long time that anyone apart from Jen had asked me how I was and laid a hand on me. And I felt a whole lot better for it. It wasn't what the eye drops contained. It was what they meant.

The resort manager, Matthew, wore a piece of volcanic rock on a string around his neck which he told us, confidentially, 'reknitted

DNA'. He also said that the Russian medicine he'd invested in, 'Ferron', could cure 'stage one and stage two cancer and AIDS' through 'magnetic pole reversal' after being 'sucked into the blood'. The Russian who'd sold it to him had also knocked up the 'natural' filtration system responsible for the water we were all drinking. I looked askance at the cup I was holding before going back to our hut to check our hep A status. Jen's yoga tutor told her to 'feel your body, focus on your senses and the sound of the sea', but all Jen could hear was an English girl on the other side of the fence complaining about losing her iPhone. As I tried to clarify my thoughts in a beachside cafe a German woman walked past shouting, 'It's too touristic here,' and, 'You people throw away too much rubbish and you burn plastic bottles.'

The owner of the cafe shouted back, 'The prime minister is coming in ten minutes. You can talk to him about it then.'

'You don't care about litter in this country. You just throw it away.'

'When were you last here? Fifteen years ago?'

'Six years ago.'

'I've travelled all around India and in fifteen years I've seen it change so much. In five years it will all be different.'

'In five years there will be less plastic bottles? You are a second-world country now; you should look after your litter.'

'In five years your twenty dollars will only be worth one rupee. Everything changes so fast.'

'It's not about the currency; it's about you burning plastic bottles.'

'The prime minister is arriving in ten minutes' time – he will tell you.'

'In other countries like China, Thailand they look after their rubbish.'

'I cannot go to China and Thailand, these countries. All I can tell you is I have been all round India. It is changing so fast.

Come back in five years.'

'In five years there will be no more plastic bottles?'

'We have plastic water bottles because people from the West want them. We have always drunk from the tap. But the politicians are changing things. In five years it will all be different.'

'It's not up to the politicians. It's up to the individuals to take responsibility.'

'Come here in five years. India is changing so fast.'

'You think so?'

'Yes. I will meet you here in five years. We will discuss it then.'

Finally, the German woman gave up. 'OK,' she said. 'See you here.'

Every day an old lady and her daughter, dressed in rags, came past our beach hut, begging. I pondered. If I gave the old woman some coins she would more than likely come back and demand more, stopping me writing short stories on my slate-and-bucket table, stories that would one day bring enormous benefits to all mankind. However, even if I donated just two rupees an hour, which I had somehow calculated was the begging rate, this would cost me less than a can of Coke. Is this how much my conscience was worth? Slightly less than a can of Coke. In the gaps between the old lady going past a coastguard helicopter would fly above us, hugging the beach, looking for white people dragged out to sea by the undertow.

'Jen, you know what?'

Jen turned to me with a look of learned helplessness.

'I think we need to keep on riding. South.'

We rode past paddy fields and green ponds full of the lotus flower, biding its time, pausing, blooming, knowing nothing.

Swami Vivekananda, the main proponent of Hinduism in the West, whilst tending towards monism (the philosophy that material and mental realms are made of the same stuff) acknowledged the place of dualism (that these are different realms altogether). From a cycling perspective we might reframe his 'you must be able to sympathise fully with each particular, then at once jump back to the highest monism' as 'you must be able to focus on each particular to see how a bike fits together and then jump back on for the ride'.

Although the lotus is a many-petalled flower, its roots sink down into the mud. And in Hindu and Buddhist meditation the lotus position, sitting cross-legged on the floor, emphasises the pure insight arising from the earth, a revelatory understanding of self that arises from an otherwise objective understanding of reality. It would be foolish to say the cyclist rides a bicycle in the same way that a Hindu meditates. Not least because a cyclist's legs are so untangled. But between the tied and untied knot, in the grounding and flight of cycling, there is a hint of another way of becoming free.

We trundled down a forest path to a crescent beach with a restaurant at one end and a few lopsided shacks at the other. I was ready to climb back on my bike when Jen persuaded me to look at the 'new hut' that was being 'personally managed' by a young man called Aarav. After a long walk Aarav showed us a hut at the other end of the shoreline with walls made of leaves and a palm tree growing through the middle. I listened. There was only the sound of the waves and the occasional chug of a fishing boat. To get water we would have to throw a plastic vase into an old freshwater well, haul it back up and pick out the leaves. There were monkeys eating mangoes from the mango trees and the occasional peacock.

'I'll take it,' I said like it was a cut-price sale on a car dealer's forecourt.

Aarav looked at me blankly. It seemed to be of no consequence to him whether 'I took it' or not. 'This afternoon,' he said, 'I will show you the secret beach.'

We locked the bikes to the palm tree at the centre of our hut, whose trunk rose through the carefully laid thatch, a lattice that showered glimpses of sky like flashes of blue feathers.

The Star Fangled Washer does not simply connect the HANDLEBARS to the fork and from there the front WHEEL. It has a subtler function. When a compression bolt is tightened through its centre, the bearings of the HEADSET are put under just the right amount of strain, such that the HANDLEBARS neither rock loosely, nor grind with stiffness. An aficionado will use a tension gauge to measure the pitch of this resistance, and some mechanics have even been known to use a fish scale. It is this carefully calibrated and balanced tension that is the secret of the Star Fangled Washer, as it digs its expanding petals into the steering tube at the top of the forks

Here is the journey of the word 'Fang' across time and continents showing its unreasonable lack of direction, West and East, through binding hospitality and toxic venom:

Latin **Pagus** village boundary ☒ Indo-European **Pag** to fasten ☒ Latin **Pax** to hold in truce

☒ ☒ ☒

Pagan   Latin **Pagina** frame
to tether grape vines ☒
☒

Page the tether of words ☒

☒

Sanskrit **Pasagati** to bind
☒

Nasalised as Old English **Fang**

☒ ☒ ☒

To imprison   To provide hospitality   A snake's tooth
☒

Fangle to make gaudy – ensnare with trim – **New Fangled**

Lying on my back in our palm leaf des res on the last empty beach in Goa, I wasn't thinking about unity and division, life and death. I was just thinking, *Ooh I wouldn't mind a glass of water.* So I went to the well and drew up the water and I poured it into a cup and I drank it down plain and cool and true.

That afternoon Aarav took us through the undergrowth behind the shack and out into the bush, twisting and turning along roughly made trails, over a hill and around a headland until we came to the 'secret beach', a tiny cove with steep cliff walls and a trickle of a waterfall in one corner where you could shower yourself after a swim. The only other visitors were the sea eagles, spiralling on thermal updraughts. Aarav cast his eye upon it all with his singular unchanging expression. It was just a beach to him, an ever-present part of his life from childhood. He repeated the same things again and again as we waded back through the scrub: 'Foreign people like the sun on their skin,' and, 'We don't want Russians here. They fight.' It felt like whatever Aarav heard he repeated without filtering, without, you sometimes wondered, even knowing what it meant. That evening he made us a fire by our shack and then, rather than leave us to a romantic reverie, sat to one side of us as the stars swung out between the palm leaves and the driftwood hissed down to its embers. It was a nod towards hospitality but also towards companionship. Jen, Aarav and I watching the world turn on its axis.

Over the following week Jen and I wandered between our new home and the last empty beach in Goa; lazing in the waves, dozing in the hammock and rocking the double bed below the palm tree, so our bikes slipped against each other, digging themselves into the sand.

Like Sufism (see TOP TUBE), Tantra appeared to offer a more accessible path to mystical or unitary experiences, being much less restrictive, in terms of caste, than mainstream Vedic religions.

It demanded less time, study, discipline and meditation, and used visualisation of gods and iconic images, reinforced by the sensual energy of emotions and sexuality, as a more direct path to enlightenment. This plug-in-and-go physical experience allowed those on the lower rungs of Indian society to not only reach an elevated awareness but to make it as gurus in the royal courts. The same physicality that appealed to followers of Tantrism, its emotion and sexuality, made it a turn-off for Western philosophy, which had long ago buttoned up its cardigans, folded down its sleeves and narrowed its focus on reason and intellectualism.

But Western philosophy is now closing in on these physical experiences from a rational perspective. Our emotional and intuitive responses to real-world situations, the quick and dirty reasoning of the here and now, are allowed an implicit role in what we call common sense, by pruning the almost infinite number of solutions to any given problem to those most applicable to its context. Do I trust this person by the side of the road directing me down an alley? Yes or no? Western reason thus admits the value of emotion, what it calls the role of the neuroendocrine axis, but only on the terms that rationality demands, in other words, 'Yeh, emotion is important, but only for giving reason a shove up the ladder.' As for sexuality – well that remains a no-go. Western philosophy might allow a bit of emotion, a tear wiped away with a knuckle, but there shall be no shagging in the temples of logic.

Tantra starts with the idea that we understand the world, not in a calm, detached way but by being immersed in the peaks and troughs of human experience. And this is the starting point. What you do changes what you understand. Not the other way around. It suggests that rituals can directly manipulate the external world, a leap into what the West would describe as magic. The chakras of the 'subtle body' with their imagined energy centres that parallel parts of our body are a case in point. But if you understand a chakra as a symbolic representation of the body, and therefore as another tool for communication with someone about their body, then it seems less threateningly magical. A consultant physician once said to me, 'Talk to the person, not the body,' and the person is as culturally various as the anatomically labelled body is generalised. In my first psychiatric outpatients' clinic my boss told me, 'Use motorbike metaphors for motorcyclists and football metaphors for footballers.' So he might as well have said, 'Use chakra metaphors for Tantric devotees and Star Fangled Washers for cyclists.' Using conventional medicine doesn't preclude an individual understanding their body in an unconventional way. What the West understands as placebo has long been understood by the East and older shamanic traditions as the power of symbols to change how we react to illness and disease, the imagined body reflecting on its physical counterpart. This isn't a sham, and it isn't hocus-pocus; it is the power of story and metaphor and myth, their ability to bewitch our mundane lives with meaning.

Tantra was originally taught as an oral tradition and passed on somewhat secretively from teacher to pupil, bypassing the orthodox Vedic texts, and wasn't associated until much later with the *pag,* the tether, of the page. The Tantric focus on sexuality and sex, both symbolically and in ritual, has often led to it being dismissed as sensationalist, a kind of acrobatic fetishism. Sex is clearly, and unapologetically, at the core of many Tantric teachings but it is also more subtly imagined than this. The Hindu god Shiva is equated with destruction but also with the balance of creative and destructive energies. Shiva is sometimes represented as a lingam, a phallic symbol not just of pleasure but of pleasure held in check, of a sexual energy channelled in other ways. Shiva's consort is Shakti, representing the female creative forces, and often represented as the yoni, a dish-shaped representation of the female uterus and vagina, with the lingam at its centre. Shiva and Shakti together represent a balanced sexual pair but also a balance and integration of mind and body. This metaphor of opposing energies holding each other in an integral balance stretches further east into the yin and yang of ancient Chinese philosophy and Taoism. And if you want to go all the way with these metaphors of symbolic mechanics, you could take off the SADDLE still attached to the SEAT POST, turn it upside down and see both the lingam and yoni of Tantric teaching. But that. Of course. Would be irrational.

The male and female parts of who we are physically and who we understand ourselves to be imaginatively cannot be separated from what they integrally represent, the human being. And the poor old bicycle, which I have knocked about into all manner of meanings and metaphors, lends itself so appositely to this representation of part and whole, polarity and unity, because it fits so well with the human body and human experience. Cyclists exude a shape-shifting sexuality, all legs and bums and shoulders, at once set free and yet contained by the revolving forces of pedalling, into a graceful unity.

If I will into existence a different couple cycling to India alongside the ones that actually did (and why not since we're in the zone of Tantric visualisation?) then we might imagine this couple revolving around each other in the space between the two bikes with the peculiar intimacy that accompanies two lovers riding together – the hushed pauses, the whirr of the wheels, the unspoken relay as one overtakes another.

Even putting Tantra to one side, there is a lot of symbolic coupling in Hindu mythology, which is often gender-bending and sexually various, with male gods becoming female and then lying down with male gods before reverting to their male form. And I've always found it interesting how cycling has been a home to nudity and a wide spectrum of sexuality in the much the same way as it has skirted around and through mainstream society. Its fluidity of physical movement can be visualised as a liberating

ambiguity in which the strict definitions of who we are and what
we're expected to be are inherently blurred, in which gender
and sexual preference are as up for grabs as Hindu mythology.
Jen explained how bikes aren't feminine goddesses, all curves
and sweeps, and nor are they masculine gods, all geometry and
angles, they are both. 'Bicycles,' she said, 'are bi.'

Cycling is approachably mundane and affordably sacred.
It is white, black, brown, girl, boy, old, young, transgender,
straight, queer, polysexual, class-ridden and classless. It requires
no confirmation, no university, no racial profiling, no evidence-
based interview. There is only a sense of ungrounded flight, of
unearthed potential, of possibility just around the corner.

When cycling first emerged as mass transport at the end of
the nineteenth century, the involvement of women was much
debated, from the erotic potential of the leather SADDLE to
the wearing of provocative bloomers. These controversies
weren't just about the sinfulness of the cycling body, they
were about the power of cycling itself, its liberating potential
for independence, its threat to the masculine order. Bicycles
reflect an inherent ambiguity not just in gender but in
sexuality and morality. They can recalibrate strength and offer
independence in a way that realigns the traditional mores of
what men and women can and can't do. (To brand this as just
the identity politics of the West is to turn away from the very
real restrictions on women cycling in the Middle East. At the
time of writing women are banned from riding in public areas
in both Saudi Arabia and Iran but are able to potter about
in designated areas.) Cycling has a radical message that is
conducted in a leggy semaphore, mile after belligerent mile.
The body is powerful and it will not be confined.

Buddhism places an emphasis on interconnectedness and
selflessness (see FREEWHEEL), and Tantric Buddhism does not
visualise the other partner as a sexual object because the self

and the other, male and female, are not separate, they represent alternative aspects of a common identity.

The Buddhist Vajra is used in Tantric ritual as a visual representation of unity and the Buddhist journey of transformation towards that unity. At one end are five lotus petals representing five poisons (infatuation, aversion, conceit, passion and envy), and at the other are five petals that represent the perfection of five Buddhas. The poisons of Vajra (in a thunderbolt of enlightenment) are transformed into perfection. With the eye of a wayward mechanic you can see in the Vajra something of the Star Fangled Washer, with its sharp, double-headed lotus petals, its linguistic transformations from fang to fellowship.

As we wandered between the palm shack and the last empty beach in Goa a peacock would suddenly emerge from the bush tracks, making a scuffling sound. Aarav would watch it respectfully and then return to his favourite conversational topic, our opinion on different nationalities and whether they would make good candidates for his palm shack. All nationalities, we tried to persuade him, would make good guests in his shack. 'But what about the Chinese people?' he would press, 'What about the Polish?'

The flightless peacock is one of the protected birds of India and symbolises the subjugation of sexual desire and piety. It is the vehicle of the god Kartikeya, the eldest son of Shiva. Kartikeya is depicted as a five-headed god fused onto a single body, riding on a peacock through the heavenly imagination. The peacock has a serpent in its claws, which it does not kill despite being its sworn enemy. Its feathers represent the blue of infinity, and the eyes in those feathers the sight by which a devotee attains supreme knowledge of self, reaching towards the Brahman of the innumerable stars.

Sitting around a fire on the last empty beach in Goa with Aarav's extended family and watching the orange embers float up towards those stars, it seemed like all things were possible. One of the benefits of travel is that it reminds you of what you've left behind by seeing it from another perspective. In other words, you only really know you've arrived when you realise it's time to go home. Whatever aspect of self I'd found in India was just a reminder of what I'd left behind and all those times I'd sat with friends in Bristol, watching cinders fly up into the sky. Jen and I stumbled away from the fire, away from Aarav, away from his family and back along the beach to our shack in the moonlight.

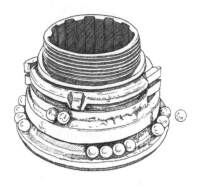

CHAPTER 20

The Freewheel

We waited out the midday sun at a roadside shrine. And as
we watched the trucks shoot by, decorated with mirrors and
primary colours, a group of women in bright saris walked past,
carrying lengths of cut timber on their heads. The eldest one,
with a few betel-stained teeth and a lined, handsome face, knelt
down, carefully laid her wood pile beside her and squatted in
front of Jen. She made gestures to indicate she wanted a drink
from Jen's water bottle. And once she'd had a sip, taking care
not to touch the lip of the bottle, she chatted to her, presumably
in the Karnataka dialect, getting Jen to repeat the names of local
places and laughing at her pronunciation. The other women had
put their loads down and were as amused as she was. Then they
all picked up their loads, helping each other, and went on their
way, chatting and smiling. It may not sound like a landmark
moment but these were the times we remembered: an unassuming
roadside stop between here and there, not so much a destination

as a lay-by to nowhere. It was a place that perhaps only a cyclist might pause and watch the world and then find that the world has come to them, under the shade of a broad-leafed tree.

The roots of the sacred bodhi tree are associated with Brahma, the trunk with Vishnu, and the leaves with Shiva, the three principal devas of Hinduism. In Buddhism it is celebrated as the tree under which the Buddha first achieved enlightenment. 'The Buddha' (meaning 'The Enlightened One') is a title given to Siddhartha Gautama, born around 560 BCE in the foothills of the Himalayas. He left the comforts of home life, his wife, his child, the ritual honours of the high Brahman priests. As a hermit he experimented with various forms of austerity including breath-holding, which gave him headaches, and extreme fasting, which caused him to keel over and his hair to fall out. It was only following enlightenment, and his recognition of the mutual interdependence of all things, that he recognised a middle way between the luxury of his home life and the ascetism of the hermit, embarking on a journey of meditation and reflection.

Buddhism rejected the caste system, the notion that there was a creator god, that there was a single underlying substance in the universe or that there could be a concept of fixed individual identity (Atman and Brahman – see HEADSET). Who we are is entirely interconnected with the rest of reality and thus, being dependent on the inevitable incremental changes of the universe, is always in a state of transience and incompletion. Our identity, in other words, is something in movement, a process rather than a fixed entity. For the Buddha this was a profound realignment of self-knowledge, which needed to be personally experienced, not just rationalised or taught, and the road to this was through meditation.

Buddhism, of all the Eastern traditions, finds most common ground with the scientific approach of the West.

But its ambivalence, its 'middle way', its ambiguity in movement, makes it hard to categorise or pin down to any one philosophical school. Indeed the Buddha saw conceptual thought as a hindrance to enlightenment (see also RAKE). Cycling, on the other hand, finds a happy home in Buddhism. The softly ticking bike can, in its uninterrupted stretches, become a form of meditation in movement, a focused reflective attention which the practitioner, the cyclist, didn't even know they had signed up for. Buddhism places great emphasis on the fact that all of existence is transient, everything is in movement, and yet to understand this you have, for a moment, to be still. The coasting bicycle puts the rider at the centre of this new reality, a self-generated stillness that turns out to be anything but still in action. And what gives cyclists this experience, what gives us the freedom to understand the world in an entirely different way? Ladies and gentlemen, I give you the Freewheel, the liberating un-clock at the centre of the WHEEL (fixed-wheel cyclists please see CRANKS for 'flow' experiences).

The Freewheel is that part of the bike that allows you to coast forward while keeping the PEDALS still. Once housed within the REAR SPROCKETS, it is now more commonly found in the hub of the rear wheel itself, where it is known as the freehub. The Freewheel is made of a set of metal tadpoles called pawls, arranged like inverted apostrophes around the outside of a cylinder. This cylinder sits within a larger cylinder which has a series of notched teeth on its inside surface called ratchets. When the bike is driven forward by the circular motion of the CHAIN around the REAR SPROCKETS, the ratchet teeth of the larger Freewheel cylinder engage with the tips of the pawls underneath them, transmitting torque to the wheel axle and the turning motion of the WHEEL. When we hold our legs still, the Freewheel ratchets are frozen, and yet the Freewheel pawls continue to revolve under the momentum of the WHEEL. This is because the pawls of the inside cylinder slide their tails underneath the paralysed lip of the frozen ratchets and then flip back up again under the tension of a spring, ready to reengage with the ratchets when the pedalling motion begins again. The flipping of these pawls against the ratchets is what makes the ticking sound of a coasting, or freewheeling, bike.

If you, counterintuitively, brush a cat's back from tail to head the fur stands up. If you smooth it in the other direction, from head to tail, the fur lies down. The spitting cat with an Afro is the pedalling bike. The purring cat with a sleek coat is the Freewheel. It is the wheel within a wheel that gives the cyclist the grace of coasting, a term often associated with laziness, but which on a bike is a kind of attentive focus, a meditation so nuanced in intuitive engineering that we barely know we are the author of our own stillness. It is a rational magic that makes time stand still, that propels the world about us rather than us around the world, that makes us the unchanging centre of a clock face rather than the turning hands themselves.

Pedalling south alongside the ocean we met Hannah, a pretty blonde German girl, and Laksh, her long-haired Indian boyfriend, who were riding to the tip of India on a motorbike. We sat together at a shack on a breakwater, where the vendor lopped off the end of a coconut, popped a straw in and then hacked the curd onto a palm leaf. Laksh handed out four-leaved clovers he'd cut from green paper for good luck. His joy seemed to rise in him like a breaking wave; he had a propulsive eloquence and an inability to stay on topic, spreading positive thoughts around him like confetti at a wedding. He gave us his phone number and told us we should stay with him in Mumbai. We told them of the kindness we had experienced on the side of the road. They had too, but they also spoke of the hatred they had encountered, travelling as a couple from different backgrounds; the flipside of kindness in the small communities of India. And then, with a final flash of their bright smiles, he and Hannah climbed on their motorbike, and were gone.

Buddhism is better thought of as a vehicle, rather than the Hindu 'darsana' or view, a way to transport its passengers to a better place, free from the suffering imposed by an everyday illusion of reality. This journey begins at a crossroads, Buddha's recognition that all journeys, however linear they appear, are actually a series of interlinked connections. Central to Buddhist philosophy is interconnectedness. A bike CHAIN may suddenly break but this does not happen in isolation. The bike's GEARS may be inadequately adjusted, leading to a stuttering shifting onto the front CHAIN WHEELS, increased wear and a final snag that snaps the links. The owner may have been working long hours to visit a sibling who lives abroad and not had the time to maintain their GEARS. And the very reason they have a sibling is that their parents met at a particular time, and grew up in a particular cultural background, and so on and so on. From this central understanding of interconnectedness follow two other points.

It is because everything is interconnected and nothing remains still that one small change leads to another in an ever-unfolding movement. Interconnectedness and transience mean that there is no such thing as a fixed self or identity, only an ever-changing or transient self. We are always in a state of becoming. In order to understand the essential non-fixity of existence, you have to stop thinking for a moment and start *being*, take a step back from the constructions that prop up the stage set of reality. And that is why meditation has such a central role in Buddhism, as a practical, physical, intuitive investigation into the nature of transience, the non-permanence that is overlooked by the grasping nature of our thoughts, which are constantly searching for a definitive end point.

We might hope to hold on to whatever we have achieved, perhaps cling to a more youthful version of ourselves, but the reality of change means that a form of dissatisfaction is always around the corner. We crave the illusion of stability, a mirage that never quite arrives.

What the contemporary West finds appealing about Buddhism is its apparent rationalism; its appeal to evidence in the form of momentary personal experience, its rejection of dogma and its refusal to consider the afterlife or a creator god. But where they differ is in later Buddhist ideas of rebirth and karma. These have been neatly separated by the West to make a secular or humanist Buddhism that the West finds more agreeable (see DOWN TUBE).

Following the road through the state of Karnataka we met two other long-distance cyclists. Oz was arched over his handlebars like a lizard, with a cycling cap at a sly angle and no top on. He explained in a relaxed drawl that for the last eighteen months he'd been cycling with his girlfriend Aida through 'Russia, Mongolia, Central Asia, whatever...' Jen was chatting away to Aida, so I was stuck with Oz, and Oz was stuck with me. Later, he explained how he and Aida had been on separate silent meditations for a week. When they saw each other again, it was as if for the first time, every word having a pristine emphasis. Oz said that travelling with someone for a year was the equivalent of ten years in 'normal' life, given that you were together twenty-four hours a day, seven days a week. That week of being away from each other and not speaking to anyone was initially terrifying for both of them but, he explained as he swerved into me, 'You got to let go of your ego, man.' I swerved to avoid him and fell into the roadside gutter.

Meditation has always been a part of Hindu tradition but the Buddha emphasised its role. Meditation is essentially an act of attention; you concentrate your focus on the present and steer away from the daydreams and mental chatter that the conscious mind gravitates towards. Its focus can be on any simple, personal, recurring process, but is mainly on the breath, the rehearsal of air through the mouth or nose. Remembering to return to this attentive focus is the mindfulness, with which the West is so presently occupied. Regular meditation, over months and years, generates a reflexive state that is at once able to observe the restless character of the mind and body, and its lack of a fixed core or self.

The Western preoccupation with mindfulness is interesting given that Buddhist meditation in Asia, until very recently, was really the province of ordained monks and not widely practised by the lay public. Natural science in the West has accepted its validity, through evidence-based trials, and it has been having a honeymoon with the third wave of cognitive psychology as mindfulness-based cognitive behavioural therapy. But its arrival now is perhaps unsurprising. There has been a general fracturing of attention in Western culture, driven both by the accelerating choices offered by consumerism and the technology those choices rely on. Loss of attention is the problem, mindfulness is the solution. Like a battery pack for extended roving, mindfulness has been marketed beyond its evident value in mental health to niche choices that consumerism itself creates: mindful trekking, mindful upholstery, mindful interior design. Sometimes it feels like the role of mindfulness, as endorsed by the West, is not to make us feel calmer and happier and more attentive (which it surely does) but to do this solely so that we can return to the world of fractured inattention and get on with being a fully paid-up member of our ever-turbulent global economy. In this way mindfulness and meditation are used as a form of mental hygiene, disconnected from their philosophical or moral context. This needn't be a problem, if all we expect from life is the ability to watch a whole TV series *and* the ad breaks. The secular mindset of the West is such that it often rejects the 'dogma' of world religion and 'irrational' Eastern philosophy yet carves out a corner for corporate-mindfulness courses and spin sessions in the gym.

Do cyclists tease out their riding experiences as metaphysical or intellectual wisdom every time they peel off their cycling shoes? Unlikely. But the radical freedom of being on a bike, the inevitable collision of people and sometimes cultures, raises intellectual questions that then bear contemplation, perhaps even insight, within the meditative framework that cycling itself encourages. For me cycling to India was not just a meditation on the nature of identity but on the astonishing role of kindness, its moral force and intimacy, in a world that I'd thought had long ago given up on caring. Virtue, wisdom and meditation, the three intertwined processes that the Buddha valued, are part of all journeys, *if* we are alert to them, if we don't just count the miles but follow the pattern of our inner lives along the way.

The non-religious man and woman on the street, rolling past the market-driven universities, the NHS Portakabins, the emergent mind and body merchandisers, have found a way to reconnect these disconnections. The bike ride, in its own quietly meandering style, rethreads a past long undone. 'But what about walking, climbing, fell running, swimming and whale watching?' Yes, those too. But nothing wanders so efficiently, nothing *ranges* as far as the bicycle. It takes you further than any other human-powered transport. And if travel broadens the mind and stillness deepens it, then cycling surely steepens it; challenging us into realms we thought insurmountable, in a way that gives us the confidence to be free, before catapulting us down the other side with that very sensation.

Oz and I eventually made peace; he stopped grandstanding and I stopped feeling like his dad. We'd learned to hang out and talk bike mechanics and surfing, a chance overlap in the orbits of long-distance cyclists. Jen and I then continued cycling south but were becoming sick of National Highway 17 (now rebranded National Highway 66 – the Route 66 of India) and increasingly convinced that National Highway 17 would soon be sick of us. And so, much like other funnelling experiences on our journey, we pulled a handbrake turn and rode east towards the cooler hills of the Western Ghats. Over breakfast a villager in a longi sarong, with a long white beard, asked, 'What is your motherland?' (For many Indians India is a motherland, the goddess Bharat Mata where religion and national politics meet in a Hindu expression of the universal.) As he was leaving, almost to himself he said, 'Yes, you are a good man,' putting his hand to his head in a blessing. In rural India faith, philosophy and morality are all at work together, alongside the cooks and the crooks, the road sweepers and the traffic policeman. To cycle here is to cycle through this living philosophy but also through a never-ending existential interview.

'Where from?'

'What name?'

'What your goodname?'

'Where go?'

'What you do?'

'Who are you?'

If we understand there is no ego and there is no 'other', then selfishness theoretically disappears. If Christianity says love thy neighbour as thyself then Buddhism says love thy neighbour because thy neighbour is you. Buddhism teaches a set of precepts based on compassion. These are not categorised as right or wrong but as skilful or unskilful, depending on their context. For example a host offering more hospitality does not necessarily mean he is able to give it; the unspoken onus may be on the guest to refuse. This contextual morality fits with the interdependence at the centre of Buddhist philosophy. Does this mean that all Buddhists are kinder people? Or that all cyclists are kinder human beings? I think the jury is out on that. I've met a lot of unfriendly cyclists and a lot of moody Buddhists. But what Buddhism and cycling share is the *potential* for human flourishing in the here and now. Buddha asked his students to follow the path of enlightenment, not into an afterlife but right into the midst of our everyday lives.

Heading off on an unmapped road, far away from the trucks, we bumped into a procession of bare-chested drummers and musicians with crescent-shaped trumpets. And at the rear an elephant. There was the sudden shock of coming up against a five-metre-tall animal in a gold mask and then the sound of drums and trumpets reaching a crescendo. It was like hitting the buffers in a waking dream.

The leader of the procession burned some herbs on a palm leaf which he laid ceremoniously in front of the elephant. But ignoring all of this, a schoolboy, with his gaze fixed on us, asked:

'Where you from?'

'What your name?'

'What is your goodname?'

Behind this procession there was a phalanx of young men shouting and chanting and hitting drums, so closely packed that there was no way to pass them. 'Come on, come on,' one of them shouted in English, waving a fist in my face. Jen squeezed me on the shoulder and we rolled onto the pavement. Cycling in India is like riding the rapids; you have to stay afloat or get dunked.

Just before midday a man with a camcorder appeared alongside us, riding a motorbike one-handed, and asked if we could stop for an interview. It wasn't an offer, more of a statement. We were fed mini pakoras and tea and asked questions such as: 'What is your job? Do you have an arranged marriage? How many kilometres do you cycle a day? What is your qualification?' And then a villager in long orange robes appeared – 'the man who looks after nature'. He shook my hand vigorously as the interviewer explained that he planted trees up and down the road. After some consultation it was decided that we too should plant a tree, so he grabbed a cutlass from the back of his bike, cut a branch off the nearest neem tree, dug a hole by the side of the road, made us crumble soil over its erstwhile roots and then crush each other's hands under the bucket of water he poured over them.

In the traditional Christian world view man has a separate, individual, precious soul. There are clear dividing lines between all living creatures, of whom man is the higher caretaker, beholden not to those creatures, but to God above. Hinduism proposes that every individual has a single soul but that singular soul is part of an indivisible unity. Buddhism says not only is there no separate self or soul but that all things and beings are interconnected in an ever-changing dependency. The fourteenth Dalai Llama, Tenzin Gyatso, goes as far as to say that 'both science and the teachings of Buddha tell us of the fundamental unity of all things. This understanding is crucial if we are to take positive and decisive action on the pressing global concern with the environment.' This provokes a different conception not just of human identity but of human kindness, an ecological compassion that reaches beyond scientist, priest, monk, philosopher and layman and out into the land.

'As in science, so in Buddhism, understanding the nature of reality is pursued by means of critical investigation,' says the Dalai Llama. In this way a more open-minded teacher becomes a kind of peace negotiator, brokering a partnership between the distancing empiricism of science and the traditions which investigate subjective and physical experiences, our very personal relationship with the living breathing world around us. This demands a lack of dogmatism on all sides. It requires reciprocal travelling. From west to east and east to west.

It wasn't just the cycling, it was the constant questioning that was tiring us out as we climbed higher and higher into the hills of the Western Ghats. Personal space has a completely different meaning in India, its orbit much less defined. It's all very well me banging on about how interconnected the universe is and how we all need to reach out beyond our comfort zone, but sometimes you just want to sit in a room and listen to your own tinnitus. You can't help thinking the reason India became the meditation hub of Asia was one of the gurus put a DO NOT DISTURB sign on the door of his cave.

Jen and I cycled past a wind farm where each turbine had a different name. The blades turned lazily in the headwind we were rolling into. 'Like a drone on a bike,' I wrote, 'just going, going.' The next day we cycled through a tiger reserve. There were birds flashing past in brilliant orange and turquoise feathers and, for a change, we could actually hear their song. A park ranger told us that it had recently rained in the dry season. He kept on rattling off the rainfall figures, as if he felt compelled to let us know. This echoed our experience in Romania when a Transylvanian family explained how the mosquitoes had come to the Carpathian Mountains for the first time in living memory (see SADDLE). People across the world were becoming united not in familiarity but in change. The seasons, which had once been locked into a generational pattern, a regular recurrence celebrated in rituals and festivals, were slipping their infallible cycle. This had created deep disorientation, with meandering thoughts like worms, trying to head to the surface hearing the drumbeat of rain.

The interconnectedness of all things, the originating principle of Buddhist philosophy, spread through non-orthodox Mahayana Buddhism to the become the 'Hua-Yen' of Chinese Buddhism. Hua-Yen highlights the interpenetration of all things; suggesting that whatever there is, and whoever we are, always represents a greater whole. Like a dew point in a spider's web our individuality cannot be understood without the web that surrounds us and transmits the shivers of each joint. This almost ineffable sense of interpenetration is the closest Buddhism gets to religious mysticism (see Sufism in TOP TUBE) and is, if you like, another expression of the ecological warp and weft we are all bound within (and interdisciplinary scientists refer to as 'Gaia'). But at a personal level it also expresses a yearning disequilibrium, the shivers in the web as those junction points stretch and give way. On a bicycle, with its spider-like crawl across the vast maps of continents, you begin to recognise how a landscape varies with latitude and longitude. And you start to understand this in a *physical* way, with a quality not unlike 'Hua-Yen'. It is at the level of personal encounters on unmarked roads, in forgotten villages, at abandoned lay-bys. Old meetings that had once seemed trivial grip again like the tack of fresh glue at the next conversation. And if you want to get really expansive about it (and why not, I set up my stall a couple of hundred pages ago), Hua-Yen suggests that our skulls don't exist. Our brains with their one hundred trillion synapses link through our senses into the changing circuits of everything and everyone around us. The fundamental alterations in the planet, of which we are a part, inevitably interpenetrate back into a fundamental sense of who we are, crackling like untethered wires in a vandalised telephone box. With our home comforts, our frozen food aisles, our stacked-up shelves, our natural identity *appears* blunted and remote, unconnected to everything that surrounds us. But, of course, those interconnections are still there.

The higher we went the more we came upon hill after hill, scalp after scalp, of skinhead number three tea shrubs. Women with patterned headscarves wandered between the rows of shrunken trees with box-shaped scissors snipping the two most tender leaves and the bud, then tossing them into sacks on their shoulders before hauling them to roadside weighing scales. If we crushed the leaves between our fingers they had the brittle quality of ruptured tea bags, and when we rode past the tea processing factories you could smell the whiff of a good English cuppa. The air was cooler and the rows of symmetrically arranged tea plants induced an easy calm.

I raised the viewfinder to my eye and clicked. And as if activated by this, two of the tea workers waded over, shouting, 'Pen, pen.' We didn't have any pens so Jen gave them two fluorescent heart stickers she'd been handing out to kids to put on their bikes. The plantation workers pressed the hearts back under the webbing of Jen's pannier bags. It's hard to know what a tea plantation worker, in middle of a tea harvest, would do with a fluorescent heart. It was Jen's attempt at creating another kind of conversation on the road, inspired by Laksh and his four-leafed clovers. But for the tea workers, witness to a hundred camera clicks a day, it was a hard-nosed, biro-based economy. Cut-out paper hearts just didn't cut it.

The fourteenth Dalai Lama had this to say about Marxism (see SEAT POST):

Of all the economic theories, the economic system of Marxism is founded on moral principles whilst capitalism is concerned only with gain and profitability. The failure of the regime in the former Soviet Union was, for me, not the failure of Marxism, but the failure of totalitarianism. For this reason I still think of myself as half-Marxist, half-Buddhist.

Marx, whilst declaring religion to be the opium of the masses, did not simply see it as a stupefying drug, rather an understandable response to the heartless machine of capital. And it was disconcerting to ride through the bonsai tea shrubs, in a romantic mist of cloud, and yet be amongst these unregulated workers who understood us as 'pen pushers' from the lowlands. And then to find myself, years later, picking a pen through a paragraph, off the back of their picturesque lives.

After a complicated series of payphone calls we arranged to stay with Mr Joseph Iype, a tour guide whose bungalow sat right in the middle of the Munnar tea plantations. Our perseverance had more to do with Dervla Murphy, the Irish travel writer and cyclist, than with our host. Dervla rode to India from Ireland in 1963 aged thirty-one on a three-speed roadster with a revolver strapped to her leg, as recorded in her book *Full Tilt*. In the 1970s she travelled with her five-year-old daughters through India and met Mr Iype, who we were now visiting in his bungalow in a kind of tangential homage to *Full Tilt*.

We phoned him again from the bottom of the hill, and he told us he would wave a white handkerchief for us to follow. And it was in this way, slowly cycling towards his tiny white surrender in the sea of green, that we came to meet him. Mr Iype had aged handsomely, with a receding tannin forehead and black plastic spectacles. His front room offered plummeting views over the plantations. There was an old sofa with patterned seat covers and a wooden ornament against one wall from which hung fly-fishing hooks, head torches, Swiss Army penknives and, somewhat incongruously, a large chopping knife, still in its original wrapping. Without even time to catch our breath we were handed a cup of tea.

'Here is your Tetley's.' Mr Iype splashed in a dollop of white. 'You English,' he said, 'need a little bit of milk.'

This, I thought, was why we had carried on cycling through India, why we had carried on riding from the 'last empty beach in Goa', in order to visit Mr Iype in this room, which reminded me of my nan and my grandfather in the West Indies and my elderly neighbour in Bristol – to drink a cup of tea from its leafy bed. From our last mug of builders' in Portsmouth through all those cups of thé, cai, chai, those pauses, those sips, those glimpses into other people's lives, to here, the silence of a hill station atop the swell of a green-leafed sea.

From that day we took tea with Mr Iype like it was a medicine, a tincture, morning, afternoon and dusk. He told us that the rains in Munnar at the end of February were very unusual. We nodded and took a sip. He said that a month or so ago a man on the road had been killed by an elephant, and that as the jungle was being cleared, the elephants were coming out for their share of the food. 'Uhuh,' we said and took a sip. Last week, just in front of his house, there had been an elephant routing up the vegetable patch and eating all his sugar cane. 'Uhuh,' we said and took a sip. Older elephants, those rejected by the herd, became rogue, he said, and then took out their bitterness on man.

'On their fellow man,' I wrote in my journal. And took a sip.

The next day we came upon a gnarly Englishman walking along a ridge of tea plants with a Russian woman. He'd saved up enough money from fruit picking in England to ride around India on a single-speed bike that he'd bought here. It was cheap to cycle in India, parts were easy to find, and he could get his bike repaired anywhere. He hated India's mopeds and cars. He also seemed to hate Indians, calling them 'fucking idiots'. He told us he had been scammed all over the place. 'No one shafts me,' he said. The Russian woman was carrying an old SLR camera that used to belong to her dad and was taking pictures as we talked. She seemed entirely at ease with herself and India, unlike this fruit-picking Englishman, carrying around his anger like a kind of self-punishing thorn.

On our last evening in Munnar I gazed out across the swooping valley beneath Mr Iype's bungalow. The light through the recent rains was like weak tea, like a stain in a developing photo.

The story of Josaphat and Barlaam, a legend from medieval Europe, purports to be the tale of two Christian saints: a prince, Josaphat, who escapes the imprisonment of his royal father and meets a hermit, Barlaam, before converting to a new faith. In fact, the tale is a reworked biography of Buddha: his renunciation of his luxurious family life, followed by his hermit-like existence, before discovering the middle way of Buddhism. The story was revised from the original Sanskrit into Manichean, then Persian, then Arabic, migrating into Europe with the Islamic invasions, before finally emerging in Georgia in the tenth century and then Greek, Latin and finally English versions in the late Middle Ages. One of the allegories it contains, 'The Three Caskets', in which the suitors of a princess must decide between gold-, silver- and lead-lined caskets, was retold by Shakespeare in *The Merchant of Venice*. The hero of the play, Bassanio, chooses the lead-lined one, signifying the unimportance of worldly desire, as a singer sings, 'Tell me where is fancy bred. / Or in the heart or in the head? / How begot, how nourishèd?'

In other words, where do desires begin – do they come from the heart or the head, the passions or the intellect? And once begun, how do they grow? Buddha would answer this by saying that craving arises in the transience of all things, in the passing self, which is as impermanent as life itself.

Mr Iype woke us at dawn for our final treatment of tea and biscuits. He prodded my knee in a friendly way. And I wondered if this was some kind of farewell blessing. The next seventy kilometres would be all downhill. Literally. I didn't have to move my knees once. And it wasn't Mr Iype's saintly blessing, or the tea, that allowed this. It was the ticking, the endless ticking power, of the Freewheel.

When the PEDALS and the CHAIN are held still and the WHEEL is moving, a bike is freewheeling; the pawls inside the Freewheel, the flickering apostrophes, spring back and forth underneath the ratchet teeth above them. If all the pawls disengage the teeth at the same time you hear a *tick tick tick tick* sound. But if the pawls disengage alternate teeth, one after the other, they make a *tick tock tick tock tick tock* sound. By the mid-1970s the Japanese manufacturers Suntour and Shimano had cornered the market in bike parts and their Freewheels have a recurrent *tick tick tick tick* that makes no concession to the alternate beat of the *tock*.

In meditation the focus is on breathing; in Freewheeling it is on a ticking movement. In meditation we still our mind and notice our sensations and thoughts travel past; in Freewheeling we keep our legs still and notice the world career past us, objects departing through our fleeting perceptions. The outcome is an inner poise, an eye within a storm.

Am I saying that every time we nip down to the shops, narrowly missing the school run, we reach a state of meditative calm, a state of absolute absorption? No, but we set off in the right direction. And on a seventy-kilometre downhill stretch through an ever-changing landscape luminous with colour and incident, we learn implicit lessons.

I would like to tell you that by the end of that long descent I had reached some kind of enlightenment. But to celebrate our freewheeling experience I had, without an ounce of wisdom, eaten a six-course curry. If coasting is an example of meditative movement, then pedalling the next seventy kilometres on a bellyful of rice is like being sick without being able to vomit.

We arrived in Fort Kochi, on the coast of Kerala, as the sun was going down, using that familiar shim of riding faster towards the night, of trying to nudge an extra sliver of illumination before there was no light left to see by. And when we finally arrived at the hotel, I discovered, slung in the glow of a table lamp, the headline news: CRICKET WORLD CUP – ENGLAND VERSUS INDIA – IT'S A DRAW.

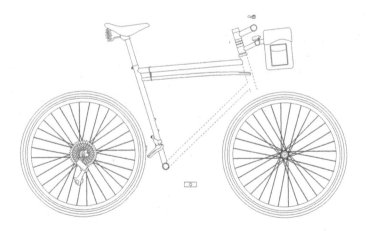

CHAPTER 21

The Rake

We followed the roads that clung to the beach, through fishing villages with Hindu statues and Christian churches, kids running towards us with their arms outstretched like planes. There were fishing webs strung, spider-like, across the backwater inlets, women weaving coconut hair into coir ropes, teasing it out from a pouch around their waist as they stepped backwards in the sand, men dyeing coir strands and lacing them with hand looms into rugs and mats, boats drawn up on the beaches between tsunami rock protection barriers.

In a string of villages there were lines of folded palm strips, hung from threads above our heads and across the road. Speakers nailed to the trees played out the same insistent tune, a tinny, jubilant, south Indian bhangra. The morning sunlight turned the palm strips into flights of birds. The India we had been cycling through was now shading into the cultural seams of south Asia, a sensual alteration.

We came to our last ferry stop on the side of an ocean inlet. Here a grandmother waited with her granddaughter, whose hair she kept stroking. Behind a rock a man slept in the shade. Gradually more and more people arrived: men in longis, boys on pushbikes whizzing around, closer and closer, shyly asking where we were from and what was our goodname. And still the boat did not come. The ferryman, it was explained, was having his breakfast. The sun ticked up into the blue sky. And, for a short time, just for a while, we became part of the village.

Finally, the ferry arrived, and then it was like a day trip, us in the hull of the boat with our bikes, passing rupees to the ferryman, festival pilgrims in orange longis on the rails above, joking and laughing, until someone explained we had cycled from Mumbai and the news was passed to them along the line. And then they were silent, and each of them bowed in turn with their palms together, and helped us with our bikes and bags off the ferry.

In Trivandrum, the last major city in the south, we booked the train tickets that would take us back to the north and Mumbai. Carrying bikes by train is a conundrum. In India they are locked away in the parcel carriage, with no guarantee they'll arrive at the other end. They will, eventually, reach their destination but not necessarily at the same time as you. This could mean a wait of twenty-four hours. It could mean a wait of two weeks. We'd booked passage on a container ship heading out from Mumbai in a week's time. Waiting around wasn't an option. Watching the SADDLES being wrapped up in paper and a label tagged to the frame was like watching your limbs being parcelled into Sunday joints at the butcher's. The booking office was a dusty, shadowy platform of randomly shaped boxes, bikes and motorbikes, wrapped in cardboard and paper like they'd been mummified before the final incarceration. No one was paying much attention to anything. Not least our bikes. I gave the porter a hundred-rupee tip to make sure they got on the train. We later saw them abandoned on the opposite platform. When the overnight express to Mumbai rolled in, our bikes disappeared behind it, and as we waddled up the platform with our bags we could only hope that they were also onboard, half a mile behind us in the parcel carriage.

To be separated from our bikes, from Billy and Bertle, was to be both released and imprisoned. We were taking the overnight train towards Mumbai over a route that had taken us six weeks to cycle. And we weren't even sure if we were travelling with the bikes that had taken us there in the first place. They either existed, or didn't exist, in a box somewhere behind us. If I, so used to being a part of the bike, began to accelerate away from the platform without it, would I feel like I was still cycling, my legs somehow paddling the air, like a stunt man who has jumped from a tall building? 'Hang on a minute,' I said to Jen, jumped off the train and ran for ten minutes back down the platform.

I shouted at a guard to open up the luggage carriage. He pointed at his watch. I made pedalling movements with my heels like the back end of a pantomime horse. He wrenched open the sliding door and I peered for a moment into the musty shadows: boxes, boxes, boxes and more boxes... I reached towards them, as if I could summon the bikes through some of kind of Jedi force. The guard swung the door closed and I pulled my arm out before the guillotine could snap on its rails. *Slam.* He pointed at his watch and blew his whistle like a snot rag. I ran the half-mile back to our carriage and hopped on a few minutes before the train pulled out. And this was how we left India's south, with a deep uncertainty that Billy and Bertle might be on their own journey, with no one there to oversee them.

People often think the Rake refers to the bend of the front forks of a bike. And the forks, when arcing forward to meet the axle of the front WHEEL, do have a rakish quality about them, the kind of gesture a card sharp might employ when picking an ace from underneath the table. In fact, the Rake, as a physical entity, doesn't exist at all. More plainly known as the offset, it is the distance between the axis of steering, the centre point around which the HANDLEBARS move, and the axle of the front WHEEL. It is this measurement, together with the angle of the HEAD TUBE, that determines a bike's trail, the distance between the steering axis and the point where a bicycle TYRE touches the ground. Which might all sound like so much engineering geekery. But the trail, the lag of a bicycle wheel behind the turning axis of the HEAD TUBE, is instrumental in how a bike steers, in other words its handling. For those of us who are devil-may-cares, it is this trail that allows us to ride no-handed.

A bicycle is in a continual state of falling sideways, even as it is moving. It may not feel like this because we make adjustments all the time. These adjustments are part of the process of learning to ride a bike, an act that has become so familiar it is part of who we are. When a bike starts to fall the HANDLEBARS lean in that direction, and the bike turns in that path, but the inertia of the rider keeps its mass moving forward over the WHEELS, realigning the centre of gravity and enabling the bike to remain upright, all as the bike is moving along. This in turn pulls the rider over in the other direction, and the whole leaning and steering process can begin again. As long as the bike is moving there is a continual act of balancing by falling. The faster the rider is going the more forward inertia there is to align the cyclist's centre of gravity and the less turning adjustments need to be made to stop the bike toppling over. This is why a bike feels more stable and easier to ride when it is moving faster. At the other end of the speedometer skilled riders and cycle couriers keep their bikes upright while stopped at traffic lights by making dramatic movements left and right with their body and the front wheel, without getting off the PEDALS, known as trackstanding.

The trail also affects how twitchy the steering of a bike is, and how readily it self-corrects the toppling effect of the rider's moving centre of gravity. A shorter rake and a long trail makes a bike more stable at lower speeds and hence less twitchy. At higher speeds the handling can become more twitchy, partly due to the gyroscopic movement of the wheels and the greater inertia of the rider. So far, so simple. But then there is the effect of the HEAD TUBE angle, the height of the BOTTOM BRACKET, the SEAT TUBE angle, and the distance between the WHEELS, all of which affect the position of the rider and their centre of gravity. And this isn't even including the overall speed of the bike and the turning cadence of the legs, influenced by the GEARS. The phrase 'as easy as learning to ride a bike' has never been so implicitly right and explicitly wrong. The more you read about the mysteries of keeping a moving bicycle upright, the more complex it becomes. The theories and counter-theories, the engineering calculations, compete with each other until the noise of algebraic chatter seems to be all that you can hear.

Zen has captured the Western imagination like no other Eastern philosophy, becoming a catch-all term for a kind of unperturbed focus. It is the elusive destination of a teaching that has long sought out a balance between thinking and doing.

When Buddhism arrived in Japan in the sixth century many of its ideas had already been shaped by the philosophy of Taoism. The Chinese philosopher Lao Tsu claimed that it was a mistake to understand reality as an underlying thing or collection of things. Tao – 'way' – is the natural flow of existence, an expression of the path of nature, a process, a movement, not a checklist. The first Buddhist teachers in China, subsequently known as the Patriarchs, developed a school of Buddhism called Chan, using elements of both Taoist and Buddhist ideas. If the foundation of Buddhist philosophy insists that everything is interconnected, that all is transient and there is no such thing as a fixed self, then Chan goes one step further and declares there is no such thing as a fixed idea, there is no such thing as a fixed concept. To rephrase this in the paradoxical terms in which Zen so delights – cyclists do not ride bikes and there is no such thing as cycling. To conceptualise in this way removes us from the true nature of reality.

Zen has made the annihilation of concepts a guiding principle; it suggests we need to be liberated from the analytical perspective of thinking, which only muddies our clarity and sets us apart from the interconnected nature of reality. In Zen Buddhism insight comes not from long philosophical debates, nor from the close reading of doctrinal texts, but in a flash of enlightenment. It can be divided into two main schools, Soto, based on a calming meditation, similar to all Buddhist traditions, and Rinzai, which also employs paradoxes, riddles, proverbs and provocative statements to shock us into a new realisation. The irrationality of the paradox often has no meaning and serves more as a way to disorientate and fragment rational thinking, cracking the mirror in which we see ourselves. The riddles of the Zen masters were often recorded as koans, of which the most well known is 'What is the sound of one hand clapping?' The Zen pupil who provides a rational answer has often misunderstood the nature of the question, whose aim is to provoke, to confound, to rattle the cages of the mind, to wake us from the sleep states of our self-centred reality and stretch us into the Buddha nature of the limitless horizon. The question for us then, after all the engineering equations have fallen to the ground like so much storm debris, is not how do you ride a bike no-handed, but how do you steer a bike with no hands?

Jen and I had two sleeping cots, one above the other, in the train carriage. The bottom cot unfolded into seats, where Jen and I sat facing each other, knees tucked in. Our window had an orange tint to filter the sun but this didn't allow India's true colours to shine through. Luckily, at the end of the carriage there was an open door through which you could see India racing by in its original golds and greens. There were no health and safety signs here, no railings, no protection to stop you falling out as the train rattled over a bridge with a river rushing a hundred feet below. An Indian traveller swung himself out of the door with one hand on the grip, watching the evening sun go down. Closer to life. Closer to death.

With enlightenment there is a profound understanding that we are indivisible from all that surrounds us, and the consequence of this is a liberating spontaneity and a more anarchic take on morality. This does not mean that the Zen practitioner acts without compassion for others. True enlightenment, by breaking down the illusory barriers between self and others, encourages compassion for all, compassion that is expressed in kindness towards living creatures. But Zen's emphasis on intuitive understanding, unrestricted by self-regarding reason and self-consciousness, encourages a spontaneous approach to living, a moment-to-moment playfulness that resists structures and definitions and defies the conventions of authoritarian rule. This living-in-the-moment spontaneity has been criticised as another way of abrogating responsibility, but Zen does not propose that we disappear into the realm of spontaneous paradox. Its followers attain insight and then return to the everyday world with a new understanding and a clearer sense of selfless purpose. The individual who seeks to free themself from the responsibilities of society and family purely as an end in itself, will not attain this same understanding. You cannot purchase enlightenment like a chocolate bar from the corner shop. There is, however, an interesting parallel between Zen and those cultures where it appears to have found its natural home. If capitalism implies that everyone has the capacity for individual gain, to seek added value through profit, then Zen emphasises, at least on a surface reading, the possibilities of individual enlightenment and self-gain for those who have the time and the money to pursue it.

The Indian man hanging out of the door, gazing at the sunset, was more likely expressing his spontaneity rather than any intuitive philosophy or moral stance. But watching him spreading his hand into the wind, it was hard not to think that this itself was a philosophy, of stepping out into the flow of the world, a way of understanding with the whole of your body.

Jen thought that train travel was more reflective than cycling, that you could glance out of the window and see a girl walk past or a woman hanging out their washing, and you could then contemplate their lives. When you were on a bike you were *in* their lives and you had your own physical pains and preoccupations. But, I replied, a train doesn't power your journey, it feels like something else is creating the picture on the other side of the tinted windows as the waiters wander up and down shouting 'Chai Tea, Chai Tea, Chai Tea.'

For those who know their bikes well and maintain them over thousands and thousands of miles there is also a loving Zen in their mechanics, in the well honed muscle memory that achieves a water-like flow of calibration, a spanner that finds its bolt before the thought makes it so. But Zen also rejects repetition and mimicry of any kind. So as soon as you saddle cycling with the label of Zen, it is no longer truly Zen, a term that is defined by its very lack of fixity. Zen is to cycling as it is to digging the soil or flying a kite or folding a piece of paper; it is a vehicle to insight, it is not the insight itself. Cycling, like many Eastern practices, creates the conditions that make insight possible, but it does not contain a separate Zen-ness, like water in a bottle. You could equally argue that it is *not* the flow in cycling that is Zen but the juxtaposition of stop and start, the sudden anger of hunger, the slap of hail on your face, the sudden illogical twists in the road that shake our contemplation into a different direction. Cycling is not the answer to a question, any more than Zen is a solution to a problem. It is just a vehicle. But it is a particularly mutable one, which refuses to remain upright unless it is moving, which will not follow the monorail of the tram track, which bucks the rider who insists on staying still, which rewards the person who is moving into stillness.

A Zen monk, when not meditating, is often engaged in some menial occupation that seeks to recover from any lapse into solipsism or introspection which might alienate the mind from the body. Cycling can be a meditation but also a mundane occupation. It is not hermetically sealed, but contains the possibility of retreat. It does not correspond to the trials of the dedicated Zen monk, but there are some cyclists who take it to that level in a decade-long discipline that parallels the persistence of the Zendo monastery. These cyclists live on little, take what is necessary and move on for tens of thousands of miles. I would not saddle them with philosophy nor would they want that. They have clearly exceeded the garden to which most of us have allotted our lives.

But that garden, our humble apportionment, of commuting to work or weekends away, can be a ten-year journey in itself. This is what Zen tantalises us with. That if we are diligent, if we push ourselves with the whole of who we are, we can see the world in a grain of sand or the infinite grains blowing across a desert road, a thousand miles from home.

I returned to my seat and watched India shutter past in the tangerine stain of the compartment window. Through the glass and in the window's reflection I saw myself, that self at one remove. I am not Anglo-Indian though I have that knocking around my genes. I am very English, socially neurotic and, I would say, lower middle class, a splitting of hairs that suggests a surrender to, but also a rejection of, the caste system of Britain.

During that train journey I began reading *Midnight's Children* by Salman Rushdie. Its narrator is an Anglo-Indian child who has Indian parents as a result of a mix-up at birth. This child, Saleem, is born on the midnight hour of India's independence from the UK with the psychic ability to hear the thoughts of all the other children born in India at that time. But the moment of India's independence is also the chime of India's partition with Pakistan, a violent segregation drawn arbitrarily in red ink.

What I took from Rushdie's book was not the treachery of British rule but something much more positive about the recombination of identity, the ability of an individual to transcend the chopping blocks of history, an imaginative metaphor that recognises no boundaries, that crosses all divisions.

If cycling to India to find myself was always going to be a circular journey, then cycling to India to understand its philosophy was even more problematic. The further east you go the more philosophy resists definition, certainly in the rational terms demanded by the West. If Zen resembles anything it is the mysticism of esoteric Christianity and Islam (see Sufism in the TOP TUBE), with its defiance of logic and reasonable explanation. But unlike those religions there is no worship of a god, there is no personal encounter with the other, there is no afterlife or before-life, and there is a rejection of scripture and dogma. What Zen does share with these mystical encounters is a dissolving of the boundaries of me and you, mine and yours, an experience of reality that exceeds the capacity of language. From a rational, or Western, standpoint it is very easy to criticise Zen enlightenment on these very grounds; what are you trying to hide if you cannot describe it? All the experiencer is left with are generalisations like enlightenment, awakening, infinite, expansive, which once repeated begin to lose their meaning. Zen argues this is because the human tongue is not an adequate organ for expressing the deepest truths of Zen. In other words, the fault lies not in mysticism but in language itself, which cannot begin to share an experience that goes beyond concepts, beyond thought and is unmediated by ideas.

'If you meet Buddha on the road kill him' (Linji Yixuan, ninth-century Chan master). This does not mean take a pistol to the fat guy, but rather destroy any notion, any concept, any belief, that you might passingly entertain. D. T. Suzuki, the major transmitter of Zen Buddhism to the West, said, 'All the Buddhist teachings as propounded in the sutras and sastras [the original words of the Buddha and their subsequent commentaries] are treated by Zen as mere waste paper whose utility consists in wiping off the dirt of the intellect and nothing more.'

Zen reframes, restates and demands that, having cycled four thousand miles to get here, the only way to really understand the philosophy of cycling is to get back on the road again and ride.

|

|

|

|

|

|

|

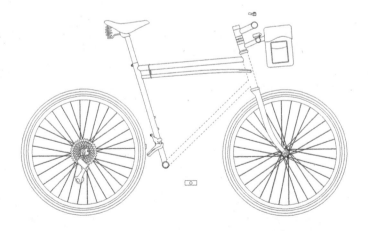

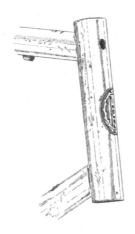

CHAPTER 22

The Head Tube

I left Jen with our pannier bags and legged it the half-mile to the other end of the platform. And there, just visible in the luggage carriage, were our bikes, hidden by parcels from the intervening stations from Trivandrum. I wheeled them back to Jen, and thence to the taxi rank, where, in a bit of a scrum, the driver with the largest people carrier claimed us. Non-folding bikes were never meant to be rammed into cars, and non-folding taxi drivers were never meant to ram them in there. Jen's mudguard was snapped off, and she shouted; no one much seemed to care, and then we were off into the chaos of Mumbai.

Zen Buddhism tells us that the best way to understand reality is not to try to understand it in the first place. Thought, reason, concepts. Gone. It is only in action that our existence can be seen for what it is. Some critics have suggested this is an overromanticised view of Zen, the one imported into America in the twentieth century and that the original Buddhist sutras and sastras were widely studied by the Zen masters before Zen practices became the dominant theme. In other words, before you reach the point where thought is no longer necessary, before concepts fail you at the last hurdle, you first have to do some thinking. And so it is that we return around the triangle of the frame, back home towards the West, our bikes rammed into the vault of a people carrier like so many broken scaffolding poles.

The Head Tube is a top slice off a triangle, the edge of a wedge of cheese whose point has been removed for a bit of a taste. It effectively makes the front triangle of the bike frame into an irregular quadrilateral. But let's not get too pedantic. The Head Tube is a nifty piece of tubing that contains the steering column of the front forks, connecting them to the HANDLEBARS by the STEM and HEADSET. The Head Tube, like the SEAT TUBE, is all about securing the comfort and position of the cyclist. A steeper, shorter Head Tube suits racers, who want a lower position and more responsive steering. A longer, more laid-back Head Tube gives a smoother ride for the touring cyclist (which sounds like a quote from an old cigarette packet). If this angle is too lazy you get wheel flop, the frame builder's equivalent of brewer's droop, where the bike abruptly oversteers past a certain point and you go round and round in circles.

Mumbai is not a place that gives up its living accommodation easily. It is, by any standard, overpopulated; 40 per cent of its people live in slums and over 50 per cent of households have one room only. Laksh, who we'd met on our bike trip south, let us sleep on his sofa in his small apartment close to the shore. Staying with Laksh was like watching a spinning top dance across a table. He was eloquent, distractable, impulsive, kind, fast, funny; moving from one topic to the next with the unquenchable joy of someone who has just bounced out of bed. 'Blanket terms are for blankets,' he would say and 'That sofa is hard to sit on. You don't sit on it. It sits on you. Like the government.' When Laksh wasn't speaking he would chant classical Indian songs softly, using an electronic drone box to harmonise with.

Laksh took us to visit his mentor and singing teacher, Asha, now in his eighties, who lived up an old wooden staircase in one of Mumbai's busiest districts in a one-bedroomed flat. Asha wore a white long-sleeved shirt and trousers. He had short grey hair, bifocal glasses and a sureness and grace. One by one his students turned up, bowed in respect as he blessed them, and then sat around the perimeter of the small room, placing their mobile phones beside them to record his songs. He enquired after our welfare, whether we'd had enough food and told us we should stretch our legs and relax if we needed. 'The health resort area is over there,' he said, pointing to a sink in the corner of the room. And then he began to sing note variations, gesturing the pitch and rhythm with the fingers of one hand. He would sing a line of raga and his audience would repeat it. Accompaniment came from a four-string tanpura and slow beats and quivers emerging from an electronic box. The men checked their mobile phones, and even Asha, as he sang the lines of a verse and demonstrated the intervals with the fingers of one hand, seemed to be texting with the other. Laksh said that when Asha was younger he was able to sing two hundred and sixty notes in a single breath.

Laksh also told us the story of how he had once rung Asha to enquire about his welfare, 'I'm fine,' his mentor had replied, only for Laksh to later discover he had been in an intensive care unit at the time of his call. 'You told me you were fine,' Laksh protested. 'Oh, I was,' said Asha; 'it's just my body wasn't doing so well.' Laksh said that Asha was the happiest person he knew, which was quite something, given that Laksh himself seemed to take so much delight in the world. But going back that night in the taxi Laksh returned to the theme he'd first raised when we'd met him by the side of the road – the hate in small Indian communities, terrible acts committed behind closed doors, the intolerance of some of his countrymen for other races and religions, their interest in Hitler and Nazism. He became more and more vocal and passionate, pointing out the Hindu and Muslim genocides in the history of his country. He wondered out loud what would happen if the rule of law collapsed, what violence would be committed and what moral codes would be violated.

I argued that the majority of people were kind, that there was violence back in Bristol and across Europe, and that the further east we'd travelled the more openness and gratitude we'd found. Laksh and his girlfriend Hannah wondered if we stayed longer whether we would see more darkness underneath the roadside stones and fewer smiles and waves. Hannah and Laksh were kind, spontaneous, heartfelt travellers, but my most-people-are-good line wasn't going to wash with them.

On the front door to Laksh's flat was the Zen line NO SNOWFLAKE EVER FALLS IN THE WRONG PLACE, and on the back a bag of the four-leaf clovers he would hand out to anyone he met. Laksh was an impetuous sower of karmic seeds, as if to undo the shadows all around him.

Of all the religions in India, Jainism has the most to say about pluralism, about the value not just of different kinds of people but of different kinds of ideas rubbing along together. Mahavira, a spiritual seeker, developed this religious philosophy in the sixth century BCE, incorporating elements of both Buddhism and Hinduism. Jainism teaches that the self is a permanent part of a wider whole (see Hinduism in HEADSET), non-permanent (see Buddhism in FREEWHEEL), both permanent and non-permanent, and to cover all the bases, inexpressible (it can't be stated either way). Jainism suggests that not only can you have your cake and eat it but you can have a slice of everyone else's too. This isn't simply a case of wanting to be all things to all people; the

Jain principle of multisidedness is a philosophical model that in its flexibility anticipates the scientific enquiry of the West. Can, for example, a four-sided triangle, as in the front part of a bike frame, still be a triangle? Well it depends on who's doing the naming. Jainism explores how all views are subjective, influenced by the observer, by our background and cultural history. Even if a philosophical point appears to be wrong, it should be ushered into the debate, engaged with and challenged. This open tolerance of other viewpoints was particularly bold at a time in Indian cultural history two thousand years ago when so many beliefs and religions were vying for dominance. You might argue that where all truths have equal status there is no central steering principle; Jainism suggests that there are 'right' answers but they have to be experienced, prodded and tested, on both a subjective and objective basis, before admitting their lasting insight. In the meantime, diversity should be respected, common ground nurtured, and bridges built.

Western academic philosophy has long since rejected its role as a mediator in our relationships or in global crises. Jainism, within the plurality of Eastern traditions, has been a part of those discussions for thousands of years and remains so.

Whether or not you believe in an animating force in nature (Jainism does), it is indisputable that our ecological systems depend on each other and the substrate of the landscape, organic and non-organic, to sustain them. For hundreds of years scientific institutions were so blinkered by their empirical findings that they failed to see the wider global shifts taking place in climate and geological systems all around them. It took a coherent metaphor, James Lovelock's Gaia, to galvanise an interdisciplinary shift in the way science engaged with the living world. This self-same metaphorical understanding, powered by an animistic awareness, was the lingua franca of our 'primitive' forebears thousands of years ago. It allowed seasonal variation and the wider biological consequences of that variation to be brought together as stories of interacting symbols. In the intervening period these stories and symbols have been dismantled into categories and boundaries we can no longer see over the top of. The Eastern traditions, within their religious systems, have preserved a respect for this widescreen view, once derided as a throwback to Neanderthal times, but now at the cutting edge of our very survival and understanding.

Jainism argues that the universe is made up of two kinds of constituents, non-living karmic matter and *jiva*, a living soul or animating force. But it does not separate the two in the same way as the Cartesian division of body and mind. Particles of karmic matter interact with *jiva* to create the complexities of material existence. Much like the animism of ancient paganism, this suggests there is a compelling, living, energy within everything. Science has long sniffed at such vitalism, that there is a force other than the chemical and physical actions of the material world. While scientists use metaphor all the time in their work they do not always see it as a primary source, as a way to yield a broader, non-empirical truth.

The multisidedness of Jainism suggests that not only should all human perspectives be heard and valued, but their non-human counterparts too, from the tiniest microbe to the largest elephant, from the geological formation of rocks and minerals to the landscapes they form. This is not just another flag-waving exercise for 'interconnection' but a surrender of human egotism, where the definition of life, of the energising units that build our universe, is broadened exponentially. Which itself leads to playful questions like, 'should the White Cliffs of Dover be given a voice on Kent County Council?' 'Should mountains have a say in the building of hydroelectric dams?' To cycle across countries is to feel the ripple of these contours, these phonemes, the imaginary voices of the valleys and rivers, a grown-up conversation that the planet, and the un-united nations, needs to have with itself.

To tune into the loss of the environment, and then to suggest that its loss is also our own loss, is to bear a kind of mystical grief and guilt (see TOP TUBE). For many, if not most of us, it's a lot easier just to bury our heads in virtual reality and set ourselves adrift from our bodies. But the price of this denial is a lack of integrated meaning; a sense of disorientation, a loss of triangulation. With the decline in religious observation, we have been left to pick 'n' choose our own meanings. The boldest choice is the existential one (see SEAT TUBE) – we accept responsibility for our lives and make up our own meanings. But in the free market of the Enlightened West many of us just buy a template off the shelf, any life-defining purpose, from celebrity watching, to sport, to New Age spirituality, available by FedEx or for immediate download. But by buying into those categories as a singular purpose for our lives, by switching off from a more unified understanding of the world, we are less able to know our place in it.

It is possible to ride your bike in Mumbai, just not very fast. Once you're in a line of taxis the honking clot of traffic shuffles forward predictably enough and you plod along with everyone else. As I rode around I saw a beggar with no legs outside a Porsche showroom, was showered with petals in the flower garland markets in the underpasses and had my glasses repaired by a man who refused to accept payment and said, 'Go with a smile.' The pavements were a torrent of people that carried everyone along, and seemed, on the surface at least, to buoy up even the flimsiest; even the beggars seemed to be borne along with all the jostling elbows and the mobiles held to ears. Everybody in Mumbai appeared to be in transit from somewhere else, from the cultural and religious demands of their childhoods, from India itself.

A short walk from Laksh's flat was the muddy foreshore with wide-open views across the bay and the city skyscrapers. Here we discovered the *shush* of the waves, lovers walking arm in arm and vendors selling peanuts cooked in hot ash. There was also the smell of shit from a slum down the road and a cow standing by itself in the flat grey ocean with a crow on its back, like an extra in a film that would never be shot.

Well over a century ago, on a rural road in mid-Wales, two of the most prominent intellectuals in British history collided with each other on bikes. The philosopher Bertrand Russell, preoccupied with his work on non-Euclidian space, according to one report, was reading a signpost on the way to Tintern Abbey, an outpost of Romantic animism (see Wordsworth's poem 'Lines written a few miles above Tintern Abbey'), when the playwright and essayist George Bernard Shaw came zooming down the hill and crashed into him, which catapulted Shaw twenty feet in the air. The playwright dusted himself off and carried on cycling. Russell, on the other hand, bicycle broken and trousers torn, had to go home on the slow train, having to endure Shaw sticking his head into his carriage at stopping platforms along the way to take the mickey.

This is the type of catastrophic crash needed to damage the incredibly strong reinforcing geometry of a bike frame, a crack that often shows just behind the Head Tube, where it meets the weaker join with the DOWN TUBE. If not properly repaired, the split can run vertically and may, with a less dramatic bump, burst open the Head Tube, releasing the forks and dumping the rider on the road. Although Russell's bike was a write-off, Shaw continued to ride his, and we might have expected it to have a few cracks. His biographer Michael Holroyd describes Shaw's tendency to 'raise his feet to the handlebars and simply toboggan down steep places' and that 'Many of his falls, from which he would prance away shouting, "I am not hurt," with black eyes, violet lips and a red face, acted as trials for his optimism.'

The playwright remained interested in cycling and transport throughout his life, and in his nineties joined the Interplanetary Society, advocating space transport.

In his early years he was a fervent rationalist and an atheist but by middle age described himself as a 'mystic' in his affiliations. He also said, 'I adore so greatly the principles of the Jain religion that I would like to be reborn in a Jain community.' He was notoriously contrary and many of his opinions were deliberately provocative. But his vegetarian, naturist, ascetic and pacifist views, his wandering multisided opinions, show a Jainist tendency that survived the collision of the opposing ideas of the twentieth century.

Perhaps not surprisingly George Bernard Shaw and Bertrand Russell did not spend much time down the pub buying each other pints, but what they did share was a commitment to pacifism. Bertrand Russell, in contrast to his aloof philosophical stance, was a vocal advocate of human rights, supporting non-violent direct action. He was arrested by police aged eighty-nine during an anti-nuclear protest and was a founder member of the Campaign for Nuclear Disarmament. And this is where his life story meets that of Satish Kumar, an activist and writer now living in Devon in the UK.

Kumar ran away from a Jainist monastery in India aged eighteen, after reading a book by Gandhi. On hearing of Bertrand Russell's non-violent campaign for nuclear disarmament he decided to embark on a 'peace pilgrimage' around the world and was on the road for four years. He and his companion travelled by foot, without money, relying on the kindness of others to give them food and shelter, delivering packets of tea leaves to world leaders as peace offerings. He went to Moscow, Paris, London and Washington DC, and it was while in England that he met Bertrand Russell. It was a partial meeting of minds, according to Kumar. Russell argued the case for nuclear disarmament from a rational perspective, the logistical madness of the bomb, whereas Kumar was advocating a wider change in human understanding, a shift from human to planetary welfare, and a conception of society that looked towards Gandhi's small-scale economics, and away from materialism. Russell argued there was no time for such idealism and that the hand of world governments needed to be forced by clear ethical principles, structured by reason.

We might now consider it naive to hand out bags of peace tea, to hope for a shift in political and philosophical perspectives towards a more unitary, non-dualistic understanding of man and nature. However, a revolution of the head, of the kind that George Bernard Shaw would have called a creative revolution, is now needed to wake us up. The foghorns on the rocks do not sound from rational logicians or travelling Gandhists, but from alterations in the land and weather, unarguable forces that threaten to tear apart the rule book of the Western imagination. The East is already in the West and has long been so, both philosophically and culturally. Any new world philosophy will have to be a philosophy *of* the world, that outstrips the binary divisions of West and East and the national borders that ostensibly separate us. The new nationalisms sweeping the West feel like hurried stage props to shore up a creaking set. Global capitalism is fast knocking down state borders but will discover not new troves of natural resources but a renegade philosophy that will spit in its eye. This will not be the wholesome holism of gentle persuasion but the arm lock of planetary change, the dust storms of the sparser fields, the wildfires stripping out the green corridors, the hard smack of the bare plate on the table.

On a petrol station forecourt, just before we left Mumbai, I rang up the agent for the container ship, the same man who had deposited us in an unruly heap in India six weeks previously. He told us we needed to pay 1600 rupees up front for 'customs fees'. He said it was 'unofficial' and, 'If you don't bring the money don't bother coming,' before hanging up. The petrol station attendant, who had been watching me rant at my silent phone, walked over.

'Is people OK?' he asked.

'Ugh,' I said.

'How you find people in Bombay?'

'Some good, some just want...' I rubbed my thumb and finger together.

The man pointed at his own fingers. 'We all have five fingers. Some small, some long, some different shapes.' He sent us on our way with a five-fingered wave.

After a short ferry trip we returned to the Uran Plaza Hotel, the same beachfront accommodation we'd used for our first few days in India. Six weeks previously, the place had made me homesick for my grandfather's house in the West Indies (see HEADSET). It was now clear why. The proprietor of the Uran Plaza, a retired navy admiral in his eighties who'd been away having a hip operation, had returned. And his hotel, which had the same ocean breeziness as my childhood memories, had been spruced up. There was a new lick of paint, the grass had been cut and the litter picked up. And Admiral Pereira was sitting by the table outside his house, reading the *Harvard Business Review*, when we introduced ourselves.

'I'm half English,' he said. 'Mother was from Stockport, father came over as an Indian soldier in World War I, shrapnel injury to the brain, met her in hospital.' He paused to take a closer look at us. 'Jenny darling, come over here. I want to see you properly. You're lean as a bean.'

Admiral Pereira was an unusual-looking Indian man, well over six foot tall, and thin with a slight stoop from his recent operation. He said he'd originally purchased the land when he'd been working at the local naval base and he'd planted all the coconut trees here himself. He'd designed his own house, which had a sweeping white triangular roof, fashioned like a spinnaker sail, directing the coastal breezes inside. It had a light, empty, playful simplicity, in contrast to the lumpen Hard Interchange, the concrete travel hub we'd left behind four thousand miles and ten months ago in Portsmouth (see BOTTOM BRACKET).

The admiral, who had no compunctions about dropping famous names, told us he'd met Lord Mountbatten, Indira Gandhi, been Jackie Kennedy's chaperone in India and designed the first ever aircraft seat belt. He tried to find the cricket on the TV to show me how poorly England were doing and addressed his hotel staff like naval ratings: 'Repeat that food order back to me.' But they all very much respected their boss, a character quite unlike anyone else we'd met.

My great-uncle Sir Arthur McDonald, my grandfather's brother, was raised on the Caribbean island of Antigua with my grandfather and, like my grandfather, educated in England. He joined the RAF and in 1936, in the run-up to World War II, commanded Biggin Hill, setting up the radar network behind the Battle of Britain. He was responsible for those map dioramas with wedges of friendly and opposing aircraft being pushed across Europe on the end of long croupier poles. Sir Arthur ended his career as commander in chief of the Pakistan Air Force, after its partition from India. When Arthur wasn't flying he was sailing, representing Britain in the Olympics and winning his last competitive race age ninety-two. As a shy teenager I crewed for him off the south coast of England and had a kind of steering dyslexia, always going hard to port when he was telling me to go hard to starboard. I'm not sure I could have piloted a plane or skipped across the ocean, but I think I found in cycling my own kind of flight. There is still in me a British pride rooted in the Victorian idea of enlightened progress, of rational exploration, of reasoned justice, of team ethics.

My bike was by now so well maintained it was in danger of cracking under the strain of its own adjustment. Just as Jen was trying to hold my hand and go for walks through the palm groves, I was retreating into the mechanics of bicycle efficiency, cleaning the CHAIN link after obsessive link. The unintended effect of this was to gather a small crowd of Uran Plaza Hotel staff, who watched silently as I gave Bertle an oil bath the like of which an Indian Hercules has never seen. 'He's eighty-nine,' the head waiter finally blurted out, as if it didn't matter how much I attention I gave my bicycle, the mysteries of growing old would always prevail.

The officials at Nhava Sheva port were kind and courteous and brought us tea and curry as we waited five hours for the port agent to come and take our 'tip' and a little bit of our dignity. We were then bundled into separate jeeps by his cronies, our bikes sticking out the rear, bouncing across the runway-sized concrete, through the customs shack and onto the portside, where we were dumped like so much unwanted baggage.

Jen and I stood with our bikes next to the monolithic hull of the ship. No one had told us what to do so we tried to pedal the last few hundred yards in the moonlight, two small somethings in a massive wasteland of everything. If the philosophy of the East tends towards the cosmic, the universal, then shipping ports do nothing to suggest it is on the wrong track. The crew leaped out of the darkness to stop us flying off the edge and then led us, and our bikes, up the gangplank. At the top of the living quarters I could see the British ensign rippling in the offshore breeze.

We were back in the UK, on a floating island of money, berthed in the harbour of India.

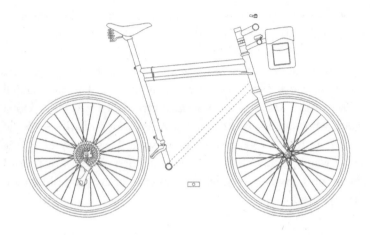

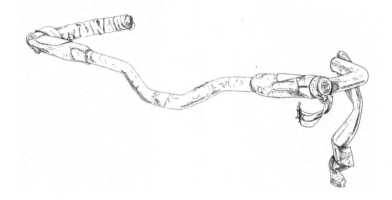

CHAPTER 23

The Handlebars

It didn't take long to find the exercise bike in the corner of the recreation room. And I began pedalling for all I was worth. Through a porthole I could see the ocean and, owing to the up-down side-to-side motion of the pedalling, it felt like the ocean was moving in jumps to my own knock-kneed revolutions. In other words, I was powering a seventy-five-thousand-tonne container ship as it chugged through the Indian Ocean. But in reverse. The exercise bike was pointing in the opposite direction. And I couldn't stop. I just couldn't stop pedalling.

We'd been on the road continuously for almost two months and the voice in my head was going, 'Look, mister, enough with the cycling. Chill out!' But the body was having none of it. 'Listen, mate,' it said. 'These muscles have been cycling almost continuously for the last ten months. We don't do stairs. We don't really do chairs. Certainly not chairs with backrests.' And so I found myself circling the exercise bike. Or rather it circled me.

And before I knew it I was on a shiny plastic seat going nowhere and everywhere at the same time. I'd become an air-conditioned hamster in the cage I was trying to escape a year ago.

The further east we sailed the more time slipped. 'All crew, please note clocks go back half an hour,' a tannoy announced. And, as if by magic, all the ship's clocks retreated by the same amount, connected by an invisible network behind the plywood panelling. This only added to the sense of unspooling what had already been spooled, day after day, mile after mile, click after click. And what surprised me was just how boring this not-cycling was. It reminded me that the actual act of revolving your legs, without any Handlebars to steer, was dull. I found myself flinging my hands in front of my chest in the open-palmed gesture of a rapper in full flow. Here I was on a boat in the middle of the Indian Ocean rapping to a SAFETY FIRST poster. Not-cycling made me realise what cycling actually is. It's not about the muscles, the kilometres, the kilojoules. It's about the steering, the control that all other transport systems try to wrest away from us.

The issue of free will has preoccupied Western philosophers for thousands of years. Do we have a distinct, individual, free choice in our affairs, or is this merely an illusion, the outcome of predetermined links in a chain – from genes to biology to society? Those who believe that we have no free choice, that our fate is pinned out like an exercise bike bolted to the floor, are known as determinists. At the other end of the scale are the libertarians, those who say we have complete free will, and that there is no such thing as predetermined fate. The chill-inducing libertarian movement, most evident in right-wing America, believes that we are all capable of reaping the material rewards of society, if only we choose to do so. This includes the poor, the neglected, the marginalised, the excluded, who according to the libertarians have no one to blame but themselves, an argument that ultimately leads to the proposal 'There is no such thing as society.' But the determinist perspective hardly seems more agreeable. If, in a simple process of cause and effect, our thoughts and intentions are merely the result of material imprints in the synapses of our brains, then all we are is a computer program running on the hardware of a genetically determined autopilot. The machine has already been nailed to the floor. Press Go and get pedalling.

The compromise, that our decisions are a bit more à la carte, with a little bit of personal freedom jostled by the hard push and shove of our biological make-up and social history, is a less radical but perhaps more reasonable explanation of what we call choice or free will. But even this compromised free will itself turns out to be compromised. In *An Essay Concerning Human Understanding* English philosopher of the seventeenth century John Locke suggests that what we call free is actually a kind of voluntary imprisonment. While we might appear to be free in our choices, it is our ability to act on these choices modified by the unseen restrictions within our environment that controls our decision-making. In Locke's analogy a sleeping man is transported into a locked room and wakes to find himself in the company of a good friend. He is happy to stay with his friend but he is not free; his choices are restricted by a door which he doesn't even know is locked.

In consumer society we are voluntary citizens of a system that encourages us to believe we have almost unlimited choice, both material and cultural. We are, apparently, free to choose our destiny and develop a lifestyle based on what we can afford. But we are free only in so far as we can choose from a set menu. To exist in any other manner would be to leave the room that has been built for us, locked in by bureaucrats and oligarchs whose keys we have no access to. To be truly free you have to find that exit and, even more tellingly, know that there is a locked door in the first place. Discovering ways to make this happen is increasingly problematic. But reaching for a bicycle is a tiny escape, which can, if we are lucky, lead us on a self-propelled journey towards a different understanding of freedom, one that is constructed by mutual co-operation and not purely by financial options. To take up cycle touring is more than just a sport or leisure option; it is a philosophical wake-up call that gives us back control by allowing us to realise how much we have lost.

Handlebars are made by bending a tubular aluminium alloy. Racers have curved 'drops', mountain bikes 'flats', while a variety of the flat, the 'butterfly' or 'moustache', is frequently found on tourers, where long hours spent in the SADDLE encourage a variety of different grips to keep blood pumping to the poor old hands, clasped around the knocks and clunks of outrageous fortune. These tubes are butted or extruded into walls of different thicknesses by forcing them over factory mandrels, solid cylindrical cores, allowing them to be thicker and stronger where they meet the STEM and thinner and lighter where less stress is applied, at the Handlebar grips. The bar is bent to shape either by hand or by machine. That Handlebars need to be steered into a bend of their own making has a pleasing circularity which mirrors the tail chasing of free will.

We hope that our decisions are based, at least partly, on our individual inclinations, predetermined opinions and beliefs; a choice without such considerations would be entirely random, like throwing a dart at a map. Whichever road we decide to cycle down is likely to be determined by our experience of the roads that came before and our preconceptions of the ones that will come after. This implies that freedom relies on a restriction of choice, a U-bend in an already circular argument. To think about free will is to risk the convolution of overthinking. Hinduism and Buddhism neatly sidestep this dilemma by calling into question the whole notion of free will in the first place. How can we have free will or self-determination if we have no separately defined self to begin with?

Jen and I had 'risers', straight Handlebars with an incline at either end where we could put our hands. Initially I bought wide ones. Then I bought short ones. Then I ordered so many lengths of metal piping from specialist Handlebar sellers the postman probably thought I wanted to rob a post office. In the end I found myself some extra-wide Handlebars that I cut down with a hacksaw. This was like war surgery, so I ended up with the left side of the Handlebars slightly shorter than the right, an inconsistency that no doubt inclined me south by south-east and eventually to the tip of India. If it had been the other way round I may have ended up in Russia. Ostensibly a wide Handlebar is more stable than a short one, but it opens up your body like a sail, ready to blow you back from where you came from like an empty crisp packet. It is also twice as difficult to ram into the back of taxi. The net result of all my hacksawing were comfortable riser Handlebars awkward to carry through normal-sized doorways. I was a prisoner of my own Handlebars. But one of the benefits of a broad-shouldered turning arc was an increase in my upper arm strength such that I was finally able to get the tops off jam and chutney jars.

Where the thickness of the Handlebar narrows, just past the point where the stem attaches, there is a weakness known as a stress riser, the result of a sudden change in the material structure of the butted tubes. This is where your Handlebars are likely to break, under the brand-new muscles of a brand-new man, confined indoors on a seventy-five-thousand-tonne container ship. If only he could find something to hold on to.

On the first morning of our voyage we pulled back the curtains to discover that our view of the sea was partly obscured by a stack of buses with SIERRA LEONE ROAD TRANSPORT stencilled on the side. The buses were wrapped in tarpaulins which flapped and unravelled in the wind, a constant accompaniment to the low-level hum of the ship's engines. But there was no escaping as we had to stay inside until the risk of piracy was over. So, I would trek from the cabin to the exercise bike and back again. Back and forth. Back and forth. Back and forth.

One afternoon I spent seeking out the buzzing sounds in the empty cabins along our corridor, set off by the vibration of the ship's engines. I opened and closed the doors and went around adjusting the furniture to various degrees left and right. With our bikes locked in the ship's office, all I could do was tinker with the interior of the CMA CGM *Wagner*, which seemed to be easier than addressing my relationship ten yards along the corridor. In the evening we watched *The King's Speech*, about George VI and the stiff upper lip of the British during World War II. The lip synch on the film was out, so an already stuttering King George no longer matched his own pursed lips, as he shuffled about England carrying the weight of the country on his shoulders. 'I love films about emotionally repressed Englishmen,' I wrote in my diary, 'they make me feel more emotional.'

The captain was worried about stowaways coming aboard at Djibouti, so even the unused cabins I was tinkering with were locked. There followed an increasing purgatory, pacing the same corridor and the same stairwell, cabin to exercise bike, exercise bike to defrosted steak dinner, defrosted steak dinner to exercise bike and thence back to cabin. I jumped into the saltwater swimming tub on the third-floor balcony, hooking out the cinders from the diesel engines with a net. The ship sailed on past Oman as the political situation was too unstable there. The chief engineer, a jolly man from Croatia with a big belly and stout arms and legs, said he wouldn't go ashore in Djibouti because they'd 'roast him like a pig'. He told us again to check our doors were locked.

When we arrived at Djibouti, a small country bordering Ethiopia, Somalia and Eritrea, we only knew it was Africa because of the black dockers on the portside. The concrete berths looked like all the other ones we'd seen and it was run by Dubai Ports World, the conglomerate that seemed to own all the ocean's mega-ports (see BAR BAG). I wondered how strange it must be for the crew to sail halfway around the world but only traverse the same three hundred yards, eating lumps of defrosted steak. Eventually we chugged into the Red Sea, and the relief among everyone on board was palpable, manifesting in an invite from Captain Jakov and his wife Marija for drinks in their cabin.

Jakov was an experienced seaman close to retirement, and the only crew member allowed to bring his wife aboard. He said there had been a real risk of piracy in the last week and only a few days before a ship similar to ours had put out a mayday after being attacked. He told us a thousand seamen were being held off the Somali coast in so-called mother ships, hijacked vessels from which Somali pirates made raids with speedboats. He said many container ships now had guards and a sniper. One day boats like his might have a citadel, a kind of fortified wardrobe impregnable to hijackers. But it wasn't only pirates Jakov had to worry about; his sister ship had had to cope with three stowaways who'd come aboard at Djibouti. They'd become aggressive and one had hanged himself. He told us that container ships now carried tasers.

He poured us some tea.

Before the advent of boxed containers, twenty years ago, a ship would stay in port for seven days and everything would be carried on and off by hand. Now Jakov's ship might be in port for eight hours in total. Seamen travelled everywhere but had no time to see anything. He felt like a prisoner on his own boat, except he'd signed a contract. He couldn't bear docking at his home port. He could see it from the bridge but didn't have the time to visit his family. And now he found himself talking about a citadel, a prison inside a prison, on a boat defended with tasers.

He poured us some more tea.

Insurance costs had risen because of piracy, but then freighter shipping costs had gone up to cover this. Everything had changed with China's accelerating manufacture of cheap goods and India joining the fray. Walmart, he told us, has its own fleet of eight dedicated container ships.

'No, thank you.' That was enough tea.

'In Croatia,' he said as he took a slug of whisky, 'tea is for when you are sick.'

'In England,' I said, 'whisky is for when you are so sick you can't drink tea.'

We clinked our glasses.

The Suez Canal can be seen from space but was only wide enough to admit one boat at a time (it has since been widened to allow two). As a result, the CMA CGM *Wagner* progressed in single file behind a line of other container ships, using the lake at the middle to pass the boats coming in the other direction. The mosques on one side and the gun emplacements of Egyptian soldiers on the other felt unnervingly close. Jakov invited us onto the bridge, where an Egyptian pilot sat next to him, looking like Ray Charles in a pair of shades.

The pilot would say things like 'Ninety-six rpm.' Jakov would repeat 'Ninety-six rpm' to an officer who adjusted the throttle to ninety-six rpm. While we were there a tiny rowing boat came alongside us, almost touching the massive hull of our ship fifty feet down. We told the first officer, who shouted over the railings.

The steering of a bicycle is entirely unlike that of a car, plane or turbine-driven ship, because the weight of the rider adds so much to its movement. The steering torque that a cyclist directs through the Handlebars isn't simply a matter of bending the elbows and moving the arms. The shifts in a rider's weight add much more to the steering. And these movements are mostly unconscious and vary with road conditions and fatigue. Attempts to model this, much like calculating the balancing forces needed to keep a bicycle upright (see RAKE), result in a glut of unmanageable mathematical equations. That the pilot of a bicycle is the master of its steering might seem obvious to us now, but to separate that pilot from the body and thence the bike, as Descartes might have once attempted, is to divide up an identity that cannot be separated.

If, as much of Eastern philosophy suggests, there is no separate self, how can there be a separate will, an autonomous choice? The closer you examine free will, the more it emerges as a fabrication of Western religion, rather than a guiding philosophy in its own right. And St Augustine may well be the guilty one (see also morality in the WHEEL). In order to absolve God from being the bearer of evil to Adam and Eve, he suggested that they must have had their own free will in the matter. In other words, they chose to take the apple from the tree and inherit the evil which they subsequently shared with all mankind. Our universe might be predetermined by a creator but man had been given free will to make his own decisions and thus had to bear moral responsibility for his actions. Even as science was sweeping religion under the carpet during the European Enlightenment, the concept of free will continued in the West, becoming the basis for our legal and political structures, in which we judge aspects of morality and criminality in light of a man's choice.

During three millennia of Buddhist and Hindu scholarship there was no discussion of free will. This does not mean that these traditions have nothing to tell us about it, rather that free will, as we understand it, was rarely discussed. The Buddha did not address such questions as they did not echo his main concern, awakening to the true nature of existence. In Buddhist philosophy everything is interconnected and because of this there is no such thing as a constant self or a fixed identity and no self to direct a choice, free or otherwise (see FREEWHEEL). In Advaita Vedanta Hinduism the self is an indivisible part of a universal and eternal substance (see HEADSET). The self cannot have a free will because it is an integral part of an underlying whole and cannot change or will; it is eternal and unvarying.

How then can we understand free choice and moral responsibility from the standpoint of these philosophies? If we have no separate self how can we make free choices? This line of questioning can end up in a kind of moral slumber: 'Hey man, we are all one, so what can "I" do? The washing-up isn't my responsibility. In fact, the washing-up doesn't need to be done. I am the washing-up.' But Buddhism and Advaita Vedanta do say our actions are accountable, but in a very different way. Although we may not have an independent, unvarying self that can will us in a particular direction, we are free to interpret the actions we make in any way we choose. In other words, it is not the choice we make but how we tell the story of that choice that makes us responsible for our actions.

In critical commentaries of Buddhism the self is likened to a chariot, which for our purposes we can make into a bicycle. The bike cannot be separated from its individual parts. We have a nominal understanding of what the bicycle is but it cannot exist as a separate thing, it is always composed of the components that comprise it. Who we are is a concept and nothing more, which merely encompasses the ever-changing parts that comprise us. And all that we are, as the philosopher Daniel Dennett puts it, are 'centres of narrative gravity'. Events are simply stories we tell ourselves of a much more complex underlying reality. The notion that there are two separate strands to reality, the simple plotline of cause and effect and a deeper interconnected structure, is not simply about the human capacity for myth-making, it is the notion that physics sells us as reality; there is a Newtonian push and shove to regular life and a deeper, underlying, subatomic relativity, in which the observations that we make change the nature of what we observe, from particle to wave and back again. Once you begin to embrace free will from a Buddhist perspective, the notion of freedom changes completely. True freedom then becomes the enlightened understanding that we have no personal freedom at all. We are all inseparably bound at a fundamental level. Once we understand this we can more honestly author the stories of our lives, tacking through those events with a clear-sighted morality.

On a bike we can escape from the material possessions of consumerism, but also, if we begin to open our eyes to a different philosophical perspective, from the notion of personal freedom itself. A different understanding of reality is that we are interconnected participants in an ever-flowing story, a play in which we have convinced ourselves we are the principal characters. Once we begin to understand this we can stop being disappointed by the lack of a Hollywood ending, the pristine unspoilt beach. And we can tell our own story in the whole-body turns, the lilting swerves, the handwritten lines of the bicycle ride.

Long bike trips are event-full because they force us out into the world in such an individual way. And yet those events are repeated again and again: the filling of the water bottles, the offers of food and accommodation, the handshakes, all echo the conditions that precede them. Cycling is the same, same, but different. It tells us a story about ourselves that we haven't yet allowed ourselves to hear. We have a destiny but that destiny is shared by all. We are not players in a single biography but in a polybiography. My history, your history, is actually the intermeshed history of all, for which we implicitly share moral responsibility. If we're all going down the pan, then we all have responsibility for that. And the sooner we realise this the sooner we will be free to tell the story of a different future, in which we all have a separate but combined role to play.

After we'd passed through the Suez Canal there was a sandstorm. The sky darkened to a murky brown smog. But as we chugged past Port Said, through the channel between the marker buoys, and out into the open water, the sandstorm parted to allow a glimpse of the setting sun. It threw the clouds into blooms of pink and violet. Then we ploughed on into the moody sea and the sandstorm closed behind us.

On our last evening there was a barbecue on the bow deck of the CMA CGM *Wagner* in honour of Marija's birthday, with a long table covered in a white cloth. The Filipino crew brought their karaoke system up to the deck, to blast out pop tunes against a video backdrop of tropical idylls and computerised dancing girls, the screen framed by the wider backdrop of the heaving ocean all around us. Jakov was manning the barbecue and kept trying to slide more squid and octopus onto my plate.

It was good to see everyone sharing the same long table, even if the crew were grouped at one end and we were at the other with the Ukrainian and Croatian officers. The chief engineer asked us how many times we'd been robbed in India. Marlon the cook told me he was interested in meditation and had I tried any of that? Well, I said, I was becoming interested in Buddhism and, what was that other one, Jainism? The softly spoken second engineer, who spent most of his time in the engine room, bellowed out 'Sailing' by Rod Stewart. Then Jen and I tried to sing 'Dancing Queen' as Marija danced in front of us. Afterwards the crew gave her some gifts and a card signed by all of them. Despite everything, the long months away from home, the dull demands of docking, the foul funnel soot, all these people from very different cultures were getting on with the business of getting on with each other.

Jen and I were wearing high-vis donkey jackets emblazoned with CMA CGM WAGNER, but we began to shiver as the sun went down. Jakob, noticing this, found some blankets to put on our knees. And so it was that we sat together, between the bow waves, like Day-Glo pensioners, watching the softly spoken engineer belt out 'Sailing' one more time, the lyrics bouncing on the karaoke screen, reminding us that we were travelling to be with 'you'. But also to be 'free'.

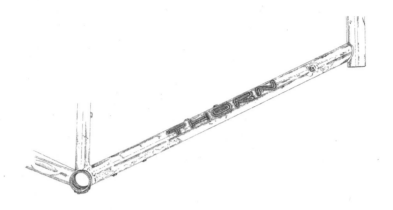

CHAPTER 24

The Down Tube

There was no customs desk, no immigration when we landed at Malta. We just rolled over a speed bump and onto the coast road with the Ferraris, Porsches and cyclists in fluorescent bodysuits. And beside us in the dust, wandering in and out of the bike lane, lines of African migrants, escapees from Libya and beyond, traipsing from their canvas tents into town.

We coasted to the British Hotel in the old port town of Valletta, with its carefree dilapidation, stepped streets and overhanging balconies. A Union Jack fluttered from a flagpole as Jen and I sat on the terrace, staring not at the boats bobbing in the harbour but at our perfect triangles of white toast.

The Order of the Knights of the Hospital of St John of Jerusalem is a Catholic military order. Fleeing the Islamic conquest of Jerusalem, they retreated to Rhodes and then to Malta. The eight points of the Maltese cross denote truth, faith, repentance, humility, justice, mercy, sincerity and the endurance of suffering. The order's creed was not to understand suffering (as in Buddhism), rather its devotional acceptance, aligned with Christ's suffering on the cross, while administering medical care to those wounded in his name.

I was baptised in the Catholic tradition and once went to Mass with my mother, aunt and grandmother in the now dilapidated Catholic cathedral on the island of Antigua. I remember boredom, the fug of aromatic herbs and the Latin chants. As a teenager I found in Anglican Christianity – in its repeating liturgies, its ritual communion – an aspiration for transcendence, something that managed to bridge the anxieties of childhood and the yearning of adolescence. In a haze of belief I applied to medical schools around the country, trying to convince them of my ability in A-level physics. St Bartholomew's in London, the college of my great-grandfather and great-great-grandfather before him, made me an offer.

Barts, as it is more commonly known, was set up by an English clergyman after a pilgrimage to Rome and later became an Anglican parish next to Smithfield's meat market. Today Barts is a specialist London teaching hospital and the Knights of St John a worldwide medical charity based in Malta, both legacies of Christian pilgrimage. It was only in the eighteenth century as the European Enlightenment began to develop the natural sciences that the healing of the body and the belief of the mind began to disentwine. Increasingly patients shared their suffering not with pastors but with the pharmacist and the physician.

I got a C in physics and Barts didn't want me. Which probably explains the metaphysical chip on my shoulder. But the University of Birmingham Medical School did (not so bothered by subatomic particles). There was no history of chivalry at Birmingham but there was a significant number of second-generation students from India and Pakistan and some Afghani refugees, one who'd been a medic for the mujahideen. I shouldered my way into Lecture Theatre 1 with a headful of biology, chemistry, misunderstood physics and a lot of coloured felt-tip pens. I was going to save the world and I was going to do it with God on my side.

The Down Tube leads from the HEAD TUBE to the BOTTOM BRACKET and completes the front triangle of the bicycle frame. It bears the torsional forces of the HANDLEBARS at the top and the relentless circular demands of the PEDALS at the bottom.

God didn't last long at medical school. Mainly because I discovered sex, or rather the lack of it, in the congregations of Birmingham. And the biochemical reactions I copied into my lever-arch file in five different colours seemed to point further and further away from a supernatural presence in the universe. The bodies in the anatomy rooms were just that. Bodies. I spent Monday mornings sawing through a cranium or unpicking the tendons of a hand while discussing who had or hadn't got off with each other over the weekend. Death was merely a precursor to life, four bottles of Newcastle Brown and, if you were lucky, a snog.

Medical school passed in a fug of booze and lecture notes rammed into carrier bags, a kind of sleepwalking trance from which I barely awoke as a junior doctor, knocked sideways by slugs of adrenaline that made me want to vomit in the sluice room. The myth I'd bought into was that medicine could raise the dead, using biblical powers; what I discovered was that doctors, like air-traffic controllers, kept the sick hovering over a busy runway, destination death. I found myself, age twenty-four, titrating morphine into an old man's arm to relieve his terrifying metastatic breathlessness, increments away from promoting the man's death from the morphine itself. He survived till the next evening and the next frightened doctor. Life happened outside the corridors of the hospital I worked in, noted down with detached curiosity as each new patient arrived; 'dancer', 'musician', 'engineer', 'cleaner', 'retired', 'pilot', 'mother'. I put my signature to the evidence-based protocols and the drug pumps of the new pharmacy. Life rates were up. Death rates were down. But nobody seemed to be asking what life was for.

Nurses said they liked the way I worked. I was a 'human' doctor. But what did this mean? That the profession, as a whole, was a machine? I awaited the first laminated flowchart on the evidence-based implementation of kindness.

One hospital I worked in was split into two halves by an A road going down the middle. On one side were modern buildings with new wards, on the other side older prefabs, alternating off a long snaking corridor. These wards were for the chronic cases, what we might call now bed blockers. And it was on this side of the A road, in the old site, that a solitary sleepwalking junior doctor would stagger from Saturday morning to the following Monday in a fifty-six-hour shift. One German doctor I knew would cycle up and down the corridor to save time. Whether his bosses approved of this I'm not sure. What I do know is that he transformed that empty weekend corridor into a place to be alive.

From Malta we took the ferry to northern Italy and cycled to Pisa and the Orto Botanico di Pisa, the botanical gardens. We wandered aimlessly between the orange trees and the ornamental ponds with their slow-paced turtles and then we lay on the grass and listened to the birds, to the soft creep and pizzicato of spring.

We cycled along the Italian Riviera, past Gucci ladies on

shopper bikes, past the neat decking of beach cafes, and then up into the Tuscan hills. Blossom littered the trees like the blush of capillaries, evergreen cypress brushed the cliffs like mascara eyelashes. To me they looked like wondrous new peaks to climb. But Jen had had enough. Enough of the unrelenting gradients, enough of watching her boyfriend clean his CHAIN again and again and again.

We came to a standstill on a terraced campsite near the perfectly named town of Bogliasco, overlooking the Mediterranean. It was pre-season, pre-Easter, and there were no other tourists around. We had our own pitch on an outcrop looking over a cypress-wooded valley. It was idyllic.

The next day the superintendent began to dismantle the abandoned caravan just in front of us. It had PROGRESS written on the side in faux black scrollwork. He tore apart PROGRESS rivet by rivet, panel by panel, with a crowbar, and then pounded at it with a mallet. I fumed and Jen fumed and we drank a bottle of cheap red wine and then shouted at each other some more. The superintendent yanked at the skin of the caravan till all that was left was its metal frame, exposing a sink full of leaves and a broken old hob that had once made tea for two.

We had travelled 14,000 kilometres to reach here. We had met people and seen sights that would have been impossible any other way. But we had also discovered how the world was changing. How a container ship burned a million dollars of dirty diesel every few months to bring tat to the West, how the sides of the roads in India were littered with plastic water bottles, how the embargoed trucks of Iran hacked out smoke like Dickensian factories, how it hadn't snowed in Transylvania for the first winter in living memory, how it *had* rained for the first time in the dry season in the Ghat hills of India. We'd started our trip in order to see the world before it changed for ever. We were kidding ourselves. The world had changed long before us and would continue its cycle of sequins and dust long after.

The word 'myth' can be interpreted in various ways: as a falsehood, an illusion that blinds us to reality or as an abstract story that reveals a greater underlying truth. We think, in our secular age, that we have stopped telling myths; that religious parables have been exposed as diversionary skits from the real deal, the hard grain of science. But the modern era has perpetuated its own myths, which steer dangerously close to that first definition, and chief among these is the myth of progress.

Buddhism contends that we have two ways of understanding the world: a conventional reality populated by apparently individuated beings and an underlying reality of interconnected change, of selflessness (see FREEWHEEL). The West is mostly content with the first reality, the conventional notion of self, which embraces self-perpetuation, self-discovery and linear progress towards a material goal. Although secular society is mostly done with religion it continues with a Christian-like notion of salvation and personal redemption. This is reinforced by economic models of perpetual growth, a fable entirely at odds with the reality of finite natural resources (see BAR BAG).

The choice in the West is not between the fantasy of religion and the enlightened progress of reason; it is rather a choice between two different myths. The sooner we recognise this – that rational progress is itself myth – the sooner we will be free to write our own stories (see HANDLEBARS), to egress from conventional reality into the freedom of our imaginative understanding. How would it be, if for the few seconds of a hawk's swooping descent, we could see through its lens? In the way that a cyclist plummets downhill with a second-to-second magnification of a valley forest into its individual trees, a shift of sensual alertness that allows us to be, for a moment, other than we expect, toppled from our pedestal of intellect into she, he, it, other, trans-human, blood, metal tubing and speed.

As soon as any network or interlinked system becomes sufficiently complex, as with the natural processes of the living world, individual parts in that network begin to interact in different ways at different times. The effects of the wider system can feed back to the constitutive parts in a way that changes the behaviour of those parts and kicks more linear models, such as the notion of progress, sideways. The falling leaves from an oak tree might be blown by a storm far from the forest, which changes the soil make-up of the forest and the insects that feed on it, with implications for tree growth and the predators that feed on the bugs. Contrary to the Cartesian model, the sum is much more than its parts. The developing system starts to display emergent properties. The overall process and pattern of interaction of the parts of a system becomes as important as the parts themselves, similar to Aristotle's ideas of entelechy, the growth of living forms towards their potential, and no news at all to Buddhism with its notions of interconnection and interpenetration.

Anomalies in the expected linear growth of complex and natural systems were first called chaotic, and methods of evaluating them chaos theory, but they are now as likely to be labelled complex systems theory. The natural world is not merely chaotic but complex.

Before the Industrial Revolution, this system was in balance through the transformation of solar energy into living organisms, their growth, and then entropic decay. Since the Industrial Revolution and the burning of carbon fuels, we are releasing more energy as disordered entropy than is being replaced by the complexity-building process of photosynthesis. The variability of our living world is becoming a more and more simple disorder. This is the failure of our monocultural agriculture, our extending desert, our rising temperatures. There is no progress towards an ever-richer complexity, rather an unbalanced decline into entropic simplicity. Cycling is a charge against the demands of economic progress. It gives to death its entropic due but only by outputting lithe old pensioners with a dynamo twinkle in their eye. It is ecologically, physiologically and culturally raging against the dying of the light.

On the second morning the caravan was gone from the campsite, leaving only its trailer and the ghost of our hangover. On the third morning the trailer was towed away, leaving only a patch of ungrassed soil, pecked at by sparrows for worms.

Caravans are, according to the National Caravan Council, worth 'more than one billion pounds to the British economy'. On the other hand, most British Romani (Romanichal) are settled in houses or static caravans. The wagons of their nearly forgotten past (known as Vardo from the Iranian derived 'Vurdon') were often burned after the owner's death, along with the owner's possessions, a Romani preoccupation with purity and the contamination of death (see DOG STICK). The Vardo was never going to be worth one billion pounds to the British economy. The economy did not want the Vardo, unless it was a romanticised set piece, because British society did not want the Romani people and their deviant path from progress. In an illusion of linear movement, the modern caravan continues to be towed to the top of a hill during the summer holidays and towed back to the concrete driveway in the working week. But the fate of the Vardo and the caravan can only ever be the same, a vanishing trick of crowbars and worms, the cyclical return of wandering energy.

Jen and I began talking again, and the talk that we were

talking was no more cycling. We caught a train to the French border and then a sleeper to Paris. I lay on my couch next to the window, watching the world sweeping past as if the summer growth, the autumn harvest and the winter death of the preceding year had never happened, and we were returning to a place and time we had left behind a year ago.

We cycled into the chalk hills of Normandy, riding through the emerging spring, the bluebell woods, the greening grass, the rape fields, the quiet villages and snoozing shops, to the narrow roads that followed the banks of the Seine, to the campsite we had stayed in a year before, Les Forges, just outside Le Havre. It had the same blossom trees, the same old-school caravans, the same hand-painted signs, the same blackbirds tucking in to worms outside our tent, the same tremolo hoot of an owl, calling through the dusk like a bike BELL. Nothing had changed. Everything was changing.

Buddhism in the West is now being stretched into forms that redefine what it, and indeed religion, is. How thin can this meaning become before it disappears? Stephen Batchelor, an Englishman who became a Tibetan Buddhist monk and then a Korean Zen Buddhist, 'disrobed' and stepped away from religion, becoming a proponent of Buddhism reworked for the modern age. He jettisoned rebirth and reincarnation in an attempt to recover a Buddhist core, the original teachings of a human Buddha. Interconnectedness and mindfulness are central to this reframing of Buddhism, which he describes not as truths but as tasks, things that you do. Truth, he suggests, leads to dogma and from there the dark shadow of fundamentalism and violence. The core tenets of Buddhism, which Stephen Batchelor and 'secular Buddhists' like him teach, is remarkably similar to the existentialism as described by Heidegger, Jean-Paul Sartre and Simone de Beauvoir (see SEAT TUBE). In existentialism there is no *a priori*, no God, to plot the path of man through an unconsoling emptiness. This is for man to decide, by what he does. There is no definitive truth out there; we make our own meaning through creative expression. We are stripped of illusion but given real freedom through personal responsibility. Secular Buddhism doesn't model itself on existential philosophy but it seems to be answering a similar question: how do we navigate life without religion? Elsewhere a different question is being asked. Is it possible to have religion back again but on different terms? We know it's an illusion but we still need the show.

Buddhism is returning to India. It has been co-opted by the Dalit movement almost as a political and social force, rather than a religious entity, as an alternative to the Hindu caste system. India's English-speaking middle classes are increasingly enamoured with its core values, which chime with the secular changes arriving in the wake of globalisation and modern science.

If you strip Buddhism down to its basics, as some secular and Zen Buddhists do, its philosophy is entirely one of process: a concentration on the moment-to-moment passing of sensations that comprises the self. Seen this way, secular Buddhism approaches a mundane mysticism, the interconnected transition of everything and everyone we are attached to in our lives, right here, right now. Stephen Batchelor hints we can retain a sense of self, as authors of our lives, while still understanding the fundamental interconnection of Buddhism, in creativity, in random collage. The writer William Burroughs and the musician David Bowie, experimenting with random collages of words and images, discovered that chance accrues a surprising interconnectedness, and that we can construct from these apparently random associations a story that mirrors the conventional notion of our lives as linear plotlines.

We might think of secular Buddhism as a bicycle ride. A cyclist finds a seemingly random conjunction of events and people at junctions, which turns into the story of their journey from A to B. The ride appears to satisfy the demands of both the secular Buddhist on the one hand, looking for a non-religious representation of interconnection, but also the rational humanist on the other, embarking on a journey of linear progress. But what this pedalling analogy does not take into account is the wayward imagination of the rider.

To strip away myth, as both secular Buddhism and hard rationalism tend, would be to kill off metaphor and its hold on our imagination. Reincarnation and rebirth imply a metaphorical cycle of change, the circularity of the seasons and, at a more personal level, the pattern of habitual thinking that Buddhists hope to free themselves from. Metaphor and myth are places where the passionate crises of religion, the yearning of man and woman for transcendent meaning, take admissible form.

We are ever torn between our irrationality, our physical and emotional instincts, and the neatly cleaved reason that science would have us believe is the inheritance of civilisation, the familiar opposition of body and mind. But what has persisted throughout human history, from paganism into monotheistic religion and the excavation of that religion from the institution of science, is metaphor, an irrational symbol grounded in the rationality of language. It has ever been the emissary between the mind and the body, between the reasonable and the unreasonable, between the headstrong and the heartfelt, helping us navigate a way between the self and the selflessness of being alive.

When we rolled off the cross-Channel ferry a bloke in an orange fluoro said, 'Follow that lorry and you're in England,' and so, with a back pedal and a *clickety clack*, we returned to Blighty, a word that I later discovered is from the Urdu and Persian *vilayati*, meaning 'of a foreign land'.

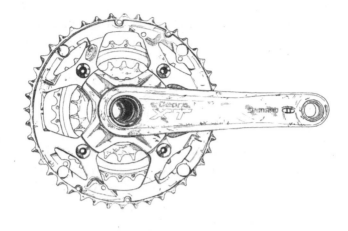

CHAPTER 25

The Chain Wheels

Our first night back in Portsmouth we stayed up till two in the morning listening to the recordings of the Master Musicians of Joujouka. This is a group of flute and drum players from the Rif Mountains of northern Morocco who've been playing improvised Sufi drone music for the past six hundred years. Our hosts Robbie and Sara had befriended them in Morocco, become their roadies in England, and were now accompanying them to the opening slot of the Glastonbury Festival. They are interesting not just for their whirligig of music, but for their part in Western counterculture, having played for the deranged novelist William Burroughs, the LSD guru Timothy Leary and Brian Jones of the Rolling Stones, who introduced them to Ornette Coleman, the jazz experimentalist.

Burroughs likened their musical performances and the pagan-like ritual of Boujeloud that accompanies them to the rites of Pan. Boujeloud is a bride baiter and ensnarer of fertile women, half-man, half-goat, who appears at marriages and festivals, bringing fertility and blessing crops. He is played by a villager in goat skins, and his bride to be by a dancing boy in drag. Dancers and musicians spur each other on in epically long sagas of hypnotic trance. Here Sufism meets the pagan rites of seasonal change. It's not hard to see why the counterculture, in its hallucinogenic resistance to the rationalism of Western society, was drawn to it. William Burroughs played with these pagan tropes in the fictionalised border town he created between West and East, the 'Interzone' of Tangier, a distorted facsimile of its international zone. Much of his fiction relied on a cut and paste of random texts, an organised chaos, partly borrowed from the Dadaist and surrealist movements of the early twentieth century. The books that Burroughs completed using this technique, *Naked Lunch* and *Interzone*, are not easy reads, but they are remarkable collisions of metaphor, a rupture of the orthodox borders between the conscious and unconscious, the mundane and the profane, the scientific and the spirited.

Theyyam is a ceremony found in Kerala, the south Indian state we had cycled through a month before. Pre-dating Hinduism and going back over three thousand years, it is pretty much uncategorisable, an all-night dance and mime ritual that incorporates tribal animism, tree, plant and animal worship. Its main protagonist, Kutty Theyyam, wears a peacock costume above the waist and a grass skirt on a box frame below. It has black pits for eyes, and twirls and spins for hours, sometimes days, to relentless drumming, entering a trance-like state, buffeted inside a sacred circle, where the dancer is kept centred by priests with palm torches.

In Padstow, in Cornwall in the UK, we have the Obby Oss, an echo of the pagan spring festival of Beltane stitched together with sailor lore. The performer of the Obby Oss wears a strange black wooden mask and below the waist a cape made of black sailcloth on a frame, which it uses to trap young women to bless them with fertility. On May Day the Obby Oss is lead by a 'teaser' with a white club, followed by musicians and drummers, who drive the procession onwards, rousing the Obby Oss into life at the start of the day and lamenting it to death at the end.

In all of these examples a myth is performed as dance, an ecstatic rhythm with natural and seasonal change at its hub, an experience penetrated with otherworldly strangeness that somehow outlasts the cynical gaze of modernism and the irony of postmodernism. To get a taste of this should we, the account managers, the mechanics, the young professionals, the shelf stackers, the coy psychiatrists of Western rational progress, don a grass skirt, a disturbing mask, and dance out a version of seasonal change every spring? I would argue that we already do, as we clamber on our bikes to welcome in the warmth. Do our bodies radiate an otherworldly presence? Not as clearly. But in thousands of blogs and tour diaries, in the compulsive outpourings of cycling stories there is a kind of chant, people sharing an experience that they find difficult to define and harder still to keep to themselves, an ecstatic, unnerving reacquaintance with the world around them. There are the trials and there are the tribulations, the violent hills, the incalculable weather fronts, the punctured defeats, the streaks of oil. This is myth-making for the secular age, persisting in ecstatic rituals of weekend escape, monthly adventure, year-long pilgrimage.

The following morning we cycled past our old pal, the Hard Interchange (see BOTTOM BRACKET). Not being quite sure which exit to take I spent the next few moments circling the mini-roundabout just beside it. To my left there was the exit to Station Approach and the Hard Interchange itself, to my right Clock Street and Portsmouth town. Just next to me, on the main road, called the Hard, there was the Ship Anson pub and the

Ship Leopard pub, where sailors would have begun their beer run ashore and thence into the Devil's Half Acre, a once-dense population of pubs. 'Hard' comes from the slipway that the earliest sailors made by dumping clay into the sea at low tide and then rolling it, a non-negotiable material platform.

There is an intriguing origin myth for 'Pompey', the slang name for Portsmouth. The city of Bombay (now Mumbai – see HEAD TUBE) was included in the wedding dowry of Catherine of Braganza, the Portuguese princess who married Charles II in 1662. As part of the bargain England got Tangier and a number of Indian territories, including Bombay. Catherine's Portuguese seaman, delivering her to Britain, saw a resemblance between the ports of Bombay (Portuguese *bom bahia* – 'beautiful bay') and Portsmouth, 'Bombay' was subsequently anglicised to 'Pompey'. 'The points of resemblance between Bombay and Portsmouth are: both are islands; both have good harbours; the two cities are flat, with the exception that Bombay has a strip of high land running from Malabar Point to Mahalaxmi, and both are only a few feet above sea level' (*Portsmouth Evening News*, 2 December 1933).

I carried on cycling around that mini-roundabout, peering into Station Approach, where I could see the restored HMS *Warrior*, the first ever ironclad warship and template for the billion-pound steel-clad frigates that now tread our coastal waters, and then I turned back to face the Devil's Half Acre, now a no-man's land of unlet offices and car parks. William Burroughs said his cut-up montages had the power of prophecy: 'When you cut into the present the future leaks out.' On the Hard Interchange the past shoulders its way through the present and then doesn't know which way to turn.

The Chain Wheel is the toothed ring around the BOTTOM BRACKET, turned by the CRANK and PEDALS. It converts the rider's pedalling revolution into the linear motion of the CHAIN, which engages with the teeth of the REAR SPROCKETS, which transform it back again into the revolution of the WHEELS. Larger Chain Wheels with more teeth create a higher gear that is harder to move, smaller wheels with fewer teeth give a lower gear that is easier to turn. Racing bikes have large Chain Wheels, while touring bikes like ours, carrying heavier loads, have smaller sets. The granny gear, the smallest Chain Wheel, allows a cyclist to spin against a low resistance, producing the torque necessary to get a bike up a hill without putting the same forces through the knees. Granny gears were first used on old diesel trucks, which were so underpowered they needed an absurdly low gear ratio to get them going, and would then crawl along as fast as a granny walked. Those truck drivers had clearly never met my nan, who was shovelling her bike up hills well into her eighties. She never learned how to drive, this being the domain of her three husbands, but she asserted her ferocious independence with an iron bicycle I could barely wheel to the end of the driveway.

The gearing on touring bikes is sometimes called a 'half step plus granny', which means there are two larger Chain Wheels for cycling on the flat, and a much smaller granny for the steeper hills. Chain Wheels wear, and run more smoothly, if they have a prime number of teeth. An assertion my nan would have loudly shared with everyone around her as she picked at an 'overpriced' fish supper with too many bones.

Between the CRANK and the Chain Wheel there is the spider. These are the metal arms at the bottom of the CRANK that transmit the power of the PEDALS through the Chain Wheel. In the good old days, instead of an aluminium spider, there may well have been a steel cotter pin hammered through the shaft of the CRANK to connect it directly to the spindle of the BOTTOM BRACKET. Although much less efficient and prone to wear, the simplicity of the cotter freed up space inside the Chain Wheel for the bike manufacturer to carve their name, using mythical metaphors like 'Phoenix' or 'Hercules' or 'Frontier'. The Raleigh DL-1 Tourist Bicycle, mass-produced from the 1950s to the 70s, had the image of a heron cut out of it (see TOP TUBE). These Chain Wheels were metaphors in drop-forged steel, circular myths that drove our forebears towards the thrill of the newly engineered future, the potential that has become our present.

Google Maps tells a hallucinatory story about the mini-roundabout I was circumnavigating on the Hard. If you click your cursor along the road through Google's street-level images, the roundabout is gone, its faint outline still there in grey where the white arrow markings and the central hump once were, but it is now a ghost of its indelible past. Then, when you turn virtually to face Station Approach, which once provided the vehicle access to the Hard Interchange, you find it has been pedestrianised with bollards down the middle. The building itself, the Hard Interchange, the portal of our bike trip, has disappeared, knocked down by the council to make way for a new 'regenerated' version. This new Hard Interchange is a see-through fantasy of ovals and glass, more like the sail of Admiral Pereira's house in Uran (see HEAD TUBE) than the endearing brutalism of old. But then, as you drag the scroll pad back towards you and move forward virtually into Station Approach, the old Hard Interchange magically reappears. The photographic stock of Google's world has not yet caught up with the council's gentrification project.

You can follow the road right around the old Hard Interchange, past the cafe, the NO CYCLING sign, the First Bus parking, until, at the end of your drive-by, a virtual reality within a virtual reality, you come across a curious flagpole atop the concrete balcony of the Hard Interchange's viewing deck. And at the top of this flagpole is a backlit sign, with cinema-like letters, spelling out SMILE. If you then zoom in you find a notice pinned to the stairwell, which explains the flagpole is a community art piece and you can submit suggestions for what should be written on the glowing sign atop. A Google image search reveals that once upon a time a resident of Pompey chose HOW SHOULD I LIVE? to be displayed above the Hard Interchange.

There is a Latin hymn by the theologian and philosopher Thomas Aquinas, 'Pange Lingua Gloriosi Corporis Mysterium'. The fourth verse of the hymn, in a plain English translation by Peter Walsh, celebrates the communion as, 'Word-made-flesh transforms the true bread / by word into his flesh; / wine is changed into the Christ's blood'.

Thomas Aquinas justified this metaphor by saying, 'Sacred scripture delivers spiritual things to us under metaphors taken from bodily things.' Metaphor is the catalyst of the physical and the non-physical realm, dissolved on the tongue. I was baptised, as many of us were, into chants of transcendence. The religious framework of the Catholic Mass and the Anglican Eucharist no longer has the same meaning for me, but the shiver of its metaphor, the dry bread on the tongue, the chill of the wine, remains.

Logos originally meant the reasoned word or argument in speech and rhetoric; it later became *logik tekhne*, the use of logic in reasoning, before becoming *logica* in Latin and 'logic' as we use it today. But the logic of Western philosophy, the use of reason in philosophical argument, is quite different to the *logos* of early Christian thinkers, the Neoplatonists and followers of Sufism. Here *logos* suggested an irrational sense of union, an undivided oneness which defies the categorisations of linear thought. For early Christians, this *logos*, in the purest sense of 'word', was a direct communication between God and man. And its metaphor wasn't just there at the beginning of God's relationship with humankind, it was, actually, the beginning: 'In the beginning was the Word, and the Word was with God, and the Word was God' (Gospel of John). It wasn't merely a bridge between God and man, it was Christ himself, God's envoy become flesh: 'The Word became flesh and made his dwelling among us.'

Central to the Christian tradition but also shared with mystical Islam and many other traditions is metaphor, the power of words to transform and connect the material and immaterial. But metaphor is also being emphasised in science, in the overwrought category of cognitive linguistics. Using analytical research, cognitive linguistics has explored the use of metaphor across cultures, languages and generations, and its tendency to be grounded in our physical conception of space and movement in very similar ways – how lemons are considered to be 'fast' in the USA, UK and India, and plums as 'slow'. How young babies innately associate rising sounds with rising objects, in the same way that we associate notes of a higher frequency with a higher spatial plane. Happy is up, sad is down. Intimacy is close. We start, stop, run and grasp in argument and cycle in biochemical, economic and ecological models. The human mind tends towards an interplay of our perception of the physical world and our spatial conceptualisation of it. What we call synaesthesia, the triggering of one sense by another, colours from music, touch from smell, is not a human error but an exaggeration of how we are already 'wired'. The hard-line separation of our senses, like the division of our material and mental experiences, becomes less and less clear when we begin to examine those categories. And so we use, and have always used, metaphor as a sensual passport.

Edmund Husserl, phenomenologist philosopher, champion of subjective experience and precursor of existential philosophers like Heidegger and Sartre, specifically saw the value of myth and fantasy. Long before William Burroughs, he used the example of a centaur playing the flute as something that exists 'neither in the soul, nor in consciousness, nor anywhere else. It does not exist anywhere.' The very unreality of a centaur playing the flute gives it an ambiguous power. Husserl, and philosophers like him, recognised the exotic power of the imagination to reframe our experience of the objective world as something that is a composite of both. And as Burroughs recognised, the best of these metaphors and myths are prophetic, they can change the world by changing our perspective on it. They are not merely descriptive but revolutionary.

Immanuel Kant, the standard bearer of the Western Enlightenment, who spoke of the power of reason to free man from his yoke of dogma, also spoke of when reason fails, when rational language cannot beat the boundaries of what has yet to be conceptualised, when the imagination has to take flight to allow the mind to reach beyond itself. And so the juxtapositions of William Burroughs' Interzone and the associations of George Orwell's Newspeak have prophesised futures that are now our present.

In Spielberg's film *ET* the boy Elliott and the alien he befriends fly in silhouette across the moon on a BMX bike, instead of landing on it. There is a transformation of outer into inner space. If metaphor represents the jarring way that we reconceptualise the physical world in our imagination, then cycling can act in the opposite direction by astonishing our imagination into soaring stories of flying down hills. Just as metaphor can change the way we see the environment, we can reinvigorate metaphor by changing the way that we interact with the space flashing past us.

'Metaphor', meaning 'carrying over', is itself a metaphor, as is 'literally', meaning 'according to the letters on the page'. In the end, as Zen Buddhism proposes, we can only escape words and the convolutions of their meaning by what we do. By where we go.

*

Jen watched me go round and round the mini-roundabout like
a goldfish with its brain shot out. 'It's this way,' she said and
headed off down the Hard.

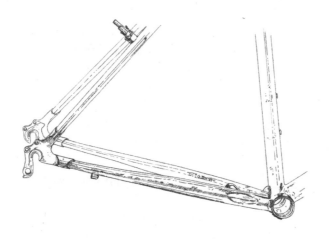

CHAPTER 26

The Chain Stays

The Chain Stays are the pair of frame tubes that join the shell of the BOTTOM BRACKET to the SEAT STAYS where the rear wheel is fitted. Together the Chain Stays, SEAT STAYS and SEAT TUBE form the rear triangle of the bicycle, the less famous twin of the front triangle. If the shadow of the front triangle makes the map of a triangular journey from Portsmouth to Istanbul to Mumbai and back again, then the shadow of the rear triangle marks a less adventurous return to Bristol and normal life – in a terraced house, in a familiar street, in unfamiliar times. It not only reinforces and completes the diamond shape, which ultimately gives a bike frame its strength and resilience (see SEAT STAYS), but holds up the tent, cooking gear, clothes and sleeping bag on which a long bike tour depends. Short Chain Stays decrease the overall wheelbase (the distance between the points where the WHEELS touch the ground), making a bike easier to move, and do wheelies, but are no good for carrying heavy loads up hills or providing the overall stability that a cargo-carrying bike needs. They brace the axle of the rear wheel into a vice, which the pedalling motion of the bike is continually trying to untwist, creating a steel-forged wishbone that the cyclist doesn't even know he is trying to snap.

As Jen and I pedalled through the county of Hampshire we passed a lush green field with caravans arranged in neat pitches. This looked like the kind of luxury that a couple of stinky bike travellers could easily collapse into. I popped my head around the door of the office.

'Hello! I was wondering if we could pitch our—'

'You do know there's no toilet here?'

'That's OK,' I said. 'We can use the ones in—'

He pointed at a sign: CAMPING AND CARAVAN CLUB MEMBERS ONLY. 'Are you a member?'

'No.'

'We only accept members,' he said and closed the book in front of him.

Further down the road we came to an unmarked field off an unmarked lane that some teenagers in the last chip shop had told us about. A man shouted through the open window of the car, leaving the field in the other direction, 'I'm undercover police. And you'd better watch out for the Dalmatians.'

'Is this a campsite?'

'Yes.'

'Is this a Traveller site?'

'Yes.'

A teenage kid bellowed from the back window in the same thick Irish accent, 'You can stay here but you have to give us ten pounds. No, twenty pounds—'

The driver interrupted him. 'Don't listen to the kid. Go tell the guy in the Land Rover that Danny sent you. He'll tell you where you can pitch your tent.'

The guy in the Land Rover was slurring his words. 'You know we're Travellers, don't you? You OK with that?'

We nodded. We pitched our tent amid the caravans and parked cars, next to some discarded butane cylinders. Some kids wandered up.

'You shouldn't be here.'

'You're lucky to be here.'

'You been to India?'

'You got any Indian money?' I dug out an Indian rupee. 'Did you cycle over the water to India?'

A young man called Pat sauntered over. 'Don't listen to the kids if they ask you for money. No one owns this land. I think it's great you're staying here. Nobody comes and stays with Travellers. They treat us like dogs. They put shit through our doors. We're on this land now and they can't move us. Are you married?'

'No,' I said, 'but we've been together five years.'

He seemed surprised. 'If I lived with a woman in my community without being married I'd have my throat cut.'

'Is it OK if we stay here?'

'Yep. We don't give a fuck what the others do. How much does it cost to cycle to India?'

'Five thousand pounds,' I said off the top of my head.

He looked at me curiously. 'OK,' he said. 'You can stay here. Any problems with the kids speak to the men.'

When Pat had gone, the kids gathered around us again. A chubby one said, 'I know what you're going to do to her. You're going to stick your thing in her hole.'

'Don't be so rude,' said Jen.

An older woman came up and scattered them. 'Stay away from the natives,' she said. 'You eaten something? You OK?'

A teenage girl said, 'You're welcome to stay here, but a kid might do something to your tent. But you can stay as long as you like.'

The chubby kid came back again. 'Do you live in that tent or in a house?'

'We live in a terraced house.'

'In a terrorist house?'

The kid who shouted at us from the back of a car said, 'You can only stay here if you give us twenty pounds.'

'Danny said we could stay here.'

'My father owns this land and you pay twenty pounds or you go.'

We went back to the slurring man who first told us we could camp there. 'You have to pay two hundred pounds,' he said, followed by, 'Don't worry – he's winding you up.' The man showed us a cut below his eye and a growing bruise. 'Did I have this earlier?' In the background there was a bare-knuckle fight going on and some bawling and shouting and bottle-throwing.

'No,' I said.

'Don't believe him,' said the kid who had been winding us up.

For some reason this seemed to break the ice. The kid shook our hands as another one told us he was going to nick our stuff in the middle of the night. In the end we locked our bikes to the gas cylinders, lobbed our baggage in the tent and fell asleep. When I got up during the night to have a piss the moon was big and full and low and dusty orange. Diesel generators puttered as cars came and went with sudden foghorns of music, as if someone was channel-hopping a jukebox with the volume turned up: Tom Jones, American country, sentimental Irish tunes, voices shouting into the dark. And then, just after midnight, silence.

When we woke at dawn to pack up the tent Pat came over to see us off. He was wearing a high-vis, getting ready to go to work tarmacking the roads.

'You sleep all right? No problems with the kids?'

'Good, thanks.'

An older man opened the door of the newest Land Rover on the site.

'Tent OK? No problems with the kids? Not too cold?'

'All fine.'

'Where you heading?'

'Salisbury.'

The man nodded slowly as if that was not just a reasonable destination but the correct one. Then they both got in the Land Rover and drove off.

Beside us was a leafless sapling next to the faded patch of grass where a Traveller's caravan had once stopped. And dangling in its branches a small wooden cross tied to a leather strap, as if deliberately left there. Part of me wanted to take it. The other part knew it wasn't mine to take.

Romani and Irish Traveller communities have been systematically persecuted and excluded from this country for five hundred years, a statelessness encountered by Romani Gypsies all over the world (see DOG STICK). For a few brief hours in Hampshire we'd met in the overlap of semi-rural England. And each of us, I think, had learned something from the other. In the past decade many thousands of nomadic eastern European Romani have migrated to England in the hope of escaping the prejudice and exclusion of the countries they have left behind (see DOG STICK), but they continue to be excluded, despised, forgotten.

A cross hangs bare in a field. It says we may be mostly done with religion but we are not yet done with belief. We may be done with divinities but we are not yet done with the divine. The beliefs of the Romani and Irish Travellers are at the intersection of Christianity, paganism and animism, throwing a frayed net over the whole of nature. This is not some romantic projection; there are no swaying corn flowers and rhyming couplets here. It is only a fading glimpse, a glance through the patio doors over the decking and the fence posts to something caught swaying in the bare trees.

We pedalled along the byroads of the Wylye Valley, next to the Wylye, a tributary of the Avon, which runs through the mythical country of Wessex, the setting for the novels of Thomas Hardy, one of my favourite and most prettily gloomy writers. The weather was warm and glowing, and quite unlike the arid heat of the Middle East or the humidity of India. We fell in and out of pubs drinking beers that we'd forgotten we'd forgotten. And several pints later we found ourselves in a country lane with no traffic about the width of our outstretched arms. We laid our bikes on the bank of the verge and then lay down too so we could feel the heat rising up from the earth beneath us, a conversation without words.

Thomas Hardy, whose childhood was steeped in Anglicanism, stopped going to church but retained a longing for religious ceremony. As his biographer Claire Tomalin puts it, 'This ambivalence made him into a poet who, in his later years, still sometimes celebrated belief alongside disbelief. He could no longer believe, but he cherished the memory of belief, and especially the centrality and beauty of Christian ritual in country life, and what it had meant to earlier generations and still meant to some.'

For Hardy redemption from suffering and death, and a compromise kind of faith, could be found in the flourishing of nature, the briars and bridleways that wove about and through his characters, an ever-branching metaphor that animated the headstone of the page. He imagined life into animals, weather and immoveable objects. God is gone, he seemed to be saying, religion and class crush us, but a living energy pervades everything.

In one of his later novels, *Tess of the D'Urbervilles*, Tess tumbles down the side of a valley, breaking into song, chanting parts of the Book of Common Prayer, infused, the reader later realises, with a pagan vibrancy: 'O ye Sun and Moon... O ye Stars... ye Green Things upon the Earth... ye Fowls of the Air... Beasts and Cattle... Children of Men... bless ye the Lord, praise Him and magnify Him for ever!' As the narrator tells it, 'the half-unconscious rhapsody was a Fetishistic utterance in a Monotheistic setting; women whose chief companions are the forms and forces of outdoor Nature retain in their souls far more of the Pagan fantasy of their remote forefathers than of the systematised religion taught their race at later date.'

Many of us have grown up falling down hillsides into green valleys, and some of us carry on doing that on bikes. It is in this submission to gravity that we half-awake to the energy of the land, half-falling over our steps, our PEDALS, in a gasp that is almost sexual, turning and tuning into the world around us.

It was Hardy's first wife Emma who was the cyclist, dressing up in a green velvet suit that matched the colour of her favourite bicycle, known as Grasshopper. Emma remained fervent in her Christian belief, and although they became estranged, in 1899, when they were both sixty, they cycled seventeen miles by moonlight from a local harvest festival, companions in a different kind of shared experience.

When Hardy died his cremated remains were buried in Poets' Corner in Westminster Abbey and his previously removed heart in the village he was born in. The story goes that although the local doctor put Hardy's heart in a biscuit tin for safekeeping, a cat gnawed it, and the cat had to be buried alongside the heart. This is undoubtedly a pub myth, but it also feels like the continuation of all that his readers demanded, that someone who breathed nature through the pores of his writing could not disappear, only perpetuate, in the body of another animal.

It has always seemed to me that writing is a kind of exploratory auger, drilling down to an underground river that leads to the future. You cannot see where the river ends, but you can feel the direction and speed of the current as it heads there. This asks of writers, artists, essayists, actors, dancers and cyclists a kind of collective foresight, sounding out the outline of the future through the myths that we are creating today. What will be our journeys in our changing seasons, on a changing planet? Where will we go and what will we return to? What will our myths become?

Cycling, like writing, offers no easy answers. The more you cycle, the more you write about it, the more you are faced with unpleasant auguries of what is to come, in the same way that the meditative unity of the natural landscape gives way to the EU FUNDED LANDFILL RENEWAL PROJECT. Our bikes are perpetual commotion machines, 'bashing-us-about-a-bit' both in the widescreen of the unsynchronised seasons and in the microcosm of the coughing CHAIN skipping on its worn-down sprockets. But this discomfort is part of our understanding and one of the ways in which cycling can be a physical philosophy, changing us through what we do.

Animism – and paganism, its more human-centred variant – pre-dates but also informs monotheistic religion and secular atheism. It suggests that the natural world has its own guiding energy or conscious purpose, a vitalism or supernatural spark that science has long since dismissed. The Rig Veda, the most ancient of the Indian Sanskrit texts (see HEADSET), is a metaphorical hymn to the strategies of the natural world, its recurrent rhythms, and generative and destructive forces, the intermingling of geological elements and energies. It makes no analytical separation of form and matter, it neither co-opts nor excludes. It is the symbolic expression of an oral tradition that reaches sideways into the natural world in an undifferentiated way and which persisted through Hinduism and into the Romani exodus from India and across Europe. The folklore of the Romani, their oral tradition intermingling with the storytelling cultures and pagan remnants they travelled through, is a perpetual retelling of passport-free travel between human- and non-humankind – fruit-bearing trees perpetuating pregnancy, women giving birth to foxes, dead princesses turning into lotus flowers, symbols impossible to separate from the landscape of which the tales are a part.

There is an alternative, animistic, take on the flickering isotope scans that light up in different parts of our brain when we give attention to nature. In this version the cracking twigs we walk upon in woods are also the firings of a neural network, a pattern that extends into the natural world from us and from the natural world into us, which is as much a part of this experience as the sensory cortex which perceives it. Animism is the quest to enlarge our empathy, to expand it like blowing into molten glass. This is not the same as saying that nature has consciousness; rather enlarging our definition of what consciousness can be – that a bird singing on the branch is an extension of our mind because we create its song in our inner ear.

Ultimately animism is the co-author of monism, the philosophy contending mind and matter are the same thing, a philosophy known to some cynics as moanism. 'There go the romantics again, firing up their William Blake visions like an old milk float.' Repetition has numbed our fascination with monism, and this is why collisions of metaphor, of image and symbol, are so powerful (see CHAIN WHEELS). They reconnect broken circuits in our understanding with the sting of incredulity.

The era of the Capitalocene or Anthropocene or Cthulucene (coined by the feminist Donna Haraway) is not just about man's role in the destruction of nature but in the destruction of its flourishing variability. From a monistic perspective, this means a diminishing of all of our options. The more we destroy, the less branches there are into which life can flow. And the convoluted ever-branching map of our biography, full of potential, to which we most aspire, becomes a map that offers no freedom at all. But the wandering cyclist remains contrary. She wills a flourishing into old roads like the bright red blood that exercise flushes through our capillaries (see the poet Attila József and his blood vessels like rosebushes in SEAT POST).

Our bikes lay side by side that afternoon on the Dorset back road, their black paintwork soaking up the sun till they too became warm to the touch. There were no cars. No passers-by. No beginnings. No endings. No in-between. There was only the tick of the insects as we lay curled beside each other on the verge, our knees up to our hips, like we were doing tuck jumps from a diving board into the unknown.

CHAPTER 27

The Chain

We got lost in Frome and pulled up outside a cottage. An old man came out, steadied himself on the doorframe and started to give us directions, while his wife shouted at him from somewhere unseen because he was now in the way of the satellite TV dish.

'Wehhhhll… if you wahhnt to go on the quiet roads –' he explained in an elongated West Country twang.

'Forward,' shouted his wife. 'Forward! It's awl fuzzy.'

He adjusted his position slightly. '– you cann go leffft… and take a right at the first junction –'

'More!'

'– but if you want to goriiiiight –' he paused for a delicious eternity '– it's a bit faarster –' another pause '– but if you want to go leffft—'

'We'll go right,' I said.

We cycled past Bradford-on-Avon, picked up Jen's mum,

who rode with us to Bathampton. She then swapped bikes with Jen's sister Sophie, who tag-teamed us to Bath, where we caught up with our friend Joe, who had a hi-fi on the back of his bike playing jive tunes as we rolled along.

Each link in a bike Chain has ten parts: two outer link plates, two inner link plates, two rollers on two bushings and two pins to hold it all together. The Chain is, in effect, a series of tiny wheels so efficient that it transfers 98 per cent of the pedalling power to the bike WHEELS. It connects the CHAIN WHEELS to the REAR SPROCKETS by looping through the rear triangle of the bike frame made by the CHAIN STAYS and the SEAT STAYS. To remove a Chain, you either have to break the frame or break the Chain with a splitter, a metal vice into which the pins of the links are wedged like agonised fillings.

A poorly maintained and lightly lubricated Chain will wear down much faster, so that the distance between its links – its pitch – exponentially increases in a phenomenon called 'chain stretch'. A slack Chain, which no longer maintains its proper tension on the CHAIN WHEELS and REAR SPROCKETS, will start to lose its efficiency, and that cherished, 98 per cent efficiency begins to disappear. But you're not just losing pedalling drive, you're in danger of losing your CHAIN WHEELS, REAR SPROCKETS and GEARS in a *cannibalistic self-devouring,* a B movie with an horrific subplot. The widening pitch of the Chain's links can no longer mesh with the teeth of the CHAIN WHEELS and REAR SPROCKETS, which it wears down with a caries-like decay. GEARS begin to slip, sprockets begin to 'cough', a tubercular rust develops over everything, and it won't be long until the whole chain set is in the grave.

This was the reasoning behind my daily Chain maintenance. But I am not alone. We are few, but we are bound, in our persistence, link by link, pin by pin, roller by roller. Sheldon Brown, the deceased patriarch of online bike mechanics, quipped that Chain maintenance was a religious problem: 'It addresses mysteries of existence, life and death to which there is no clear and obvious answer, as long as the chain is exposed to dirt.'

Although a Chain will only maintain its 98 per cent efficiency in laboratory conditions, the whole point of cycling is to escape those sterile conditions and take on life in all its grit and grind. Our Chains set us free. But the consequence of this, for me at least, was excessive fretting, cleaning and lubing, eternal worrying at links, bearings and bushels in a world that was always cascading towards chaos. And it was while using an old toothbrush to scrub the tarnish inside each link that I wondered if it would have been a lot easier to take the train.

Jean-Jacques Rousseau, eighteenth-century author and philosopher, opens his essay *The Social Contract* with 'Man is born free, and everywhere he is chains.' Each of us, he explains, is born with a natural freedom and kindness but is then trammelled by society with all its iniquities. However, if we examine this quote more carefully, as if we were about to oil each part with a cotton bud, we discover that 'Man is born free, *and* everywhere he is chains.' Rousseau does not say '*but* everywhere he is chains'. Our chains are not meant to be simply thrown off, they are part of the human condition, the bonds that make society, into which we must all grow as we become adults. To mature fully our innate kindness has to encompass the relationships within that society. There is no ejector seat; we cannot simply opt out of society because it corrodes our innocent kindness; a new balance has to be struck. Jen and I appeared to be self-sustaining in our simplicity, but we also had to reach out to those around us, a community that didn't even know it was joined together by our ride – atheist to Christian to Jew to Muslim to Hindu to Buddhist.

In the online emporium of obsessions that is Sheldon Brown's Technical Bicycle Info you can find various recipes for cleaning a bike chain which famously include: frying it in detergent in a pan; feeding it like a worm into a plastic bottle of citrus oil, capping the bottle and shaking it like a magnum of champagne; disassembling the whole chain into its links, and then cleaning each part with a cotton-wool swab, before using separate, specific lubricants for each pin and roller and bushing.

I would have willingly submitted myself to this but we would never have made it to India or indeed have maintained a loving relationship. As it was I had to admit time and wear into my Chain and then, at exactly the prescribed distance of three thousand miles, when we arrived in the United Arab Emirates, I broke it (intentionally) with a chain splitter.

The two Chains, the one I had just broken, blackened by the aluminium oxide of the CHAIN WHEEL, and the new one, pristine and cooked in premium grease, lay alongside each other across the British newspapers we'd just bought. Those papers, inevitably, were full of the pervasive unkindness of others. We knew no one in the Emirates apart from the hospitable Rachel who we were staying with, and England seemed so far away. I threaded the new Chain about the REAR SPROCKETS, CHAIN WHEEL and GEAR derailleurs, through the rear triangle, and then pressed in a pin to join it all together, bending off the tip, the 'stalk', with a satisfying snap.

Midway through medical school I began to ruminate obsessively about blood, which, if you place a diagnostic grid over it now, would be called obsessive compulsive disorder. I'd just come out of a very messy relationship and stumbled into depression. Having obsessive ruminations about blood may have been tenable if I'd been an English student or a lawyer or a historian, but the life of a medical student meant taking blood and inserting drips, hurried swabs of cotton wool and, for me, frantic handwashing in a basin for specks of red that never seemed to disappear, seen through the eyes of a tired young man trying to keep a perpetual motion machine going everywhere and nowhere.

My GP recommended antidepressants, and when I declined, insisting that I was training to be a doctor and therefore couldn't be depressed, he suggested instead a 'friendly chat'. In today's NHS this would have meant a swift dose of cognitive behavioural therapy, the cure-all of talking cures, but for reasons that still remain unclear to me I ended up having a year of Jungian psychotherapy. Like a good student doctor, I got up at five thirty in the morning, cycled to my Jungian counsellor, lay down on an easy chair and prepared to have the ruminations syringed out of my brain.

Even in the 1990s, when I was training, the go-to talking cure for OCD would never have been Karl Jung, a mystical physician from a pre-rational age. Behavioural therapy was the thing, repeatable tips like shouting, 'Stop!' and pressing the tip of a drawing pin, or flooding the preoccupied mind with the calamity it was so averse to. In behaviourism there is no emphasis on meaning. Neurosis is scooped out. But human blood just seemed to stain everywhere; beyond behaviour, beyond cognition, beyond reason, it sat in the creases of my hands like unmarked trails. And no amount of handwashing, no amount of self-help, could remove it. Carefully, judiciously, curiously, non-prescriptively, the Jungian therapist searched for meaning in these worries. And the preoccupations lessened and then disappeared.

Was it the easy chair that wanted to be a couch but couldn't afford the extra yard? Was it the therapeutic hour at student rates? Was it the simple passing of time and the remoulding of post-synaptic neurones? I will never know. But what I learned at that pre-dawn hour, when most of my peers were sleeping off their hangovers, is we don't just feel pain. We express it. It pours out of us as meaning.

Just before World War I Karl Jung severed his relationship with Freud and looked towards the East. His reading of Hinduism with its broader conception of self (see HEADSET) enlarged Jung's definition of ego into an identity integrated with everyone and everything around it. His metaphorical interpretation of karma, as a recurrence of symbolic patterns, was formative in his development of the collective unconscious and mythical archetypes. His collective unconscious is not, as some would have it, a reservoir of ideas to which we all have access. Instead, he suggests, we share a predisposition to mythic outlines, symbolic shapes – archetypes which we then flesh out into the fully fledged stories we tell ourselves.

Jung believed that this tendency towards symbolic forms was innate; we didn't learn it during childhood. For this heresy he was excommunicated from mainstream psychology. But his emphasis on humans' mythical tendency, their drive to generate meaning, their healthy predisposition towards some kind of religious form, is a useful counterpoint to the more arid schemas of cognitive psychology. 'An idea is psychologically true in as much as it exists,' he said. And for Jung, God, in whatever flavour of religion, was the overarching archetype, a coherent symbol, a unifying principle, a living metaphor that integrated the disparate parts of a man and woman in their internal model of themselves and the world (see also CHAIN WHEELS). Mystical awareness, as found in the religions of West and East, was the recognition of this integration, which was not a 'primitive' experience but the highest order towards which all men and women could aspire.

Jung reintroduced the idea, at least to the West, that the mind has a much more fluid boundary – that it is transpersonal. And our oldest understanding of transpersonal, of an imaginative landscape without borders, is ancient pagan and animist beliefs, still tilting towards us in the standing stones of Salisbury and Avebury, as the A roads curve away in their passage to clearer destinations. To wish for a meeting of pagan animism and modern rationalism is to risk the ridicule of both, but to dismantle the whole of our understanding into ascetically sealed parts is no understanding at all.

Jen, Sophie, Joe and I pedalled to an abandoned train platform on the bike path into Bristol where we found our friends Ed and Izzie, their son Stan and my friend Mike. Together we rolled through Staple Hill, Fishponds, Clay Bottom, Easton and back into Bristol. Sam, who'd been staying in our house while we'd been away, had written FINISH on a roll of wallpaper which he held across the bike path with another pal, Liz, amid a larger crowd of friends and family. I sped up to be alongside Jen, and then we cycled together, no-handed and holding hands, through a sheet of paper intended to cover up the cracks in walls.

CHAPTER 28

The Cranks

On the day we cycled into Bristol the police had cleared a squat, Telepathic Heights, on the pretext that firebombs were being made there to attack the supermarket on the other side of the road. The location was smack bang in the middle of Stokes Croft, an area of inner-city Bristol that lies somewhere between the retail malls of the city centre and the middle-class housing of the suburbs. It has long been an unruly mix of nightclubs, homeless hostels, massage parlours and bars, middle-class bohos mixing with city-centre drinkers, drug addicts and students. And it was, for a while, a small-scale Interzone able to resist the lumbering advance of corporate capitalism. Parachuting in a Tesco Express was never going to go unnoticed.

We woke during the night to the *thwack* of police helicopters. In the riot that followed cars were set alight, stones thrown and trailers tipped over. It's not clear where the petrol-bomb rumour started. But the volatility had been a long time brewing, and its ingredients were a lot more complex than a dash of Tesco unleaded and a twist of economy doilies.

Where do you begin to unpick the causes of a riot? Do you start with the police knocking down the door of a squat? Do you start with the booze and late-night clubbing of a spring bank holiday? Do you start with a coalition of anti-Tesco activists in a year-long fight against a planning process that seemed not to care? Do you start with the disparity between rich and poor and a local environment of street homelessness? Do you start with the Bristolian history of street protest, which extends through its anarchist co-ops, the Golden Hill Tesco land occupation of 1992, the nearby St Paul's riots of the 1980s and the political radicalism and mobs of the nineteenth century? Do you start with capitalism and cheap labour (see BAR BAG)? With a couple of cyclists on a floating warehouse of tat bound for supermarket shelves (see HANDLEBARS)? Or with the very forces of disorder, the carnival of the unconscious, given an even break by its rupture through the Interzone of Bristol's city centre (see REAR SPROCKETS)?

In the looping video that shows the front of Tesco Express being spider-webbed by a boot there is a sign at the side. It says BRISTOL'S BEST BIKE SHOP. And up and down that street, back and forth between the traffic light junctions, there have always been hundreds of bicycles, trying to avoid the lumbering lorries, the inner-city traffic. In Bristol, a city not built for bikes but alive with them, you are political by just sitting on a SADDLE, announcing that there is another way of doing things, another kind of power transfer.

The Cranks are the arms of metal that connect the PEDALS to the spindle of the BOTTOM BRACKET, which allow their turning force, or torque, to be transmitted to the CHAIN WHEELS and the CHAIN, thence the turning motion of the WHEELS. Enormous forces are applied through the lever of the Crank to the BOTTOM BRACKET spindle. The turning forces here are up to twenty times those at the PEDAL. And if the Crank is made of a softer alloy metal, then the hard steel of the BOTTOM BRACKET spindle can bore it out like a drill.

Basic human motions such as running, skipping, walking, jumping and hopping all rely on energy released from the elastic push and shove of muscles and tendons against gravity. Cycling involves the suspension of the human body above the ground, free floating, and the use of our legs and the largest muscles in our body in an entirely different way, using circular forces. The original leg-powered cranks of the textile spinning wheel only emerged during the Renaissance five hundred years ago. If Copernicus's replanting of the sun at the centre of the universe was a realignment of cosmic perspective that shook religious orthodoxy to its core, then the Crank was the lesser heresy; not only was God absent from the centre of the universe but man could turn its revolutionary surfaces with his legs.

Buddhism understands karma as a mental intention rather than a good or bad deed. It involves moral choices which have moral consequences, but these choices do not have a linear outcome and there is no simple lever between cause and effect. What we call action and consequence, cause and effect, is a much more fluid aggregation of interactions that has no clear beginning and end. Some Buddhists compare deeds to seedlings that lie dormant or flourish depending on the prevailing circumstances and whose ongoing growth or trajectory requires a formal nurturing. This is a long way from a push and shove determinism, a deed and the misdemeanour, born of the Enlightenment, which runs alongside the question of free will in Western philosophy (see HANDLEBARS).

Another way of understanding karma, at least from a Buddhist perspective, is to reframe the propositions of rebirth and reincarnation as *punabhava* – rebecoming. For a Buddhist there is no permanent self only self-transformation. The consequences of our intentions don't just have an impact on those around us and the outside world, they act to continuously change our own identity. To intend good for others may well result in a positive outcome for them but it also changes the shape of our own ever-rolling identity. This puts a different light on the seemingly insurmountable problems of our age. Cycling all the way to India amid the unfettered belch of Iranian lorries, the cinders of bunker oil container ships, the roadside plastic bottles, the inexorable march of 'progress', it felt like there was little that two tiny human beings on bikes could do. But once you begin to understand what you do as a form of intention that changes your character by its very action, then however far away the goal appears to be – rolling back the rising tides, overhauling the seasons, reintroducing diversity – then the means, the action, has its own intrinsic value, both personal and environmental. The colloquial understanding of karma – what goes around comes around – is not just that one good or bad deed begets another, but that it changes who we are as we employ it.

Cycling is an action which, if we intend it so, has a karmic outcome, not only as cleaner transport but in evolving the characters we are continually becoming. It is both creating change and changing us in its creation.

We are not always aware of the habitual patterns we fall into, which can have such consequences for us and those around us. Hence the emphasis on meditation in Buddhism, the reflective awareness of our intentions and the focus on kindness as a direction for that intention. We might not always be able to escape the ever-dominoing consequences of karma, Buddhism tells us, but we can escape our ignorance of it. The path to environmental action requires a revolution of the head, as well as a revolution of our material circumstances. This demands a pragmatic engaged philosophy that has the same urgency in our lives as Indian philosophy once held in the East; an understanding that creates not just insight but outcomes; freedom from the habitual patterns that are devaluing not just our own lives but the richness of the flourishing world around us.

Is it possible for there to be a social*ism*, an anarch*ism*, even a benign conservat*ism*; a fiercely engaged physical philosophy? A political radical will often suspect the reflective philosopher of being a wet flannel, and the reflective philosopher treats the radical with a benign pity. Cycling has a go at travelling between both. We may not see its effects after just one bike ride, but we may see them in the unravelling future of a cyclist's life. It doesn't matter if meditation is plumbed into an evening class, a business consultancy or a bike ride into the hills, irrational intuition can, and will, usurp and depose our habitual understanding.

Much of the debate about cycling falls into familiar polarities: either we change our roads or we improve cycling culture to thrive on the roads that have already been built. In moments of freewheeling reverie I imagine a *kaboom* moment when the two meet, a tipping point that is neither materially kerbside nor in our imagination, a cycling reality that is as engagingly hybrid and interrelated as the world we are trying to navigate.

Any forward-looking alliance of our human strengths has to wander 'abroad', neither rationally preoccupied with the technological revolutions of science nor mystically 'out there' in utopian communities hidden in the countryside. And all of this has to be engaged through the social action of politics.

And bikes, yes bikes, can be at the heart of this meeting. The proof is the countless bike workshops across the world which are meeting places for fellow wanderers, refugees, immigrants, the excluded, the imprisoned, the marginalised; those getting themselves back on their feet and then back on a bike after breakdowns and homelessness. Putting what is broken back together again. Building a bike from its parts and then riding it. The metaphor is in the making. It leaps off the page and onto the road.

After the Tesco riots, graffiti artist and flagbearer for Bristol's alternative status Banksy created a souvenir print of the event, showing a Tesco Everyday Value petrol bomb with its fuse alight. The print was sold in a limited edition by the organisers of Bristol's anarchist book fair, raising money for the legal costs of those arrested. You can argue about the rights and wrongs of this, but it highlighted an important fact. Actions have unexpected consequences. And one of those consequences is a print that now sells for five hundred pounds on eBay: 'Putting this up for auction,' one seller notes, 'as it really is sat in a tube in a drawer and I would rather go on holiday.'

Banksy is a slam dunk in metaphor. His juxtaposition of the material and the imaginative, the rioter throwing a bunch of flowers, the policeman dressed up as a teddy, the peace wall that cracks into a package holiday destination, is a symbolic crash. You can sneer at him for the blasé fault lines he sets up (and he's an easy target for those who like to wield the mallet of 'high' art on 'low') or alternatively see his stencils as a Day-Glo decorator's brush that brings out the street-level collisions already there, which we ride through every day: the disparities between a supermarket selling products to the poor for shareholder gain and freewheeling past a Tesco Express selling economy booze to street drinkers who beg for cash from the tourists who buy Banksy prints to put on their walls.

Bristol finds itself at the confluence of hippy Wales, channelled over the Severn Bridge, and the secular hard-headedness of the London corridor, trundling down the M4. It has a history both of inner transformation and hard-nosed political radicalism. And it has taken, and given, a lot of hard knocks.

Following the English civil war, in the 1640s, there was a space into which a new kind of English radicalism flowed. Workers forced out of the countryside by the land enclosures of the wealthy created a mobile working class, and institutional religion, battered by the war and the Reformation, was hanging on the ropes. Quakerism, one of the radical Christian sects that moved into this space, suggested that everyone could come to Christ 'in their own hearts', without the authority and power of the Church, and that sin was just another way to control believers through the institutions of religion. In 1656 the Quaker radical James Nayler rode on horseback into Bristol, while his followers sang hosannas and threw clothes before him in what many took to be a blasphemous re-enactment of Christ's entry into Jerusalem. Nayler was imprisoned and branded with a B for blasphemy. He had his tongue pierced with a red-hot poker and was made to repeat his procession through Bristol backwards, facing the rear of the horse. Quakerism never quite recovered its radical hold on the wandering population, and its families, excluded from formal education and state power, invested instead in factories and businesses in Bristol, the most well known of which is Fry's chocolate, which later merged with Cadbury's.

Around the end of the nineteenth century there was a resurgence of enlightened radicalism in Bristol; a newly politicised class that was looking for both inner and outer transformation and found itself increasingly at odds with religious notions of God or Christianity. In her book *Rebel Crossings* Sheila Rowbotham tells the story of two of these Bristol radicals, Helena Born and Miriam Daniel, and a Scottish unionist, Robert Nicol. Helena was one of a number of Christian socialists living in the middle-class suburb of Clifton, high up in the city, who were trying to make links with the working-class areas of Bristol 'down in the floods' next to the River Frome, a river now hidden by the M32. Helena rubbed shoulders with atheists and anarchists at a time when anarchism was more closely allied with socialism, and found kindred spirits in Miriam Daniel, an avant-garde poet and socialist, and her partner Robert, a Scottish agitator. The trio left Clifton and moved into a slum in the St Philip's area, hoping to create a utopian community dedicated not just to socialism but to a different way of understanding reality. Miriam and Robert's publication *The Truth about the Chocolate Factories or Modern White Slavery its Cause and Cure* was, on a surface reading at least, a criticism of the (Quaker-owned) Bristol chocolate factories and their working conditions. But it also contained the following aspirational lines:

> Hail the great Sun; the source of energy which brings joy to the hearts of countless of your despairing brothers and sisters. No, as you are noble men, gentle women, true maidens and youths, you will come out from the West where the day dies, and turn to the East to welcome the splendid Light of Love and Liberty which are not two, but one and Indivisible.

Miriam had Robert's child Sunrise, and they all moved from Bristol to America's east coast. Here they went in search of the transcendentalism and naturist anarchism of Ralph Waldo Emerson and Henry Thoreau, nineteenth-century 'seekers' and philosophers much influenced by Eastern philosophy. Their story is just one example of the hybridisation of politics and spirituality at the time, when anarcho-socialism, individualist-anarchism, democratic-enlightenment and anarcho-sexology, love-ins of hyphenation, were living realities and not just nooks in New Age bookshops.

In nineteenth-century Britain Fabian socialism had alliances with anarchism and theosophical schools of spiritual seeking at a time of growing faithlessness. Fabianism eventually threw off its hyphens and entered the material world of politics that was to become the Labour Party of the twentieth century. And just as all of this was happening the bicycle was gathering working-class solidarity, a marriage of body and politics, allowing young couples a fluidity in sexual relationships a good distance from the prying eyes of tenements and city parishes.

The song 'Daisy Bell' was written in 1892, a year after Miriam, Robert and Helena escaped Bristol for America, and just as the 'safety bicycle' was making a name for itself across the West. 'Safety' hid the thrill of more earthly delights.

Daisy, Daisy, give me your answer, do
I'm half crazy all for the love of you
It won't be a stylish marriage
I can't afford the carriage
But you'd look sweet upon the seat
Of a bicycle built for two.

Later in the same song, there are the lesser-known lines

When the night's dark we can both despise
Policemen and lamps as well

In 1895 the Clarion Cycling Club was set up for the 'freedom and fellowship' of working-class citizens. It had sections all over the country, and still exists today with two thousand members. At the same time 'rational dress', the right of women to wear more practical clothing, and not just on bikes, was gaining ground, something which for many men was an uncivilised assertion of female freedom. Cycling was stripping away gender, social and sexual codes in a sacrilegious 'Woo-hoo!' an ecstatic and unifying experience freewheeling into the future.

When Miriam, Robert and Helena arrived in Cambridge, Massachusetts, perhaps unsurprisingly they didn't find the utopia they were looking for but an industrial town with its own problems and infighting. They drifted towards the individualist anarchism of Benjamin Tucker, who gave Miriam Daniel a forum for her poems and allegories of free love and radical feminism in his paper *Liberty*.

Anarchy is commonly thought of as chaos and violence, when in fact it's a much more considered meeting of activism and philosophy, beginning in the mid-nineteenth century. Pierre-Joseph Proudhon, a French philosopher, struck out for mutualism, the idea that individuals should be able to own the fruit of their labour rather than factory owners or the state. His violence comes not from any material call to revolution (see SEAT POST) but from paradox and contradiction, with statements like 'Anarchy is order, government is civil war.'

Benjamin Tucker was influenced by Proudhon and allowed Miriam a way to combine freedom in personal relationships and identity with the wider ideals of socialism. Increasingly her ideas drifted into the outfield, into what Sheila Rowbotham calls extreme antinomianism, where there are no moral laws and no single theory or category of understanding in political, personal or spiritual terms. Miriam then fell out with Benjamin Tucker, moved to a ranch in California and distanced herself from Helena Born, before dying prematurely from breathing problems. Robert Nicol stayed in California with Sunrise to immerse himself in the alternative ideas, communes and magnetism of what would become the hippy lifestyle of the west coast.

Helena went back east, where she befriended and mentored a younger woman, Helen Tufts. Helena and Helen went on long bike rides together, advocating rational dress. And it was in Boston that Helena became the lover of a married socialist and anarchist organiser, William Baillie, their affair consummated on a meandering bike ride to visit a Walt Whitman convention, a poet of nature, mysticism and unhindered sexuality. When

Helena died, her friend Helen married William Baillie, and they continued their own criss-crossing journey of politics and personal liberation well into the twentieth century. Their daughter, also called Helena, became a professor and civil rights supporter.

Murray Bookchin, born in the New York Bronx in 1921, the son of Russian-Jewish immigrants, was originally a communist who was thrown out of various groups before discovering ecology and becoming known for his own take on ecological anarchism. He argued that society needed to be organised along lines that reflected the sustaining networks of the environment itself, rather than top-heavy decision-making. The degradation of the environment was a result of this top-down power and the pursuit of profit. He wrote, 'Ecology clearly shows that the totality of the natural world – nature taken in all its aspects, cycles and inter-relationships – cancels out all human pretensions to mastery over the planet.' Unlike a lot of radical dreamers from the 1960s and 70s Bookchin got to grips with his own ideology, building an experimental 'school of social ecology' and ignoring his fellow anarchists' rejection of democracy by organising small assemblies and green jobs in his local elections. He campaigned alongside a young Bernie Sanders, the socialist democrat who fought Hillary Clinton for the Democratic presidential nomination. Sanders won the election but then distanced himself from Bookchin's eco-anarchist assemblies. Later in life Bookchin believed that anarchists were becoming too preoccupied with individualist-anarchism. Those who looked inward to, say, the mystical preoccupations of Miriam Daniel and the Bristol radicals were ignoring the political struggle that lay at the forefront of their own ideology. He went as far as saying that the movement had been reduced to 'lifestyle anarchism', the appearance of anarchy for appearance's sake, a criticism that that has been levelled at identity politics more generally and has cast its net over Banksy's stencillism.

The various social and individualist philosophies that lap through modern culture have proved most potent when each has held the other in check, preventing radical social movements lurching towards dogma or inward-seeking individualists drifting into self-indulgence, like the yippies of 1960s America, whose anarchic socialism met the transcendent practices of the East. The academicisation of philosophy, the 'victory' of capitalism and the inward-looking tribes of the New Age may have made these combinations, these hyphenations, less likely, but they are still there to be made, as new generations forget the paths behind them and instead move forward, a healthy balancing act seen in the unceasing momentum of cycling.

Cyclists and cycling movements are continually making and rebreaking these connections wherever they go, and in my corner of Bristol there has been an anarchist collective since 1995, where the original squatters turned a bank into a housing co-op. It has long had an open-access bike workshop and spaces for environmentalism, anarchist activism and print making.

The central feature of Banksy's anarchism is not his graffiti but the continually paradoxical nature of what Banksy, or the idea of Banksy, has become. Banksy is the manufacturer of his own myth at a time when the manufacturing industry is dead and the service industry is a cafe full of Banksy prints. But it would be wrong to place him and his work slap bang in the funfair of postmodernism and money (see PEDALS). His up-yours contradictions, his wormholes of irony, have more in common with the absurdism of the early twentieth century and people like Alfred Jarry, myth maker and cyclist extraordinaire.

In 1891, the same year Miriam Daniel was writing odes to free love in the name of individualist-anarchism, Alfred Jarry, foul-mouthed teenager and libertine, was cycling into Paris. The first performance of his play *Ubu Roi* led to a riot. Ubu, its principal character, obscene king and destroyer of civilised manners, would become the template for Jarry's own life. He combined fascination with the hard mechanical sciences of the day with the table-turning fantasies of his own imagination, taking flight in increasingly uncompromising bike rides, with a rifle over his shoulder, two pistols down his belt and a tramcar BELL riveted to his handlebars. If Banksy brokered his myth with anonymity, Jarry pedalled his on the streets of Paris with a loudhailer. His life and his writing defied separation and his bicycle cycled between the two.

He inaugurated a sham school of philosophy which sought to leap beyond metaphor and into 'pataphor', paradoxical fantasies that existed in a universe of their own making. Jarry, the 'pataphysician', went all-out to explore this new philosophy by bike, on a rocket fuel of wine and absinthe. If the smart intellectuals of the nineteenth century had pedalled about on the safety bicycle, Jarry was out to prove how unsafe any fixed notion of rationality could be. Pataphysics allows for reason but immediately juxtaposes it with the impulsive and the irrational. What we believe to be *the* truth, Jarry proposes, is simply another illusion. In this way pataphysics has more in common with the face-slapping koans and paradoxes of Zen Buddhism than with Western philosophy.

The conclusion of these investigations, on and off the bike, was that there was no difference between the psyche and the body, and that reality tended towards a singular unity, subjectively experienced but rationally observed. Pataphysics playfully sent up the certainties of science by taking the reader into this reality, to a place where machines were living entities, capable of love and being loved.

Jarry's contemporaries were mainly idealists and symbolists, who elevated imaginary experience above objective reality while keeping objective reality, the bread and butter of putting food on the table, quite separate. Jarry, on the other hand, let this symbolism out of the box and rode it through the streets of Paris. He lived his contradictory philosophy of pataphysics to the full, with the same vividness that Eastern philosophy is expressed in the chaotic street life of India. He found not formal enlightenment but an irrational delight, a guffawing unity with the godless universe, whose mathematics pointed not to a box of tools but to a momentary transcendence, afoot the pedals of his track bike.

Jarry did not meet H. G. Wells, but he was an admirer of his work and wrote his *Commentary and Instructions for the Practical Construction of the Time Machine* shortly after reading the French translation of Wells' original story *The Time Machine*. Wells, like Jarry, was a keen cyclist and directly influenced by the radical politics of his time, being a Fabian socialist and 'free lover'. But Jarry's *Commentary*, written under the pseudonym Dr Faustroll, was more playful, concluding time should be based on a subjective sense of duration, rather than simple increments of seconds, minutes, hours and days.

Jarry was very much influenced by Henri Bergson, an early tutor, who considered time in terms of duration. Duration was not extended, in the sense of a line passing from A to B, neither was it a series of discrete events that occurred one after the other. Duration was a continuous unity, a unified flow that had no beginning or end. To try to separate it out would be like trying to pull apart the rolling waves of the ocean. Duration could only be understood intuitively, in states of flow. Bergson saw in this an indivisible stream of consciousness, a term coined by his colleague the American philosopher William James, a stream that rational science had lost sight of in its empirical quantification of experience.

Jarry's 'tempomobile', or time machine, was his beloved Clement Luxe track bike, with no gears and no brakes to interfere with the ever-flowing unity of time. It had an enormous CHAIN WHEEL, and an exhausting gear ratio, estimated by his biographer Alastair Brotchie to be 36:9, generating the kind of torque used in modern sprint cycling. To get it moving would have been torture, but when it got moving it really would have *flown*. Jarry died in a paupers' ward from TB of the brain, an infection thought to have spread from his lungs after a cold contracted on a bike ride. But his wild cycling, the duration of his experiences, has long outlasted his autopsy report on the mortuary table. Pataphysics is still a guilty pleasure in Western universities, a hip flask of irrationality between formal seminars, but his influence reaches far wider than this, and is evident in the feints and sucker punches of modern art, the street happenings of 1960s situationism and the foul graffiti on the side of walls.

The individualist anarchism of the end of the nineteenth century enlarged into the identity politics of the 1970s: feminist, gender, sexuality, race and single-issue causes that struggled to find a coherent unity in the way that Bristol socialists like Helena Born had hoped for. The Californian theorist and provocateur Donna Haraway tried to make (non)sense of these dilemmas in her 'Cyborg Manifesto' of the 1980s, an academic paper of perverse intent, as playful and contradictory as Jarry's, which deploys the jargon of technical language in order to undermine it. Haraway proposed no anarchist utopia but instead a 'cyborg' future. Her creature, a mixture of organism and machine, was the anti-Schwarzenegger of those seemingly contradictory forces, with sexuality, gender, gay rights and socialism mashed up in new ways, where 'people were not afraid of their joint kinship with animals and machines, not afraid of permanently partial identities and contradictory standpoints'. Rather than despair at the retreat of identity politics into its multiple silos, she rejoiced in a cyborg that was all of these things at once, 'monstrous and illegitimate', a creature not born of old institutions or new-wave politics, but of them all welded altogether, a collision of mind and metal and of metal-tasting blood.

I grew up with bikes. As a three-year-old I had a tricycle, as an eight-year-old I had a Chopper, as a teenager a racer in kingfisher green. Then, somewhere along the line, the bikes disappeared. Work, it turned out, demanded a car. And it was only much later, as an adult, that I bought a second-hand Raleigh Explorer, a prototype for the now-commonplace expedition bicycle, a sort of mountain bike used for touring. There followed a new-found obsession with all things bone-rattling. I embarked on long journeys all over the place, rediscovering the landscape I'd grown up with. The first proper conversation that Jen and I had, on our first ever date, was side by side down the bike path into Bristol city centre.

And if our bikes ever had a mechanical problem we sought out Bike John. The doorway to his terraced house was like Mark E. Smith's mouth, bits of wood and plaster knocked out all over the place. The ground-floor corridor and living room were punk hymns to cycling, the white walls scuffed and streaked with oil and rubber. Having your bike repaired by John was a lot more than just having your bike repaired by John, it was a digressing conversation into politics, the online globalisation of bike parts, local grocery prices and how, if you weren't prepared to pay a proper price for getting your bike repaired, you weren't prepared to confront the fault lines in your own hypocrisy. Bikes were John's lifeblood and his extended family. He took his repair stand to festivals, schools and youth clubs. But this didn't mean that he *loved* them. He resented the way they'd gatecrashed his home and his cash flow. He remained as belligerently contradictory as the machines that took lumps out of his wall and stacked up in his front yard like oversized bunches of keys.

Once, as he launched my Raleigh into the stand, he told me the story of the bike he'd built for Banksy, who frequented his local boozer and couldn't find a frame big enough to ride on. John earmarked a clunker that was the right size and then built it up into a working ride. The artist couldn't afford to pay John at the time but exchanged it for one of his early stencilled prints. John told me it was now his pension. One day, he said, he'd use it to rent a proper workshop and reclaim his house from the bikes.

As soon as Jen and I decided to ride to India, we figured that our workaday rides might not be up to the job and, somewhat sheepishly, began looking at more expensive models rather than going to John for refurbished ones. I continued to bump into him at the corner shop, and, we agreed, he was looking much trimmer, having laid off the booze and cooked breakfasts. It turned out John had pancreatic cancer and died six months before we set off. The last time I saw him I felt bad I'd spent so much on my new bike. John said it didn't matter. How you spent your money didn't matter. He'd cashed in the Banksy print, bought a Harley-Davidson and ridden across Europe with a mate, dosed up on morphine. I admired his Harley and he admired my new expedition bike. And then he went into his house. And I cycled off up the hill.

John's funeral was standing room only. The congregation cycled there together. I am now the same age as John, and it seems to me that a life lived with bikes and the friendship they bring is one of the richest you can have. Bikes are more than tools, more than transport, so much more than sport; they are part of what it means to be alive.

CHAPTER 29

The Seat Stays

The Seat Stays are the pair of narrow-gauge tubes that run from the top of the SEAT TUBE to the CHAIN STAYS. They transmit much of the shock from the rear wheel to the rider and act as the point of attachment for the rear BRAKES. The brake cable often loops down over the join between the TOP TUBE and Seat Stays in its path from the HANDLEBARS towards the rear BRAKES, a thread of seamless continuity across the tube welds of a bike's architecture. But more importantly the stays complete the rear triangle and the integral structure of the whole frame. In this way they bring the frame 'home' to a more singular notion of what a bike, and cycling, is (see VIRTUAL TRIANGLE).

If you look at a bicycle from the side, you can see it consists of two triangles: the front triangle, which comprises the SEAT TUBE, TOP TUBE and DOWN TUBE (more of a trapezoid if you count the HEAD TUBE), and the rear triangle, which includes the CHAIN STAYS and Seat Stays, sharing the SEAT TUBE with the front triangle. Looking down at a bike, there are two additional smaller triangles. One is made by the two Seat Stays and the rear axle, another by the two CHAIN STAYS and the rear axle. The corners of these multiple triangles act like pinned joints so that when one edge is tensed or compressed, the adjoining sides compress or tense in compensation, distributing these internal forces around the structure as a whole. It is not the individual elements that contribute to a frame's strength and lightness but the composite. This, together with its spoked WHEELS, gives a bike its airiness and flight. Rather than being frozen, a bike frame is in a constant ebb and flow. Its parts might define it, but it is the whole, the tense composition, that makes it come alive.

On our return I fell back in love with Bristol's inner-city brokenness, its crazy-paving paradoxes; the lopsided paving stones, the terraced houses toppling down the sides of hills, the boom-box BMWs accelerating down the narrow streets, the punk pubs playing trad jazz, the prim estate agents with chewing gum on their heels, the organic cafes nailing blackboards over laminated menus for full English breakfasts, the first, second, third and who's counting generations of families from the Middle East, Asia, eastern Europe, Caribbean and sub-Saharan Africa.

Later, in a basement room expressly hired for the purpose of writing this book, I started to notice something unusual about my heart, or rather the way it beat, like a skipping rope that catches and then flies with the pace of a boxer's jump cord. At about one hundred and fifty beats per minute. I fretted at my pulse this way and that, as if it were my fingers that were at fault and not the heart itself. The possibilities of imminent death were innumerable. Could it be the hacksaw pulse of ventricular tachycardia? Or the shrivelled snake skin of ventricular fibrillation? Whatever it was, I was dying, I was doomed, I was dead.

'Press one for results. Press two for appointments.'

'*Badoom, badoom, badoom, badoom, badoom, badoom...*'

'I'd like to speak to my doctor.'

'*Badoom, badoom, badoom, badoom, badoom, badoom...*'

'Your doctor will ring you back between the hours of four and six p.m.'

'*Badoom, badoom, badoom, badoom, badoom, badoom...*'

'Do you have chest pain?'

'*Badoom, badoom, badoom, badoom, badoom, badoom...*'

'No.'

'*Badoom, badoom, badoom, badoom, badoom, badoom...*'

'Your doctor will ring you back between four and six p.m.'

'*Badoom, badoom, badoom, badoom, badoom, badoom...*'

I pressed the big red button. 'I am a doctor.'

'What do you think?' the GP asked me as I limped into his office as if only a heart this fast could make a man this lame.

'An SVT?'

He put two fingers on the artery that runs either side of the neck and gave it a little massage which for some patients can be a safe way of stimulating the vagus nerve and switching off the *badabadabooms* of SVT. The skipping rope paused, hung in midair like a high-wire act and then returned to its more familiar, plodding, beat.

'Yes,' he said. 'A supraventricular tachycardia.'

I had just cycled to India for crying out loud. My heart was invulnerable. It was Agincourt, the Battle of Britain, the Channel Tunnel.

A supraventricular tachycardia is a super-fast heartbeat that begins in the upper chambers of the heart known as the atria. (It does not come from the larger chambers below, the ventricles, with their more worrying inclination to a deathly and disordered stampede.) And it can be triggered, as in my case, by the body's electrical impulses doing a U-turn into a feedback loop, driving the heart at twice its normal pace.

One heart tracing and a dose of beta blockers later, and I was back on the bike with a diagnosis of 'paroxysmal supraventricular tachycardia'. It wasn't the 'supraventricular tachycardia' I minded so much as the 'paroxysmal', which sounded like a dose of hysterics quite unamenable to smelling salts. The beta blockers gave me strange dreams. I would find myself trapped in an endless circular bike tour to India. Jen watching me go past. Again and again and again.

The heart was out of bounds in Birmingham Medical School dissection room. The skull was considered simple enough, but the heart demanded a finesse thought to be beyond first-year medical students. To compensate we were taken on a guided tour by an anatomy prosector. Our heart lay on a metal tray a good distance from the ribcage it had been taken from, pinned with wire markers and paper flags like a diorama pulled out of a map.

'What's this?' said Dr Hatch, the unfeasibly eccentric anatomy tutor, pointing to a green paper flag.

'Mitral valve, Dr Hatch.'

'And this?'

'Tricuspid valve, Dr Hatch.'

'And these?'

'Um.'

'Chordae tendineae. Heart strings. Lyre of Orpheus and all that.'

'Yes, Dr Hatch.'

'And what runs down here?' He pointed to the dividing wall, the interventricular septum.

'Electrical system, Dr Hatch.'

'Name the parts.'

'Sino atrial node. Atrioventricular node. Bundle of His. Left posterior bundle. Right bundle and... and...'

'Purkinje. Dear boy. Purkinje fibres. Purk-in-je.'

Jan Evangelista Purkinje discovered both the Purkinje muscular conduction fibres of the heart and the brain's coordinating Purkinje cells, at either end of the long wandering trail we call the autonomic nervous system. Purkinje was a Czech anatomist, physiologist, poet, philosopher, activist and monk. He left his monastic order, studied philosophy at the University of Prague, specialised in the natural sciences, became an anatomy prosector at Prague Medical School and eventually an expert in the experimental physiology of the senses. He was a translator of German poet, philosopher and physician Friedrich Schiller, sheltered writers in his home and promoted Czech democracy and free speech. He saw the physician as an artist rather than a repair man, whose role was not just to sustain life but to help people make the most of the lives they had left.

Three months on from my first episode of paroxysmal supraventricular tachycardia I was still experiencing, lo and behold, paroxysms of supraventricular tachycardia. I didn't feel unwell so much as disorientated.

'Can I cycle a hundred kilometres this weekend?' I asked the heart specialist at my first outpatient appointment.

'That's just ridiculous,' he said. 'The heart was never meant to be pushed that hard. You should consider having an ablation.' And with that he was gone along the corridor to the next patient.

With prolonged exercise the volume of blood in our circulation increases. This enlarges the return of fluid to the heart and stimulates a more forceful contraction, a greater output per beat. This causes the heart muscle to change: it thickens and strengthens, and the underlying, or resting, heart rate reduces as it becomes more efficient. But some of this decrease is also explained by an increase in parasympathetic tone, modified by the parasympathetic nervous system.

The more flamboyant and, let's face it, better known sympathetic system is responsible for fight or flight, our reaction to perceived threat, with increases in heart rate and diversion of blood to the muscles. The humbler parasympathetic is responsible for rest and digest, with reductions in heart rate and the diversion of blood from the muscles to the stomach.

These two autonomic pathways regulate each other and our basic physiological functions, balancing each other out. And the balance of this finely tuned system drifts after prolonged exercise, with an increased parasympathetic tone and a lower resting heart rate. But this increased tone can then have a surprising and paradoxical effect. The slower conduction of the electrical circuits in our hearts can offer a window into which rogue electrical impulses can sneak and set off the racing heartbeats so disturbing to writers of books on cycling and metaphysics. The thickening muscle of the exercising heart, while undeniably more powerful, can shape the nerves that spread through it and set off fickle trigger points where these rhythms begin, the so-called hot spots, which catheter ablation, recommended by my heart specialist, can burn away. By cycling to India I could well have changed the structure of my heart in such a way that it was now signalling its distress in a flapping rhythm. But the linear story of cause and effect was never going to be that simple.

I was stressed, I was tired, I was drinking more booze and caffeine. I was jumping into cold winter lakes. And there was something changing between Jen and I. All of these were undoubtedly tonal triggers for the vagus nerve. And it seemed to me that going in to ablate the radical factions in my heart was not the right solution. So, I thought, I might as well try another approach. I might as well just chill out. And, having been convinced by the rather convoluted diversion of a four-thousand-mile bike ride to India that meditation might be worth a go, I closed my eyes. And breathed.

The vagus nerve is named from the Latin, meaning 'wandering'. It's a long ambling highway made of mixed sensory, motor and parasympathetic nerves that eventually enters the skull near the cerebellum, the part of the hind brain involved in motor coordination. This is also the seat of Purkinje's other great finding, the Purkinje nerve cells, which network the higher cortical regions associated with consciousness with our body movements. The vagus wanders from the heart to the brain, calling from door to door in a gathering communication that speaks to our breathing, our pulse, the branching canopies of the brain, and consciousness. Is it any surprise that if we regulate our breathing, if we calm and monitor our thoughts, if we narrow the concentration of our focus, we can affect the heartbeat at the very centre of our life?

Our perception is built around twin modes of attention so interwoven as to be inseparable, a narrow focus and a wider vigilance. In the mindfulness of Buddhism these two attentive states are being used together in a heightened way. There is a focused attention on repetition, such as in breathing or the ticking of the FREEWHEEL, and a simultaneous monitoring that is wider, a vigilant awareness of the travel of our thoughts. Our ability to meditate improves the more we do it; we focus for longer and with more ease, while our self-monitoring gets better. Our ingrained patterns of thinking, our emotions and our consequent behaviour become more accessible to us. In other words, we begin to reconnect, like an engineer in a frazzled telephone exchange sticking skinned wires back together.

It is unarguable that our attention is being changed by digital technology. Our ability to do more is matched only by our capacity to concentrate less. This is partly driven by the demands of economic growth, which has largely switched from factory production to virtual aggregation – the strip-mining of our online lives for profit, the data-harvesting of our imaginative and social worlds to feed warehouse algorithms. The social media we so readily inhabit are actually a prizefight, where the trophy is our attention. If, as Eastern philosophy supposes, the way we attend to the world cannot be separated from the way we understand it, then what is at stake here is not only our credit rating but our ability to wake up to reality. Our enlightenment, in other words, is being bought for dollars. Facebook's mission statement used to be 'making the world more open and connected'; now it is to 'give people the power to build community and bring the world closer together'. Yet Facebook's own digital filters manufacture identity cul-de-sacs, groups which frame themselves in opposition to the groups around them, all in the service of more clicks and more distraction. Facebook doesn't care about connecting us or creating 'communities', it cares about money.

This is where radical politics and subjective philosophy can meet (see CRANKS). If the way that we attend to the world is up for grabs – and there is a very real land grab going on, being driven by these economic forces – then the fightback begins with how we attend to and understand the world. Metaphysics, our ancient investigation into the nature of reality, becomes no longer a relic of Greek learning (see BELL), but *the* most important way to meet the forces that seek to alienate us. Meditation becomes not a lifestyle option but a singular point of resistance.

Cycling reconnects people, yes actual people, across continents. It is not algorithmically inclined, it does not filter out our differences but instead discovers a common kindness. The Muslim, the Christian, the Hindu, the atheist do not announce their allegiance before offering water or the shade of a pomegranate tree or a bed for the night. The rolling back roads and not the rolling news are the community that we share. And out there on those roads, the wind, the leaves, the sky, the sun, the birds sustain and prolong our attention, re-concentrate our focus, rebuild our understanding. To close your eyes and feel the sun and the wind on your face is not advanced technology. To have the space and the solitude to do so is not a discovery of the last ten years but of thousands of years of philosophy and learning. How then have we reached the point where we need to be told to close our eyes and breathe by the National Institute for Clinical Excellence? How have we allowed philosophy, excavated from religion and science, to become so separate from our relationships and our working lives? I have no answer to these questions other than to get back on my bike, a turning outwards and inwards that is surely one of the balances needed right now in a fraught world of distraction.

As the vagus nerve enters the brain it splays into a number of fine threads that lead through the medulla and into the cerebellum. The cerebellum has long been associated with motor coordination, the checks and balances of muscle memory which allow us to move with intent and purpose rather than the slapstick of near-hits and misses. It undoubtedly helps with the intuitive balance needed to ride a bike. But it is only more recently that scientists have investigated its magnificent Purkinje cells, showing how they connect with regions all over the brain. The cerebellum might be solidly linked with the motor control of our muscles but it also connects with nervous pathways involved in attention, language, emotion and the higher cerebral processing we call consciousness. To ask where the vagus nerve begins and ends is like asking where the tide meets the shore.

That the Purkinje cells of the cerebellum are integrated with our 'higher' conscious but control our 'lower' limbs will come as no surprise to many Eastern philosophies, or to continental existentialism, where to be is to do (see SEAT TUBE). That cycling and staying balanced on a bike has a much wider effect than on muscle tone and stamina, that it encourages a balance in the way that we understand the world, is simply another way of reaffirming the interconnectedness of all that we are.

A mixture of 'ridiculous' cycling, some attentive breathing in a quiet room, a disappearing dose of beta blockers, one less pint at the boozer and swearing off coffee meant that my racing pulse became less racy. I don't know if the heart remodelled itself on the mind or the other way round, but I began to notice that I no longer noticed my heart at all. If I was aware, it was only in contrast to the waywardness that had gone before. As the journalist Michael Blastland has noted of his own paroxysmal arrhythmia, 'Our pulse is part of who we are. It is normality. It's safe. The steady rhythm from which spring the unsteadying intoxication of music, poetry, love, fear. And I think the joy of the skipped beat comes from that contrast. Adventures are exciting but who doesn't want to go home afterwards.'

Abraham Maslow, one of the founders of humanist psychology, the bedrock of talking therapies in the West, was drawn to 'peak' experiences (man's mystical encounters or ecstatic states of unity), but he also believed we have 'plateau' experiences – encounters that approach such peak states and then continue to offer a sustaining and fresh sense of perspective in our lives.

> The great lesson from the true mystics, from the Zen Monks, and now also from the Humanistic and Transpersonal psychologists, is that the sacred is in the ordinary, that it is to be found in one's daily life, in one's neighbours, friends, and family, in one's back yard, and that travel may be a flight from confronting the sacred.

My paroxysmal supraventricular tachycardia, which started the second autumn we got back, stopped the following spring, when our son was born. And in the delivery room I wasn't thinking about cycling, philosophy, religion or the nature of reality. All I was thinking about was the pulse of his one-hundred-and-fifty-beats-per-minute heart as I held him in the chaotic blood of birth, to my chest.

René Descartes, the philosopher and polymath who I've spent so much of this book undermining, located the bridge between mind and body in the pineal gland, in the centre of the brain. But perhaps, just perhaps, he intuitively located it in what we *feel*, in our relationships with each other and the environment, the inwardly tuned sensitivity of the pineal gland to the outward turning of the sun. Russell Shorto, in his book *Descartes' Bones*, describes how the philosopher's last work was a treatise on the 'passions of the soul'. And how, at the final count, he decided the bridge between mind and body wasn't to be found in the pineal gland after all, but in passion. In the 'heart'.

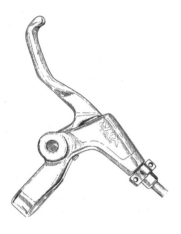

CHAPTER 30

The Brakes

When our son started cycling it wasn't balancing he found difficult, it was braking. He could pedal forward well enough but couldn't see how to bring that movement to a close and would wobble off into a verge. He would try to use his feet only to find that his heels didn't quite reach the ground, until one day his hands discovered and then trusted the Brakes. Cycling demands a leap of faith – that the bike's rolling momentum will maintain our forward progress. But getting off the SADDLE requires another kind of faith entirely, that what we set in motion can be stopped somewhere along the road, a hopeful pessimism, which all things considered is probably the best way to approach the unknown.

On the trip I had V-brakes, two metal arms that gripped two rubber pads about a pivot and pressed against the metal rim of the WHEEL. So the WHEEL is part of the braking system, and if the rim is out of alignment a bike cannot properly slow down or may even stop you rolling along the path in the first place. Stopping, in other words, is part of starting.

You will not be surprised to learn that I *needed* top-of-the-range XTR Shimano Brakes, solid forged levers of alloy metal with a gantry join, looking like the dockside cranes on Bristol Harbour. But I just couldn't get them to work. I fiddled, back and forth, up and down, endlessly noodling at the spring tension that aligned them until suddenly they would slip again and begin rubbing on the WHEEL. After four weeks of scratching my head and sending the parts back and forth, I sheepishly discovered that the reason my top-of-the-range Brakes didn't work was because I hadn't properly fitted the WHEEL. The Brakes were slipping because the WHEEL itself was moving in the frame.

In rim braking the energy of the moving bike is turned into heat energy, which is dissipated throughout the WHEEL. When you're going down a mountain pass on a fully loaded touring bike the rims can get hot enough to cause a blowout in the INNER TUBES. Experts will tell you to 'pump' the Brakes – alternate the front and rear Brakes, balancing your speed and stopping power in a way that allows the rim to cool.

I've never met anyone who's had a blowout, but I've met a fair few who've 'endoed' during emergency braking. This is when the sudden locking of the front wheel causes the rear wheel to lift off the ground, pitching the bike and rider over the point where the front tyre touches the ground. The bike and rider effectively become a turning circle so that when the rider's centre of gravity tips past the axis of the front wheel, they are flung over the HANDLEBARS and into the unyielding arms of fate.

But a somersault over the HANDLEBARS can easily be avoided if the cyclist braces her arms and sits back in the SADDLE. Touring bikes like ours, which have a long wheelbase or frame, are much less likely to endo than a racing bike, or a penny farthing, where the rider sits over the front wheel. The best technique is to grip the front Brake hard, while shifting your weight back on the SADDLE, and then, a moment later, snatch the rear Brake to stop the rear wheel skidding and fishtailing ahead of the HANDLEBARS. Brakes work best when they are modulated – alternated – using the feel of the bike, its momentary levitations from the ground, to judge which lever to press and when. We learn how to use them rationally, but they have to be applied intuitively, using left and right brake levers – in the metaphor of pop psychology, left and right hand, right and left brain dominance, alternating synthetic and analytic ways of acting and learning. Stopping is every bit as complex as our first wobble from the kerb, yet it is an afterthought, which we only confront when we most need it.

Brakes were once pushed onto WHEELS by solid rods and levers. Then Bowden cables were introduced, flexible steel cables that move inside steel-wound tubes to remotely pull the brake pad onto the WHEEL rather than push it with a plunger. They use fixed levers at either end of the cable to increase the 'mechanical advantage' that braking requires. The force of the brake pad on the rim is exponentially greater than that at the HANDLEBARS because of the different distance the levers travel at each end of the cable. We move the brake control levers a few centimetres at the HANDLEBARS, whereas the brake pads travel only a few millimetres onto the WHEEL. Conservation of energy means that the same amount of work has to occur at either end, so although the brake pads move a shorter distance, they do so with much greater force, allowing us to decelerate and, hopefully, prevent a crash.

Our son learned to ride on the path that runs alongside our house in Bristol, the same unused railway track on which we headed to India six years before. I held onto the seat stays at the back of his frame as he made stops and starts, working the pedals, clutching the brakes, until the bike began to strain at my fingers.

And for once I wasn't worrying about the bottom bracket, the bell, the seat tube, the front hub, the rear sprockets, the tyres, the seat post, the gears, the saddle, the top tube, the pedals, the wheels, the inner tubes, the bar bag, the stem, the headset, the star fangled washer, the freewheel, the rake, the head tube, the handlebars, the down tube, the chain wheels, the chain stays, the chain, the cranks, the seat stays and the clutch of the brakes, all I could feel was the tug of his bike in my hand.

'It's OK, Dad,' he said. 'You can let go now.'

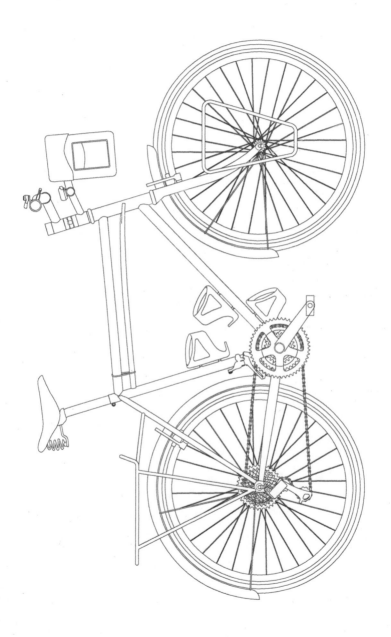

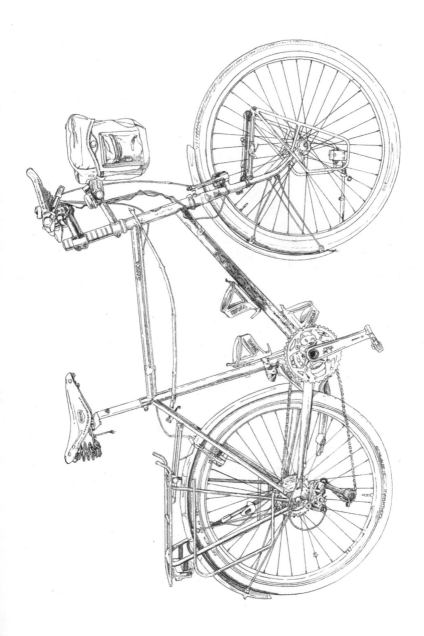

Bibliography

Abrahams, Sir Adolphe, *The Human Machine: An Analysis and Description of the Human Body, and its Structure and Functions, in Terms of Inanimate Machinery*, Penguin, Harmondsworth, 1956

Adamson, Peter, *Philosophy in the Islamic World: A Very Short Introduction*, Oxford University Press, Oxford, 2015

Adonis, trans. Judith Cumberbatch, *Sufism and Surrealism*, Saqi Books, London, 2016

Armstrong, Lance, *It's Not About the Bike*, Yellow Jersey Press, London, 2001

Aurelius, Marcus, trans. Maxwell Staniforth, *Meditations*, Penguin Classics, London, 1964

Aveni, Anthony F., *Empires of Time*, Tauris Parke, New York, 2000

Bainbridge, David, *Middle Age: A Natural History*, Portobello Books, London, 2012

Baldock, John, *The Essence of Sufism*, Arcturus, London, 2004

Ballantine, Richard, *Richard's Bicycle Book*, Pan, London, 1984

Bartley, Christopher, *An Introduction to Indian Philosophy: Hindu and Buddhist Ideas from Original Sources*, Bloomsbury, London, 2015

Batchelor, Stephen, *After Buddhism: Rethinking the Dharma for a Secular Age*, Yale University Press, New Haven and London, 2015

Bathurst, Bella, *The Bicycle Book*, Harper Press, London, 2011

Baudrillard, Jean, trans. Bernard Schutze and Caroline Schutze, *The Ecstasy of Communication*, Semiotext(e), South Pasadena, 2012

Beattie, Andrew, *The Danube*, Oxford University Press, New York, 2010

Beeley, Serena, *A History of Bicycles*, Studio Editions, London, 1992

Bertram, Christopher, *Routledge Philosophy Guidebook to Rousseau and the Social Contract*, Routledge, London, 2004

Blake, William, *Songs of Innocence & of Experience*, Tate Publishing, London, 2006

Boyce, Mary, *A Persian Stronghold of Zoroastrianism*, Oxford University Press, Oxford, 1977

Brandt, Jobst, *The Bicycle Wheel*, Avocet, Palo Alto, 1993

Broome, Matthew R., and Lisa Bortolotti (ed.), *Psychiatry as Cognitive Neuroscience*, Oxford University Press, Oxford, 2009

Brotchie, Alastair, *Alfred Jarry: A Pataphysical Life*, The MIT Press, Cambridge, Massachusetts, 2011

Brotton, Jerry, *A History of the World in Twelve Maps*, Penguin, London, 2013

Brown, Sheldon, *Sheldon Brown-Bicycle Technical Information*, https://www.sheldonbrown.com, accessed Oct 2018

Butler, Christopher, *Postmodernism: A Very Short Introduction*, Oxford University Press, Oxford, 2002

Camus, Albert, trans. Justin O'Brien, *The Myth of Sisyphus*, Penguin, London, 2005

Carroll, Anthony J., and Richard Norman (ed.), *Religion and Atheism: Beyond the Divide*, Routledge, Abingdon, 2017

Cartwright, Garth, *Princes Amongst Men: Journeys with Gypsy Musicians*, Serpent's Tail, London, 2005

Cioran, E. M., trans. Ilinca Zarifopol-Johnston, *On the Heights of Despair*, The University of Chicago Press, Chicago, 1992

Cipolla, Carlo M., *Clocks and Culture 1300–1700*, W.W. Norton, New York, 2003

Clarke, Michael, *Flesh and Spirit in the Songs of Homer: A Study of Words and Myths*, Clarendon Press, Oxford, 1999

Conrad, Peter, *Mythomania: Tales of Our Times, From Apple to Isis*, Thames & Hudson, London, 2016

Coverley, Merlin, *Psychogeography*, Pocket Essentials, Harpenden, 2010

Coward, Harold, *Jung and Eastern Thought*, State University of New York Press, Albany, N.Y., 1985

Cox, Gary, *How to Be an Existentialist, or, How to Get Real, Get a Grip and Stop Making Excuses*, Continuum, London, 2009

—, *Sartre: A Guide for the Perplexed*, Continuum, London, 2007

Czigány, Lóránt, *The Oxford History of Hungarian Literature: From the Earliest Times to the Present*, Clarendon Press, Oxford, 1984

Damasio, Antonio R., *Descartes' Error*, Vintage, London, 2006

Daniel [*sic*], Miriam and Nicoll [*sic*], Robert, *The Truth about the Chocolate Factories or Modern White Slavery its Causes and Cure*, Facts for the Times (Vol 1), Bristol, no date (pamphlet)

Dasti, Matthew R., and Edwin F. Bryant (ed.), *Free Will, Agency, and Selfhood in Indian Philosophy*, Oxford University Press, New York, 2014

De Botton, Alain, *The Art of Travel*, Penguin Books, London, 2003

Debord, Guy, *Society of the Spectacle*, Black & Red, Detroit, 2010

Dehaene, Stanislas, *Consciousness and the Brain: Deciphering How The Brain Codes Our Thoughts*, Penguin, New York, 2014

Department of Islamic Art, 'Vegetal Patterns in Islamic Art', in Heilbrunn Timeline of Art History, The Metropolitan Museum of Art, New York, http://www.metmuseum.org/toah/hd/vege/hd_vege.htm, pub. Oct 2001, accessed Oct 2018

Descartes, René, trans. Desmond M. Clarke, *Meditations*, Penguin Books, London, 2010

Donoghue, Denis, *Metaphor*, Harvard University Press, Cambridge, Massachusetts, 2014

Engels, Frederick, trans. Clemens Dutt, *Dialectics of Nature*, Wellred, London, 2012

Ernst, Carl W., *Sufism: An Introduction to the Mystical Tradition of Islam*, Shambhala, Boston and London, 2011

Enzina, Wez, 'Bizarre and Wonderful', '*Ecology or Catastrophe: The Life of Murray Bookchin* by Janet Biehl', *London Review of Books*, Vol. 39 No. 9, 4 May 2017

Evelyn-White, H. G., *Hesiod, Homeric Hymns, Epic Cycle, Homerica*, Loeb Classical Library Volume 57, William Heinemann, London, 1914

Fakhry, Majid, *Islamic Philosophy: A Beginner's Guide*, Oneworld, Oxford, 2011

Fechner, Gustav Theodor, trans. Malcolm Green, *The Comparative Anatomy of Angels*, Atlas Press (Journal of the London Institute of Pataphysics Number 1, Sable 138), London, 2011

Flanagan, Owen J., *The Bodhisattva's Brain: Buddhism Naturalized*, The MIT Press, Cambridge, Massachusetts, 2013

—, 'Varieties of Naturalism', Chapter 26 in Clayton, Philip, and Simpson, Zachary (ed.), *The Oxford Handbook of Religion and Science*, Oxford University Press, Oxford, 2009

Foley, Michael, *The Age of Absurdity: Why Modern Life Makes it Hard to be Happy*, Simon & Schuster, London, 2011

Fonseca, Isabel, *Bury Me Standing: the Gypsies and their Journey*, Vintage, London, 2006

Freud, Sigmund, trans. ed. James Strachey, *Three Essays on the Theory of Sexuality*, Basic Books, New York, 2000

Fulcher, James, *Capitalism: A Very Short Introduction*, Oxford University Press, Oxford, 2015

Gallagher, Shaun, *Phenomenology*, Palgrave Macmillan, Basingstoke, 2012

Glaskin, Max, *Cycling Science*, Frances Lincoln Limited, London, 2013

Goldberg, Michelle, 'Iyengar and the Invention of Yoga', *New Yorker*, New York https://www.newyorker.com/business/currency/iyengar-invention-yoga, pub. Aug 2014, accessed Oct 2018

Grant, Friedel, and Andrew Grant, *Heinz Stücke: The Interview*, Travellingtwo: Bicycle Touring around the World website, http://travellingtwo.com/6553, pub. Oct 2010, accessed Oct 2018

Gray, John, *The Silence of Animals: On Progress and Other Modern Myths*, Penguin, London, 2014

Griffiths, Jay, *Kith: The Riddle of the Childscape*, Hamish Hamilton, London, 2013

—, *Pip Pip: A Sideways Look at Time*, Flamingo, London, 2000

—, *Wild: An Elemental Journey*, Hamish Hamilton, London, 2007

Groome, Francis Hindes, *Gypsy Folk Tales*, Abela Publishing, London, 2012

Gupta, Bina, *An Introduction to Indian Philosophy: Perspectives on Reality, Knowledge and Freedom*, Routledge, New York, 2012

Hagenbach, Dieter, and Lucius Werthmuller, trans. William
    Geuss and Linda Sperling, *Mystic Chemist: The Life of
    Albert Hofmann and his Discovery of LSD*, Synergetic
    Press, Santa Fe, New Mexico, 2013
Hamilton, Sue, *Indian Philosophy: A Very Short Introduction*,
    Oxford University Press, Oxford, 2001
Hancock, Ian F, Dileep Karanth (ed.), *Danger! Educated Gypsy:
    Selected Essays*, University of Hertfordshire Press,
    Hertfordshire, 2010
—, *We are the Romani People*, University of Hertfordshire
    Press, Hertfordshire, 2002
Haraway, Donna Jeanne, 'A Cyborg Manifesto', in *Manifestly
    Haraway*, University of Minnesota Press, Minneapolis,
    2016
Hugill, Andrew, *Pataphysics: A Useless Guide*, MIT Press,
    Cambridge Massachusetts, 2015
Humphreys, Alastair, *Moods of Future Joys*, Eye Books,
    London, 2007
—, *Thunder & Sunshine*, Eye Books, London, 2009
James, Simon P., *Environmental Philosophy: An Introduction*,
    Polity Press, Cambridge, 2015
József, Attila, trans. Peter Hargitai, *Selected Poems*, iUniverse,
    New York, 2005
Kandel, Eric Richard, *The Age of Insight: The Quest to
    Understand the Unconcious in Art, Mind and Brain*,
    Random House, New York, 2012
Kast, Verena, trans. Norman M. Brown, *Sisyphus: A Jungian
    Approach to Midlife Crisis*, Daimon-Verlag, Einsiedeln,
    1991
Keown, Damien, *Buddhism: A Very Short Introduction*, Oxford
    University Press, Oxford, 2013
Kirk, Robert, *Mind and Body*, Acumen, Chesham, 2003
Krabbé Tim, trans. Sam Garrett, *The Rider*, Bloomsbury,

London, 2002

Krane, Jim, *Dubai: The Story of the World's Fastest City*, Atlantic Books, London, 2015

Kumar, Satish, *You Are Therefore I Am: A Declaration of Dependence*, Green Books, Foxhole, Dartington, 2013

Kyabgon, Traleg, *Karma: What It Is, What It Isn't, Why It Matters*, Shambhala, Boston, 2015

Lakoff, George, and Mark Johnson, *Philosophy in the Flesh*, Basic Books, New York, 1999

Lambert, Tim, 'A Brief History of Portsea, Portsmouth', localhistories.org website, http://www.localhistories.org/portsea, pub. 2007, accessed Oct 2018

Lee, Jessica, 'An Ancient Path of Kindness', Maptia Website, https://maptia.com/jessicalee/stories/an-ancient-path-of-kindness, accessed Oct 2018

Liiceanu, Gabriel, trans. James Christian Brown, *The Paltinis Diary: A Paideic Model in Humanist Culture*, Central European University Press, Budapest, 2000

Lilwall, Rob, *Cycling Home from Siberia*, Hodder & Stoughton, London, 2009

Locke, John, *An Essay Concerning Human Understanding*, Digireads.com (eBook), Kansas City, 2004

Lovatt, Catherine, 'The Mioritic Space: Romanian National Identity in the Work of Lucian Blaga', *Central Europe Review* 1 (18), 1999, see http://www.ce-review.org/99/18/lovatt18.html, accessed Oct 2018

Lutz, Antoine, Heleen A. Slagter, John D. Dunne, and Richard J. Davidson, 'Attention Regulation and Monitoring in Meditation', *Trends in Cognitive Sciences* 12 (4): 163–169. doi:10.1016/j.tics.2008.01.005, 2008, accessed Oct 2018

MacKenzie, Jeanne, *Cycling*, Oxford University Press, Oxford, 1981

Mardia, Kanti V., and Aidan D. Rankin, *Living Jainism: An Ethical Science*, Mantra Books, Alresford, Hants, 2013

Marino, Gordon Daniel (ed.), *Basic Writings of Existentialism*, The Modern Library, New York, 2004

McDonald, Ian, *River Dancer: New Poems*, Hansib Publications, Hertford, 2016

McGilchrist, Iain, *The Master and His Emissary : The Divided Brain and the Making of the Western World*, Yale University Press, New Haven and London, 2010

—, 'Attention and the Hemispheres: How Attention Changes the World', The Skeptical Brain blog, *Psychology Today*, New York, https://www.psychologytoday.com/us/blog/the-skeptical-brain/201012/attention-and-the-hemispheres, pub. 2010, accessed Oct 2018

McGrath, Melanie, *Motel Nirvana: Dreaming of the New Age in the American Desert*, Flamingo, London, 1996

McGurn, James, and Mick Allan, *Cyclorama*, Company of Cyclists Ltd, York, 2012

McGurn, James, *On Your Bicycle: The Illustrated Story of Cycling*, Open Road, York, 1999

McNerney, Samuel, 'A Brief Guide to Embodied Cognition: Why You Are Not Your Brain', Scientific American Guest Blog, *Scientific American*, Springer Nature, New York, https://blogs.scientificamerican.com/guest-blog/a-brief-guide-to-embodied-cognition-why-you-are-not-your-brain/, pub. 2011, accessed Oct 2018

Mehta, Suketu, *Maximum City: Bombay Lost and Found*, Review, London, 2005

Metcalf, Thomas R., *Ideologies of the Raj*, The New Cambridge History of India: III.4, Cambridge University Press, Cambridge, 2001

Millar, David, *Beyond Dubai: Seeking Lost Cities in the Emirates*, Melting Tundra Publishing, Alberta, 2015

Milson, Fred, *Complete Bicycle Maintenance 5th Edition*, J. H. Haynes & Co Ltd, Yeovil, 2008

Moran, Jim, 'Three Challenges for Environmental Philiosophy', *Philosophy Now* 88, 2012, see https://philosophynow.org/issues/88/Three_Challenges_For_Environmental_Philosophy, accessed Oct 2018

Müller, F. Max (ed.), *Sacred Books of the East: translated by various oriental scholars and edited by F. Max Müller Vol I*, Clarendon, Oxford, 1879–85, see https://en.wikisource.org/wiki/Sacred_Books_of_the_East_-_Volume_1, accessed Oct 2018

Murphy, Dervla, *Full Tilt: Ireland to India with a Bicycle*, The Reprint Society (by arrangement John Murray), London, 1966

O'Brien, Flann, *The Complete Novels*, Everyman's Library, New York, 2007

Orr, Emma Restall, *The Wakeful World: Animism, Mind and the Self in Nature*, Moon Books, Altresford, Hants, 2012

Özdemir, Adil, and Kenneth Frank, *Visible Islam in Modern Turkey*, Macmillan Press, Basingstoke, 2000

Penn, Robert, *It's All About the Bike*, Particular Books, London, 2010

Phillips, Adam, and Barbara Taylor, *On Kindness*, Hamish Hamilton, London, 2009

Plant, David, 'Biography of James Nayler', The British Civil Wars, Commonwealth & Protectorate 1638–1660 website, http://bcw-project.org/biography/james-nayler, pub. 2009, accessed Oct 2018

Polt, Richard, *Heidegger: An Introduction*, Cornell University Press, Ithaca, 1999

Prentice, Nick, *Thomas Hardy's Tragic Vision: Writing Towards Proto-Modernist Modes of Fiction*, PhD, University of

West of England, 2016, available http://eprints.uwe.
ac.uk/28121/, accessed Oct 2018

Quarmby, Katharine, *No Place to Call Home: Inside the Real Lives of Gypsies and Travellers*, Oneworld, London, 2013

Rose, Jenny, *Zoroastrianism: An Introduction*, I.B. Tauris, London, 2014

Rowbotham, Sheila, *Rebel Crossings: New Women, Free Lovers, and Radicals in Britain and the United States*, Verso, London, 2016

Rushdie, Salman, *Midnight's Children*, Vintage, London, 2006

Russell, Bertrand, *History of Western Philosophy*, Routledge, London, 2004

—, *Mysticism and Logic, and other Essays*, Ockham Publishing, Aberdeen, 2015

—, *The Problems of Philosophy*, Oxford University Press, London, 1946

Russell, Gerard, *Heirs to Forgotten Kingdoms: Journeys into the Disappearing Religions of the Middle East*, Simon & Schuster, London, 2014

Saroyan, William, *The Bicycle Rider in Beverly Hills*, Faber and Faber, London, 1953

Scheerbart, Paul, trans. Andrew Joron, *The Perpetual Motion Machine*, Wakefield Press, Cambridge, Massachusetts, 2011.

Scheffler, Samuel, ed. Niko Kolodny, *Death and the Afterlife*, Oxford University Press, New York, 2013

Sekula, Allan, *Fish Story*, (Catalogue) ebook edition, Witte de With Centre for Contemporary Art, Rotterdam, and Richter Verlag, Düsseldorf, 2014

Seneca, Lucius Annaeus, trans. C.D.N Costa, *On the Shortness of Life*, Penguin, 2004

—, trans. & ed. Moses Hadas, *The Stoic Philosophy of Seneca*, Doubleday & Co., New York, 1958

—, trans. Aubrey Stewart, *Minor Dialogs Together with the Dialog "On Clemency"*, Lazy Raven Publishing, 2017

Shabistari, Sa'd ud Din Mahmud, trans. Florence Lederer, *The Secret Rose Garden of Sa'd Ud Din Mahmūd Shabistarī*, John Murray, London, 1920, available at https://archive.org/stream/ TheSecretRoseGardenOfSadUdDinMahmudShabistari/ secretrosegarden-shabestari_bw-en_djvu.txt, accessed Oct 2018

Sheldrake, Rupert, *The Science Delusion*, Coronet, London, 2013

Shorto, Russell, *Descartes' Bones: A Skeletal History of the Conflict Between Faith and Reason*, Abacus, London, 2013

Siderits, Mark, *Buddhism as Philosophy: An Introduction*, Ashgate Publishing, Aldershot, 2007

Singer, Peter, *Marx: A Very Short Introduction*, Oxford University Press, Oxford, 2000

Smith, Melanie K., *Issues in Cultural Tourism Studies*, Routledge, London, 2003

Sorell, Tom, *Descartes*, Oxford University Press, Oxford, 1988

Steger, Manfred B., and Roy, Ravi K., *Neoliberalism: A Very Short Introduction*, Oxford University Press, Oxford 2010

Stevens, Thomas, *Around the World on a Penny-Farthing*, Arrow, London, 1991

Storr, Anthony, *Freud: A Very Short Introduction*, Oxford University Press, Oxford, 2001

—, *Jung*, Fontana Press, London, 1990

Suzuki, D. T., *An Introduction to Zen Buddhism*, Grey Arrow, London, 1959

Thomas Jones, Dhivan, 'Review: *Confession of a Buddhist Atheist* by Stephen Batchelor', https://thebuddhistcentre.

com/westernbuddhistreview/review-confessions-buddhist-atheist-stephen-batchelor, pub. 2012, accessed Oct 2018

Thompson, Mel, *Buddhism: Key Ideas*, published by Mel Thompson (ebook), 2013

—, *Understand Eastern Philosophy*, Hodder Education, London, 2012

—, *Understand Philosophy*, Teach Yourself (Hodder Headline), London, 2010

Tomalin, Claire, *Thomas Hardy: The Time-Torn Man*, Viking, London, 2006

Urry, John, *The Tourist Gaze: Leisure and Travel in Contemporary Societies*, Sage, London, 1996

Van der Plas, Rob, *Simple Bicycle Repair: Fixing Your Bike Made Easy*, Cycle Publishing / Van der Plas Publications, San Francisco, 2010

Van der Plas, Rob and Stuart Baird, *Bicycle Technology: Understanding the Modern Bicycle and its Components*, Van der Plas Publications, San Francisco, 2010

Visser, Wayne A. M., and Alastair McIntosh, 'A Short Review of the Historical Critique of Usury', *Accounting, Business & Financial History* 8 (2): 175–189. doi:10.1080/095852098330503, 1998

Vivekananda, Swami, *Raja Yoga*, CreateSpace, California, 2015

Vogel, Steven, *Why the Wheel is Round: Muscles, Technology, and How We Make Things Move*, The University of Chicago Press, Chicago and London, 2016

Warburton, Nigel, 'Augustine's Cogito Argument Pre-Dates Descartes' Cogito', http://virtualphilosopher.com/2006/12/augustines_cogi.html, pub. 2006, accessed Oct 2018

Wessels, Tom, *The Myth of Progress: Toward a Sustainable Future*, University Press of New England, Hanover and London, 2013

Wilkinson, Robert, *Minds and Bodies*, Open University, Milton

Keynes, 2002

Williamson, Adam, 'Biomorphic Art, The Art of Arabesque', http://artofislamicpattern.com/resources/introduction-to-islimi/, accessed Oct 2018

Wilson, David Gordon, with contributions by Jim Papadopoulos, *Bicycling Science*, MIT Press, Cambridge, Massachusetts, 2004

Wynter, Harriet, *The Clockwork of the Heavens: An exhibition of astronomical clocks, watches and allied scientific instruments* (Catalogue), Asprey and Co., London, 1973

Yeats, William Butler, *The Celtic Twilight*, Historical Books Limited, Shipston-On-Stour, 2008

Acknowledgements

Jen for the whole journey. Our families. Special thanks to Mum, Dad, Annie, Archie and the McDonald family.

This book would never have been possible without Jo Heygate, agent, kindred cyclist and friend.

Jay Griffiths. Imogen Denny, Hugh Davis, Mark Ecob, Sarah Barlow. Dawn Painter. Christina Petrie. Jane Stables.

Klara Papp for her translation.

Clive Cazeaux for that first chat about philosophy.

Mel Thompson for his comments on philosophical aspects. I thoroughly recommend Mel's eloquent and thoughtful introductions to Western, Eastern and comparative philosophy, mel-thompson.co.uk

Boneshaker Magazine – a true labour of love and a worldwide cycling community. Some of the chapters in this book began as articles for the magazine. Particular thanks to editors James Lucas and Mike White and creative director Chris Woodward, boneshakermag.com

Pi Manson and Chris Woodward who created the bike plan layout at the end of each chapter and to Bike Cad for allowing us to use their software, clandestine.cc, chriswoodwarddesign.co.uk, bikecad.ca

Bristol Bike Project for their tools and parts. Martin Callingham for photography.

Ryan Downes, wheel builder extraordinaire, ryanbuildswheels. co.uk

Jake at Jake's Bikes for that first red Raleigh Explorer, bristolbicycles.co.uk

Ben Dowden for the video, bdfilm.co.uk

Rob Wall at Roll for the Soul, Nick Hand and all of Bristol's bike community for helping out in so many ways I cannot even begin to list them.

Pip Taylor for blazing the trail and a copy of *Full Tilt*.

Special thanks to Jimmy Leach, Anton Marrast, Satish Kumar, Simon Nurse, Robin Mather, Ian Street, Laura and Tim Moss, Kim Harding, Phil Taylor, Carine and James at 'Ride with a View', David Weight, Martin Skelton for their help during the crowdfunding campaign.

This book was powered by the music of Matt Elliott on a loop.

Unbound is the world's first crowdfunding publisher, established in 2011.

We believe that wonderful things can happen when you clear a path for people who share a passion. That's why we've built a platform that brings together readers and authors to crowdfund books they believe in – and give fresh ideas that don't fit the traditional mould the chance they deserve.

This book is in your hands because readers made it possible. Everyone who pledged their support is listed below. Join them by visiting unbound.com and supporting a book today.

Jane Bull
Kevin Bull
Sophie Bull
Adam Burgess
Dominic Burton
Rob Bushill
James Butcher
Charlie Butt
Julie Cameron
Ali Campbell
James Campbell
Rich Campoamor
Paul Carlon
Richard Carne
Nadia Carpenter
Anthony Carrick
Patrice Carter
Deborah Casson
Smiler Darren Castle
Ben Cave
Rob Chambers
Jit Chauhan
David Chedd
Laura Chessar
Andy Chester
Abb-d Choudhury
Kelly ChowChow
Pete Clarke
Svein Clouston
Fran Coates
Rachel Cocking
John Coe
Allison Cole
Karly Coleman
Michael Coleman
Liz Collier
Tommy Commane
Sean Condon
Stephen Connolly

Ben Cook
Gary Cook
Toby Cooles
Giles Cooper
Claire Copley
Irene Corcoran
Sean Coulter
Michael Coupe
Jules Cox
Lee Craigie
Leighton Crane
Giles Cudmore
Mark Culmer
Cycle Miles
Adam Dacey
Eleanor Dale
Brian Davidson
Ben Davies
William Davies
Diego De la Hoz
Natalie De Luca
Aniello Del Sorbo
Peter Denheen
Chris Devaney
Damien Digonnet
Adam Dolling
Hans Dols
Alison Donaldson
downlandcycles.co.uk
Ollie Downward
Piotr Drabik
Sarah Eagle
Paul Eaton
Chris Elliott
Sam Ellis
Ian Emmerson
Frank Erler
Lynnette Evans
Mark Evans

Tony Fahy
Andy Farndale
Edie Fassnidge
Scott Ferguson
Dominic Field
Chris Fieldsend
Mike Fitzgerald
Ian Fitzpatrick
Bård Fjukstad
Paul Flower
Elizabeth Forrester
Barbara Fowler
Jerry Fox
Luke Francis
Jeremy Frayn
Timothy Frost
Mog Fry
Angela Fryer
Jonathan Fulford
Ella Furness
Carrina Gaffney
Sophie Geschke
Juergen Ghebrezgiabiher
Julie Gibbon
Jon Gillard
Glasgow Bike Station
Andrew Goldney
Mark Gonsalves
Ann and Ken Gough
Dave Graham
Lucy Greaves
Cay Green
Paul Gregory
Mike Grenville
Jay Griffiths
Zoe Grimes
Paul Groom
Mike Grove
Susan Guest
Sam Guglani

Luke Guilford
David Haddock
Adrian Haldane
Sam Halmarack
Nick Hand
Matt Harcourt
Kim Harding (Edinburgh
    Festival of Cycling)
Robert Keith Hardy
Jason Hares
Marie Harris
Wendy Harris
Caren Hartley
Steven Harvey
Christine Hastie
Jack Hatfield
Oliver Hayles
Thom Heald
Thomas Heller
Ellie Henderson
Catherine Heygate
Hildegard Heygate
Joanna Heygate
Kevin Hickman
Martin Hickman
Michael Hill
Kathy Hinde
Karl Hobbs
Chris Hoe
Anna Hope
Frank Hopkinson
Jeff Horne
Stephen Hough
David Houghton
Rob Howard
Jennifer Howells
Joe Howells
Ken Huggins
Joel Hughes
Matt Hulse

Rick Hurst
Richard Ireland
Mary Isaacs
Isca Frameworks
Pam Isherwood
Alexei Ivanovich
Helen Jackson
Melinda Jacobsen
Nick James
Mandy Jamieson
Sally Jeffery
Adam Jenkin
Jenny & Sol
Dylan Joffre
Elle Johnston
Adrian Jones
Richard Jones
Thomas Joy
Kat Jungnickel
Andres Kabel
Patric Keller
Lawrence Kelly
Jonathan Kendall
Sarah Keogh
Christian S. Kern & Tati
  Otaka
Virpi Kettu
Dan Kieran
Jill Kieran
Rob Kilner
Owen Kimm
Anna Kissell
Laurence Koster
Evan Kwan
Franck Lamamra
Christopher Larraz
David Lawlor
Garth Leder
Daren Lee
Fred Leefarr

Tony Leonard
Sean Lester
Laura Lewis
Rob Lewis
Rozi Leyden
Sam Leyden
Margaret Leyland
Tara Li-an
Simon Linde
Clare Linton
John Lister
Bryan Lock Smith
Mildred Locke
Rachel Louis
Stuart Lowe
Eleanor Lowenthal
Ian Lowry
David Lucas
Brian Lunn
Benjamin Mack
Jon Macklin
Manifique7
Elliott Mannis
Pi Manson
Edward March-Shawcross
Claude Marthaler
Duncan Maxwell-Lyte
Alessandra McAllister
Declan McCallion
John McCarthy
Martine McDonagh
Archie and Wendy McDonald
Ian McDonald
Robin McDonald
Fiona McGowan
John McGuire
Joe Medler
Fergie Meek
Julian Merriman
Luke Milbourn

Millican Team
Darren Mills
Duncan Mills
Laura Millward
John Mitchinson
Thomas Moody
Sarah Mooney
Greg Moore
Tom Moreton
Curtis Morgan
Ben Moss
Laura Moss
Richard Moulton
Bernd Müller
Ciaran Mundy
Neil Munro
Darren Murray
Simon Nash (Green Oil UK Ltd!)
Marco Navarro-Genie
Carlo Navato
David Neill
Bruce Nicholls
Gary Nicol
John Nightingale
Katherine Nightingale
Philip Nixon
Bruno Noble
James North
Simon Nurse
Michael O'Connell
Denis O'Keeffe
Peter Oberholzer
Matthew Olden
Steven Olsen
Rick Orme
Brian Palmer
Duncan W.J. Palmer
Nep Pangilinan
Stephanie Papa

Andrew Patrick
Ed Patrick
Jesse Paul
Adrian Pavey
Joseph Paxton
Michelle Payne
PeloBros
Robert Penn
James Perrott
Abigail Perrow
Owain Perry
Dan Petley
Christina Petrie
Neil Pike
Rita Platts
Justin Pollard
Miranda Polr
Katherine Potsides
Alex Poulter
David Priestley
Monica Purkis
Paula Purkis
Emma Pusill
Edward Quartly
Juan Rae
Herman Ragan
Nick Raistrick
Chris Randall
Lydia Rattray
Kit, Anna & Pete Redmond
Jason Reeves
Craig Reilly
Malachy Reynolds
Aine Rickard
Andrew Riddington
Ridewithaview
Kent Riggs
Susan Rios
Diane Rissik
Victor Manuel Rivera

Katy Rodda
Sarah Rodger
Linda Rodgers
Polly Rodgers
Julien Roger
Wojciech Rogoziński
Anita Roy
Ryan @ RyanBuildsWheels
Kate Sandel
Andy Santegoeds
Julian Sayarer
Martin Schuster
Clare Scott
Will Sefton
Charlotte Selby
Laurence Shapiro
Sue Sharpe
Sarah Shaw
Sue Sherrington
Oly Shipp
Martin Silvester
Mark Simmons
Ollie Simpson
Rohan R. Singh
Martin Skelton
Rosie Sleightholme
Neil Smailes
Simon Smart
Robert Smith
Tony Smith
Michael Spencer
Quentin Spender
Ralph Sperring
Peter Spinner
Kate Stables
Craig Standage
Lisa and Darrin Stead
Joe Steele
Zoe Steley
Jenny Stolzenberg

Mark Summers
Hyojung Sun
Wil Symons
Dave Taylor
Jon Taylor
Tom Taylor
Susan Taylor-Searle
John Thackara
Pete Theelke
Charlie Thelu
James Thomas
Douglas Thompson
Jonathan Thompson
Ken Thomson
Titchmarsh
Jeremy Toynbee
Nick Tracey
Richie Troughton
Nico Tyabji
Kate Unsworth
Clive Upton
Jennifer Uzzell
Lily van den Broecke
Craig Vaughton
Chris Venables
Miranda Ward
Graeme Watson
Jim Watson
Neil Webster
David Weight
Paul Wells
William Wells
Dan Weltman
Mike White
whiterosemodelworks.co.uk
Matthew Wicks
Jessica Widdows
Molly Williams
Pete Williams
Gemma Wilson

Robbie Wilson
Ben Winter
James Wise
Gretchen Woelfle
Nico Woitzel
Ed Wolstenholme
Garrett Wood
Thomas Woodbury
Graham Woodcock

Steve Woodward
Tom Woolner
Madeline Worsley & Siobhan
    Dolan
Chris Woudstra
Hongyan Wu
Frank Zappa
Morris Zwi